REVERSING THE LENS

D0168151

The Defiant Ones, MGM/UA Studios, 1958

REVERSING THE LENS

Ethnicity, Race, Gender, and Sexuality Through Film

Jun Xing and Lane Ryo Hirabayashi

UNIVERSITY PRESS OF COLORADO

Published by the University Press of Colorado
5589 Arapahoe Avenue, Suite 206C
Boulder, Colorado 80303

The University Press of Colorado is a proud member
of the Association of American University Presses.

The University Press of Colorado is a cooperative publishing enterprise supported, in part, by
Adams State University, Colorado State University, Fort Lewis College, Metropolitan State
University of Denver, Regis University, University of Colorado, University of Northern Colorado,
Utah State University, and Western State Colorado University.

∞ This paper meets the requirements of the ANSI / NISO Z39.48-1992 (Permanence of Paper).

Library of Congress Cataloging-in-Publication Data

Xing, Jun.
  Reversing the lens : ethnicity, race, gender, and sexuality through film / Jun Xing and Lane Ryo
Hirabayashi.
      p. cm.
Filmography: p.
Includes bibliographical references and index.
    ISBN 0-87081-724-8 (alk. paper) — ISBN 0-87081-725-6 (pbk. : alk. paper)
    1. Minorities in motion pictures. 2. Race relations in motion pictures. 3. Racism in motion
pictures. 4. Sex role in motion pictures. I. Hirabayashi, Lane Ryo. II. Title.
    PN1995.9.M56X56 2003
    791.43'655—dc21
                                                                                    2003002123

Design by Daniel Pratt

to
Barbara Black and Cris Johnson
Video Library, Information and Technology Services
University of Colorado, Boulder

and
Wendy Eades
Media Specialist, Office of Instructional Services
Colorado State University, Fort Collins

with our collective appreciation and thanks

CONTENTS

Contents

Part IV Retrospect and Prospects

FOREWORD: REVERSING THE LENS

Charlie Chan is dead. So are Willie Best, Butterfly McQueen, Tonto, and a thousand other one-dimensional media "banditos," the ghosts of our cinematic subordination. Or so we've been told. Certainly *Bamboozled* (2000) argues otherwise, calling for vigilance, admonishing that a new, golden age of neominstrelsy is always just a pilot script, a season's deal, or an audience fad away. But it seems that for the most of it, the art of the blatant, racist stereotype has pretty much faded. Debates have moved on to become more complexly theoretical, evolving away from early critical "search-and-destroy" missions aimed at the mere analysis of images and their "positive versus negative" attributes.

Additionally, though, the media presence of "minority" leadership as public intellectuals, social activists, and elected politicians making and redefining power relations while combating discriminatory social structures and regimes has also diminished. In the brave new world of overdevelopment and overconsumption, as Guy Debord and Aldous Huxley so correctly forecast, censorship and propaganda have become less overtly the business of authoritarian states but rather are more subtly overdetermined, veiled by the velvet glove of market economics. "How much 'free speech' can you afford?" seems more the question of the day. Now the power agendas of the spectacular technoculture are mainly carried out by displacement and distraction. The political voices and spaces of social activism that were once the stuff of "breaking news" have been displaced and are now occupied by celebrities, athletes, rappers, and entertainers full of vacuous opinion and looking for that necessary patina of social depth and commitment that covers the dull glow of narcism radiating from their screen personas. As for the consuming public of developed societies, it is all mediated distraction, "bread and circuses" endlessly disseminated through 500 vapid cable channels. Debate and critical choice do not occur on the tube or in the voting booth but rather in the shopping mall, where it's all about the freedom to choose between competing brands of celebrity-endorsed sports shoes.

In light of these recent political and cultural turns, it seems that the famous and often cited W.E.B. DuBois diagnosis—that the problem of the twentieth century was the *color line*—has morphed with terror and clarity at this, the

Charlie Chan in Egypt, Fox Film Corporation, 1935

dawn of the twenty-first century, more broadly into the problem of the *difference line*. Certainly, many of these *differences* have always been with us in one brutal form or another as dark historical nightmares, genocides, socially structured oppressions, clashing religions, class struggles, homophobic persecutions, and so on. The list is necessarily long. But what has changed, especially here in the United States as we rush into this new century/millennium, is that the "problem" once defined and brutally contained under the binary model of *color* (with "black" versus "white" being the absolute poles of disenfranchisement and privilege) has shifted toward a more complex "multicultural" model. The hard-won, stingy "progress" that came with the end of the Civil Rights Movement benefited and changed the entire society in unanticipated ways. One admirable result ensued when a variety of emergent groups, classes, genders, and sexual identities adapted the valuable lessons about politics and identity shaped by the movement's legal strategies and social activism. Consequently, these emergent social formations have identified, organized, and actively staked their claim for more political power and cultural presence on the U.S. social landscape.

Moreover, this process has been greatly enabled by two tangible forces of our postindustrial, and now so problematically "globalized," planet. First, we have experienced overall growth and acceleration of the mass-mediated image-idea stream driven by the almost total pervasiveness of our techno-cyber-informational system. Second, as a result of mass migrations, dislocations, and movements of populations (much facilitated by modern air travel), we are experiencing a general confluence and compression of multiple, cultural, and social *differences*. Broadly, this movement has been from the agrarian South toward the advanced, technologized nations of the North, from underdevelopment and malnutrition to overdevelopment and overconsumption—the restless many searching for survival, sustainable wages, or some version of the consumer "good life" among the privileged few. Ironically, then, the countries of the developed world—particularly the United States—have become more accelerated, electronically mediated, interconnected, and compressed social environments. Yet simultaneously and paradoxically, these developed consumer societies are both more integrated and divided by *difference* and as a result are more complexly contentious than ever.

In an electronically mediated technoculture where one's screen image determines so much about one's political fortunes and collective fate, one of the central, pressing needs of emergent social formations has got to be to construct a distinct and clearly articulated pedagogy concerned with teaching the media of *difference*. This should be a multifaceted endeavor aimed not only at media production but, as importantly, at audience building and creating a historicized, theorized critical discourse about the media. As an anthology exploring the modalities of color and *difference* in media through a pedagogical frame (in a society pushed by accelerating technological and demographic change toward a "multicultural" inclusiveness), *Reversing the Lens* stands out as a significant contribution to this urgent project. That is to say, *Reversing the Lens* covers new territory, fills the important space of the book that hasn't been written until now.

As an opening gambit, part of the solution to the mis- or underrepresentation of people of color and *difference* in commercial and independent cinema has been to push for more *different* faces on our screens, as well as for the making of more independent media productions by the emergent groups. In dominant cinema the prime example of this approach would be the colored "triple play" at the 2002 Academy Awards with Sidney Poitier, Denzel Washington, and Halle Berry all winners. We must learn from our experiences in mass-mediated representation, however, that it is never enough to see merely *different* faces on our screens or in celebrity or executive circles. Dominant media is so overwhelming, penetrating every aspect of consciousness, that any nonwhite or *different* face or film is instantly positioned, contextualized, interpolated within the ideological frame and values of the dominant media system, the "ideological octopus," the "society of spectacle," and so on. What is needed is for all of these emergent, *different* cinemas and media, no matter what their orientation toward the norm, to view a group's work as an overall project in discourse building—

from securing more people of *difference* and color in dominant cinema and its attendant business and "star" systems, to producing more independent films, to building a pedagogical, critical, discursive apparatus. In other words, it is not enough to celebrate the doings of nonwhite stars or the flood of flicks for, by, or about people of color made as fodder for expanding crossover and multicultural markets. We must build a conscious, enlightened audience, broadly through education at all levels but also through the intellectual pursuit of film history, criticism, and theory from our unique points of view. This must start with a pedagogy of representational emergence focused on the media. And *Reversing the Lens* is a much-needed move in that direction. The words of the late, brilliant James Baldwin about the black audience—that it is struggling to awaken—can be extrapolated here, applied to all emergent audiences struggling to awaken, create, and apprehend the images that define and overdetermine so much of their lives.

ED GUERRERO
CINEMA STUDIES, NEW YORK UNIVERSITY

PREFACE

Reversing the Lens: Ethnicity, Race, Gender, and Sexuality Through Film grew out of a regional conference that focused on the use of video and film in studying multiple dimensions of ethnicity and race. Several premises guided the way we organized the conference; an exposition of these premises will help to clarify the nature of this anthology.

We decided to limit our initial call for papers to universities, colleges, and community colleges along Colorado's Front Range. Although we recognize that most representations of ethnic studies come from one or the other coast, we also know how many of our colleagues in Colorado regularly grapple with issues of ethnicity and race and how they intersect with class, gender, religion, and sexuality. Moreover, colleagues in a wide range of departments in Colorado have developed innovative and detailed perspectives about how best to teach film and video in this regard. Our vision grew out of our involvement with our respective ethnic studies departments, but we have been very open as well to Colorado colleagues in other fields who have been working with film in the classroom in a similar way.

The contributors to this anthology are trained in a wide range of disciplines including history, English, communications, American studies, anthropology, sociology, and political science. Nearly all of them also have ties to ethnic studies and women's studies. As we began to pull the anthology together, we happily discovered that it had the potential to be of interest to a wider audience than we had originally imagined. Rather than being limited to the classroom, *Reversing the Lens* is relevant to anyone who is curious about how video and film can be utilized to probe ethnicity and race. Three related premises frame this book.

First, we take a broad ethnic studies standpoint. We focus, that is, on how racialization is either sedimented or contested in the popular imagination and the different ways video and film can be utilized to expose "race" as being (1) a social construction, (2) subject to political contestation, and (3) a phenomenon that varies through time and space.

Second, analytically speaking, we cannot and do not look at racialization apart from other potential forms of difference including ethnicity, class, gender, and sexuality.

Finally, given our collective interest in global and transnational linkages, we have not drawn a hard-and-fast line among local, national, and international. Although our main focus is on racial and ethnic representation in the American context, broader perspectives are relevant here for two main reasons. First, ethnic and racial representations do not necessarily fall neatly along national boundaries. "For example," as film historian Carlos E. Cortés put it in his essay "The History of Ethnic Images in Film: The Search for a Methodology," "it may make analytic sense to separate screen images of Korean-Americans, other Asian-Americans, and Koreans in Korea. However, for purposes of impact on audience perceptions, such distinctions make little sense because viewers' perceptions of Korean-Americans may be influenced by the screen treatment of other Asian-Americans and of Koreans" (quoted in Lester D. Friedman, ed., *Unspeakable Images: Ethnicity and the American Cinema* [Champaign: University of Illinois Press, 1991], 70). Similarly, in their study *Unthinking Eurocentrism: Multiculturalism and the Media,* Ella Shohat and Robert Stam have argued for a "relational strategy" or a "dialogical [Mikhail Bakhtin's term] approach" to media representation—"one that operates at once within, between, and beyond the nation-state framework" (New York: Routledge, 1994, 9).

We agree with the points these authors make. They allow us to address issues of deterritorialized identities and hybrid sensitivities often reflected by the students and filmmakers we teach.

ACKNOWLEDGMENTS

First and foremost, we acknowledge the support of the Center for Applied Studies of American Ethnicity (CASAE) and its staff at Colorado State University, Fort Collins. In particular we thank Irma Woollen, then an administrative assistant at CASAE, for her logistical work in support of the conference that inspired us to prepare this anthology.

The Fort Collins Fort Fund provided financial support for the conference, for which we are grateful.

We also appreciate the sponsorship and support of the Department of Ethnic Studies at the University of Colorado, Boulder, particularly Karen Moreira, Jose Martínez, Danette Petersen, and Chelsea Lane.

Editorial consultants Karen Wuest and Claudia Manz helped us prepare a solid manuscript. We thank Executive Director Darrin Pratt and the staff at the University Press of Colorado—especially Dan Pratt, Laura Furney, and Cheryl Carnahan—for their enthusiasm and their work on production and other final stages of this book.

We collectively thank the artists, producers, and organizations that have allowed us to reproduce stills from the films we treat herein. We hope readers will consult the Filmography at the end of this book and will rent or purchase films of interest to them. This medium is very expensive, and we—the audience—have to do our part to keep these programs in circulation.

Finally, Jun Xing would like to thank four locally based independent filmmakers: David and Irene Foxhoven, Steven Wong, and Kenneth Holubeck. Over the years they have come into his classes numerous times, shared their experiences with students, and made their works available to his students.

REVERSING THE LENS

Secrets of Chinatown, Northern Films, Ltd., 1935

PART I
BEYOND THE IMAGE

INTRODUCTION

LANE RYO HIRABAYASHI AND JUN XING

The central purpose of *Reversing the Lens: Ethnicity, Race, Gender, and Sexuality Through Film* is to show how visual media can be used to facilitate cross-cultural understanding and communications, particularly with respect to the thorny topics of ethnicity and race. In this anthology we will demonstrate why and how visual media are useful in this regard, delineating how various forms of critical visual thinking can help us move more carefully and systematically when we cross cultures through video and film.

We believe that, although much enjoyment is associated with visual media, we must be vigilant so our encounters do not become voyeuristic or an end in themselves. Although ethnicity and race may be constructs, they remain the locus of serious division and inequality in the twenty-first century. Video and film can play an important role in facilitating understanding of how personal commitments and social movements foster progressive change. This anthology offers both students and teachers ways to use the powerful tool of film to study a situation themselves and then move on to consider how to change the difference and division that confront us all.

THE EDUCATIONAL VALUE OF VISUAL MEDIA

By the 1960s it had become clear that visual media—especially popular film and video—play a critical role in forming ethnic representations. Many authors have documented the pernicious dimensions of such processes. Although we agree with this thesis, we also believe film and video can be powerful tools to *expand* avenues of learning within and across cultures.

Film has tremendous potential to motivate people to recognize how cultures differ in both verbal and nonverbal patterns of communication. We believe this potential stems not only from the power of television and cinema in Western cultural formations and indeed globally but because of the seeming immediacy of film and its seeming evidentiary power. As Jun Xing points out in Chapter 2, film can encourage viewers not only to develop empathy for others but also to be moved to action—recognizing and confronting stereotypes and sometimes even unlearning them. This is particularly true if teachers use supplementary readings, lectures, and thoughtfully designed discussion questions along with the film. Furthermore, video documentaries may inspire viewers to study social issues more deeply and become critically engaged in them.

These facts justify an anthology that initiates a more sustained examination of ways to pursue learning through video and film. At the same time, these issues are far too important to remain in the university classroom. Just as we have found that video and film provide a springboard for our students to become more aware of themselves—of how their background and experiences shape their perceptions and feelings about ethnicity and race—we invite anyone from the general public to peruse *Reversing the Lens* to facilitate their self-awareness. Most of the films discussed in this anthology are readily available for rental (see the Filmography at the back of the book for a complete list of the videos and films discussed and for information about how to order them). *Reversing the Lens* invites readers to consider our analyses, view the videos and films discussed, and critically evaluate the various approaches offered.

ORGANIZATION OF THE ANTHOLOGY

Reversing the Lens can be read on a number of levels. The anthology is divided into four parts, and it can be read, first, along these broad topical lines.

Part I includes this introduction and Jun Xing's chapter on using media to smash stereotypes and develop empathy. These two chapters frame the book as a whole as well as framing each individual chapter.

Part II focuses on a number of racialized communities and how they are represented in video and film. Malcolm Collier and Lane Ryo Hirabayashi discuss how to use the documentary *Monterey's Boat People* to study continuities among the different Asian populations who have worked and fished in that picturesque area of central California. Ward Churchill surveys the way Hollywood cinema has captured and presented stereotypical images of American Indians throughout the history of moving and still images. Carmen Huaco-Nuzum uses the film *El Espejo/The Mirror* to discuss the construction of Chicana feminist space and place in urban settings. Adeleke Adeeko and Brenda Allen bring the intersections between ethnic and racialized populations to the foreground. Adeeko utilizes the feature-length production *Mississippi Masala* to examine the interface between the African American and the new immigrant South Asian (Asian Indian) communities in the Deep South. Allen uses the documentary *Skin Deep,* which focuses on university students, as a vehicle for discussing the challenges the increasing diversity of the United States poses to American society.

Part III expands upon the theme of racialized communities by examining how ethnicity and race are represented and played out vis-à-vis a range of contemporary social issues. Marilyn Alquizola and Lane Ryo Hirabayashi discuss how the video documentary *Slaying the Dragon* can be used to deconstruct racialized and gendered stereotypes of Asian and Asian American women. Lee Bernstein considers several feature-length films to juxtapose Hollywood's representations of race and crime against what the research records reveal. In a fascinating chapter on Chicana queer studies, Elisa Facio demonstrates the merits of independent film in conveying insiders' views about the intersections of sexual, political, and ethnic identity. Jeffrey Ho tackles the problem of teaching Eastern mysticism to Euro-Americans by discussing the popular Hollywood film *The Matrix.* Finally, Brett Stockdill, Lisa Sun-Hee Park, and David N. Pellow utilize the award-winning production *The Panama Deception* to discuss the way U.S. foreign policies are sometimes manipulated to cover up greed and imperialistic designs to the detriment not only of people of color in both the United States and Panama but also to the polities of both countries.

Part IV features a chapter by Jun Xing about selecting, introducing, and reinforcing critical visual thinking in crossing cultures through film and video. Although this might appear to be a pedagogical piece, we recommend that readers work through it to heighten their reflexivity—that is, to examine how they might personally select and watch films to gain greater self-awareness and sociological insight. The anthology concludes with a short chapter that raises additional issues and questions we feel are important but that will have to wait for a new cohort of viewers and presenters to be fully discussed.

Inherently, *Reversing the Lens* aspires to pose as many issues as it is prepared to resolve fully. Nonetheless, we can affirm that video and film are uniquely powerful tools that can raise both individual and collective consciousness. We realize that we have only initiated what we hope will become a long-term, collective dialogue, but we are proud to be among those who have called for a systematic study of the uses of film in ethnic studies within a broad, interdisciplinary perspective.

Broken Blossoms, Connoisseur/Meridian Films, 1919

THEMATIC INTERSECTIONS

Because this anthology is a multifaceted enterprise, we need to address thematic intersections that crosscut the topical setup of *Reversing the Lens.* These themes provide the critical framework that knits the chapters and parts of this anthology together as a collective whole.

The first theme concerns the strong emotions that pertain to ethnicity and race in the United States, along with the prospects—and pitfalls—of using video and film to explore these issues. The second theme relates to representation and construction, since we believe that to analyze films effectively we must pay attention to what is featured, what recedes into the background, and what is hidden. The third theme emerges out of the relationship among visual media, social issues, and engagement.

The Power of Emotions

Video and film are especially useful media for exploring our consciousness at both overt and tacit levels because they speak to our emotions as well as to our intellect. For this reason we must seek to understand films that raise both positive and negative feelings within viewers, asking how the emotional reactions a film evokes can be transformed from threats, challenges, or confrontations into opportunities for discussion, self-examination, and learning. More specifically, those who use film in the classroom need to overcome students' conscious and unconscious inhibitions and biases to encourage honest assessment of and dialogue about racial and ethnic issues.

To this end, we believe video and film should not be used alone, even if it seems students would understand a film without additional instruction or explication. To take a proactive approach to critical visual thinking, we seek to implement strategies that will create opportunities for students to explore personal and collective sentiments about ethnicity and race. During this exploration, instructors need to be aware of the emotions that may be unleashed as students view particularly affecting films or videos. Viewers may moan, groan, sigh, cry, or express disgust, enthusiasm, or rage. At the same time, video and film may serve unique functions in exploring ethnicity and race. At its best, film can facilitate significant qualitative insight into other people's worlds, especially when a production is able to capture insiders' standpoints and perspectives. In effect, this takes the burden of representation off the shoulders of students and faculty of color, even as it brings certain issues to nontarget populations (e.g., Euro-American, male, heterosexual, Protestant) in a way that is probably less alienating to those populations than face-to-face confrontations.

In this light, we are interested in determining what kinds of philosophies and methodologies are most effective for both teaching and viewing film and video substantively to promote critical visual thinking. *Reversing the Lens* addresses such issues, including how to identify, evaluate, and contextualize films using introductions, study questions, readings, and so forth; how to develop related writing assignments, including impression pieces; and how to relate to the social issues and theoretical debates a given program or set of programs embodies or presents.

The Power of Representations

The discussion of film among film historians and critics is inherently theoretical. Although our primary purpose is not to debate film aesthetics, the creative artistry of a film is not irrelevant. Professors may need to inculcate their students with a higher level of visual literacy by encouraging them to think more critically when watching nighttime television, for example, analyzing not only the images they see but also the language and context. Also relevant are the theoretical concerns of cultural, literary, and linguistic studies, such as questioning the positioning of subjects, voice, authority, and representation.

Although video and film can certainly be used to promote critical visual thinking about the representation of people of color, this issue is more complicated than it may appear. Students should be encouraged to think about such questions as, Who has the authority to represent a given community? Does one have to be an "insider" in that community or experience to represent it authentically? Can sympathetic, well-informed outsiders be as effective, or even more effective, precisely because they have both empathy and a modicum of detachment from the group being represented? We have no ready answers to these questions, but we think they must be asked to encourage an active and analytic approach to visual data.

Actor H. T. Tsiang as the stereotyped "Jap," early 1940s

We must also consider the ways "truth" and "reality" are represented on the screen, particularly in documentaries. Not everyone, of course, will want to read Deleuze or other high-level theorists on the topic of representation, but the key elements of critical film theory should be glossed with interested viewers.

From *Topsy and Eva,* Feature Productions, 1927

These tools will enhance not only students' critical assessment but also their appreciation of how a given production is constructed.

The Power of Personal Change and Social Movements

In our classes we have seen that film can break through barriers, giving viewers the opportunity to think about and discuss controversial topics that might otherwise be ignored or avoided in a relatively safe environment. Even more important, film can serve as a catalyst, illustrating interaction among cultures on the screen and, at the same time, in the classroom. The discussions and interactions that occur as a result can provide a field for cross-cultural exchange, interaction, and learning. Film and video can also explore the ways social relations cut across racial and ethnic boundaries by examining the development of multiracial grassroots organizations and coalitions, the experiences of biracial and multiracial individuals, or the ways in which people of color are impacted by transnational and diasporic linkages engendered by global capitalism and international migration.

Furthermore, film and video can be used to teach about social issues and social movements while also inspiring students to actively confront twenty-first-century issues such as the dimensions of ethnicity, racialization, gender, and sexuality, and how they intersect. By studying not only successful campaigns but also struggles that appear to have "failed," students can learn about progressive organizing strategies, logistics, politics, and so forth.

In sum, this anthology explores a variety of productions from mainstream feature films to lesser-known but still significant independent videos and films. By advocating a critical orientation to the content, production, reception, and impact of these films, we submit that viewers can sharpen their critical visual thinking skills even as they explore a range of issues having to do with the social construction of "race."

2
MEDIA EMPOWERMENT, SMASHING STEREOTYPES, AND DEVELOPING EMPATHY

JUN XING

As American society has become increasingly driven by technology, many educators have embraced numerous innovations in teaching and research. Since the introduction of video technology, for example, an increasing number of faculty have successfully incorporated film in their classes. Given the convenience of a "smart" classroom, film has become even more popular. To the delight of both instructors and students, the preinstalled overhead film projector can show any VHS tape on a large screen. Computer-aided teaching and multimedia technologies are also being integrated into many U.S. university classrooms. These media-based innovations have expanded traditional venues of learning. In ethnic studies, a growing number of scholars have embraced film as an effective teaching tool. James A. Banks, for example, has provided a list of multicultural films suitable for classroom use in his widely adopted text *Teaching Strategies for Ethnic Studies* (1997). The Avery Fisher Center for Music and Media at New York University published *A Map Guide to Independent Video by and About African American, Asian American, Latino, and Native American People* (1992). More recently, National Video Resources has put out a series of publications under the title *VideoForum,* including *Viewing Race: A Videography and Resources Guide* (1999).

With its increasing popularity, film presents both opportunities and challenges for teachers. (Note that the term *presenters* may be substituted for *teachers*, since the same general principles hold for community leaders, organizers, and so forth, who might also want to shows films to educate and sensitize their constituencies.) This chapter grew out of my experiences teaching film in American, Asian American, and ethnic studies over the past ten years. I will share observations concerning some of the social, theoretical, and pedagogical issues involved in a film-oriented course. For clarification, I will start by discussing three key premises.

First, my discussion will focus on independent films made by and about ethnic minorities. Over the years, minority film and video artists have produced hundreds of social-issue documentaries, dramas, and experimental films dealing with various aspects of the ethnic experience. The growing ranks of independent films have addressed significant issues of racial representation, countered old and new stereotypes, challenged the universal mainstream standards of art, and established an intertextual dialogue with Hollywood films. As alternative media sources, they have become a powerful pedagogical tool for teaching ethnic and multicultural issues. As Barbara Abrash and Catherine Egan wrote, "And it is precisely these non-mainstream productions that most consistently challenge traditional perceptions, question conventional wisdom, and posit alternative ways of representing and interpreting history and culture."[1] My discussion will focus specifically on these "non-mainstream" works.

Second, for the purpose of this chapter, teaching film in the classroom should mean more than a supplement to lectures and readings. Although film is clearly an established teaching resource, it is used in many different ways. Some teachers simply use film as an add-on, a "teaser," or a way for a busy professor to take up class time. To use film as an effective teaching medium, teachers must exercise careful and thoughtful planning and methodology. Film should not be used merely as a supplement, but it should be an integral part of the thematic and pedagogical focus of a course so it will be "firmly embedded in an instructional unit."[2]

Third, in a film-based course, emotions are an important part of the learning process. The films we use to raise topics related to ethnic studies are often emotionally charged and highly sensitive. In addition to the inherently controversial subject matter of race and ethnicity, film as the main medium of instruction often evokes strong student emotion. It would be a serious mistake for an instructor to exclude the sharing of perceptions and feelings and emphasize a strictly intellectual approach. One of the main pedagogical questions discussed here is how to "teach" films that raise strong emotions—both negative and positive—in our students as well as in ourselves as we teach.

Taking these premises as a point of departure, I will focus my discussion here on two key topics: media empowerment and the elements of visual literacy. In the final chapter of *Reversing the Lens,* I will discuss teaching strategies for a film-based course that highlights ethnic studies issues.

MEDIA EMPOWERMENT

Carlos E. Cortés, a film historian who has long used film in his history classes, called for developing student media literacy, or the ability to critically read and analyze the visual media.[3] He wrote, "When applied to the mass media, this school multicultural empowerment would include strengthening student knowledge about the media, developing student skills in critically analyzing the media, and helping students become more action oriented when dealing with the media."[4] Indeed, this social dimension of the film experience represents the greatest opportunity for ethnic studies classes. Almost all of the independent films by ethnic minorities carry important social messages. For the majority of filmmakers, the notion of filmmaking as a method for social change instead of as a showcase for artists has understandably meant incorporating an activist component into their work. For that matter, these films can be used effectively both to teach students about social issues and to inspire them to engage in struggles for social change, especially those dealing with ethnicity, racialization, gender, sexuality, and their interactions.

There are many different paths to this lofty goal. In my class I have adopted two effective approaches—one analytical and the other activist—that I will describe in detail in the next two sections.

Smashing Stereotypes: An Analytic Approach

It has become a cliché to say that visual media, especially popular film, play an important role in ethnic representation. As the most powerful media in contemporary society, film has obviously contributed to the stereotyping of different cultures and ethnic groups. Because of this, minority filmmakers have produced works that showcase and critique those stereotypes, such as Marlon Riggs's *Ethnic Notions* (1987) and Deborah Gee's *Slaying the Dragon* (1988). Accordingly, defusing ethnic stereotypes should be a primary goal for ethnic studies classes. Almost every chapter in *Reversing the Lens* addresses this issue at some level.

Controversy has long raged among teachers, however, over the impact of screening stereotypes in the classroom. On the one hand, some argue that film could sensitize students to stereotypical depictions of ethnic and cultural groups. On the other hand, some have serious reservations about showing derogatory images that may reinforce stereotypes for students not previously exposed to them. Although I do think this is a legitimate concern, I argue that these reservations are often caused by misinformation or a lack of confidence in students' critical abilities. The instructor must make sure that the viewing experience in the classroom is never passive because to counterbalance the weight of depicting stereotypes, students must be trained in how to critically view a film.

13

New conceptual studies (in psychology and linguistics) on ethnicity in film have yielded new and interesting discoveries about the relationship between media and spectators, particularly with regard to prejudice and stereotyping. Scholars in social psychology, for example, have applied a social-cognitive approach to the film-viewer relationship. Film audience members, as social cognizers, "actively select, organize, transform, and interpret film information, at times in a biased or distorted way, guided by their needs, values and beliefs, especially those concerning 'self' and 'others.'"[5] This alternative reading of the spectator's role is further developed in the field of linguistics. Film scholars have borrowed the critical concept of "dialogism" from Russian scholar Mikhail Mikhailovich Bakhtin in the study of race and ethnic representation.[6] For Bakhtin, language, text, and media are essentially a matter of utterances or voices rather than sentences and images. "Each cultural voice," he claims, by nature "exists in dialogue with other voices."[7] Even though listeners, readers, and spectators do not speak from the film itself, they are inherently in the conversational process with it. Thus the Bakhtinian formulation of dialogism posits an active role for audience members, who are not passive recipients of the film's message but rather are in constant internal dialogue with the film they are viewing.

Along the same line of argument, Stuart Hall offers a new interpretation of representation. In contrast to the "old" notion that representation merely "represents" meaning that is already there, Hall posits that there is no single fixed meaning of media images. To him, the signifier and signified in representation are not solely reflective but "constitutive"—a process by which the viewer is drawn into the image in an active way, through interpolation. Hall's new understanding of representation is profound in the sense that it offers a new way of looking at how to perceive what is being represented. Thus the reception of visual texts becomes a dynamic and dialectical process between filmmakers and the audience.

If we take his model seriously, instructors and students can contest gender and racial stereotyping in the classroom even though students may be exposed to those stereotypes for the first time. I have used Hall's two lectures on video, *Representation and the Media* and *Race, the Floating Signifier,* alternately to initiate discussion about what Hall calls "the practices of signification" in the media.[8] For example, after screening *Representation and the Media,* class discussion focused on "identity, identification, and the viewer," one of its fourteen headings. Through concrete examples from sports to advertising, Hall demonstrates how the viewer is drawn into the process in an active way through identification. Similarly, as viewers we can open up the practice of representation and make it less natural. By "getting inside" the stereotype and asking questions about how stereotype works, students are able to recognize and unlearn stereotypes. In this process of critical engagement, stereotypes begin to lose their reality and validity, or, to use Hall's words, they become "uninhabitable."

Used effectively, film provides a relatively safe environment for students to talk about racial and ethnic stereotyping. In real life it is hard to take on issues of race, ethnicity, gender, and sexual orientation. Discussing racial stereotyping publicly can be rhetorically difficult and emotionally harrowing. Beverly Tatum, for example, has precisely pinpointed three problems in public discourse about race:

a. Many students, regardless of racial group membership, have been socialized to think of the United States as a just society;

b. many students, particularly white students, initially deny any personal prejudice, recognizing the impact of racism on other people's lives, but failing to acknowledge its impact on their own; and,

c. race is considered a taboo topic for discussion, especially in racially mixed settings.[9]

In contrast to public space where there are no ground rules, a university classroom can provide a dynamic and safe learning environment. With careful pedagogical preparations, which I will discuss in Chapter 13, students often feel more comfortable expressing themselves openly on the sensitive subject of stereotyping because they know such a discussion is part of a serious educational process or a constructive dialogue as opposed to a political debate where the goal is to gain points.

Film also helps to bring real-life situations into the learning environment. As the main medium of instruction, film has two inherent advantages in studying and abolishing ethnic stereotypes. First, film provides a sense of immediacy and richness the printed word often lacks, evoking in students the sense that they are "right there." Whereas abstract discussion of stereotypes can be flat and uninspiring, film often provides concrete examples of stereotyping in our everyday environment. Pam Tom's black-and-white narrative film *Two Lies* (1990), for example, has been very effective in helping students recognize the impact of media stereotypes on our daily lives. It provides a disturbing and eerie look at a Chinese American teenager's identity crisis as a result of her mother's cosmetic eye surgery. Although the film focuses on a Chinese American family, during a postscreening discussion of this film, students of various backgrounds volunteered stories about the ways standards of beauty had shaped their lives. *Two Lies* demonstrated a drama and personification with which my students could easily identify. In this environment, the classroom can become a site of natural and dynamic exchange of ideas and experiences without the risk of conflict and misunderstanding.

Based on my experience, I am confident that if we prepare our students well and equip them with the right skills, they will not become victims of the stereotypes we are trying to smash. Instead I assert that film helps to break through barriers, giving students the opportunity to discuss stereotypes in a relatively safe environment while also empowering them analytically.

From *Two Lies,* a film by Pam Tom. Courtesy Women Make Movies

Developing Empathy: The Activist Approach

Ethnic cinema is a direct outgrowth of the civil rights movement and political activism in the 1960s. From the beginning, ethnic filmmakers tried to build a so-called triangular cinema of community, storyteller, and activist.[10] Their films have the potential not only to teach students about social issues but also to inspire them to engage in political activism. In ethnic studies we are familiar with the debate about balancing scholarship and advocacy in our teaching and research. For many activists, Italian Marxist Antonio Gramsci's concept of the "organic intellectual" has become a model of practice. As "organic intellectuals" we are all obligated to help our students learn to be effective advocates of social justice, especially with regard to race, ethnicity, gender, and sexuality. I have experimented with some different strategies to develop students' empathy and critical engagement with social issues.

John Bodnar, in an essay on the debate over public memory, has identified two kinds of history in ordinary people's consciousness: the official and the vernacular.[11] Official history, according to Bodnar, relies on "dogmatic formalism" and represents the past "on an abstract basis of timeliness and sacredness." Vernacular history, on the other hand, "represents an array of specialized interests" and "views of reality derived from firsthand experience in small-scale communities rather than the 'imagined' communities of a large nation."[12]

Produced outside the traditional mode of storytelling, ethnic films—especially documentaries—become a powerful medium to record "vernacular history." This practice of using film as a vehicle for confronting racism and addressing injustice is a trademark of those works. They give agency to minorities who throughout history have been viewed as subjects rather than objects. Christine Choy and Renee Tajima's *Who Killed Vincent Chin* (1988) and Elaine Kim's *Sa-I-Gu: From Korean Women's Perspectives* (1993) are two films I have often used in my class. In both, history is presented as a process people live through. *Who Killed Vincent Chin* is the story of a twenty-seven-year-old Chinese engineer who was brutally murdered with a baseball bat by two white unemployed autoworkers in Detroit in 1982. This film takes a process-oriented approach to the story rather than an event-oriented one. By the end of the eighty-seven-minute film, when the murderers walk away free after five years of struggle in the courts, the audience is left with lingering questions about the case and its legal implications.

During the Rodney King civil unrest in Los Angeles from 29 April to 2 May 1992, Korean American businesses were specifically targeted in the violence and suffered about half of the $800 million in property damage. Many community leaders and activists believe the mainstream media contributed to the destruction of Koreantown. "When Korean Americans were thrust in the spotlight in April 1992," said Elaine Kim, co-director of *Sa-I-Gu*, "the enormity of misunderstanding about them was brought into play. The media reduced Korean Americans to images of screaming women and men on the roofs with guns."[13] To counter the mainstream media's biased coverage, three women of Korean background—Dai Sil Kim-Gibson, Elaine H. Kim, and Christine Choy—recorded the statements and life histories of Korean American women in Los Angeles. The film does not pretend to portray balanced and objective views on both sides of the conflict, but it offers an essential perspective from those Korean immigrant women about the riots, ethnic relations, and racism in U.S. society.

On the surface, such documentaries leave the audience little to celebrate. They do, however, demonstrate to students that ordinary people, even those with relatively little power, are actively addressing injustice and modifying their social environments. Further, the films emphasize historical processes more than immediate results, affirming the significance of struggle, decisions made, and consequences accepted. Put differently, the films have provided students with a sense of advocacy in the struggle for social justice and equality.

Students' empathy with the struggles for justice presented on the screen, however, is by no means automatic or uniform. A key element in encouraging student empathy is to bridge the sometimes uncomfortable gap among general topics, personal lives, and community issues. Several recent studies have shown that students have different frames of reference in understanding social issues and therefore may require different learning modalities. For example, Thomas Kochman discussed classroom modalities for black and white students. According to him, the black mode is "high-keyed: animated, interpersonal, and confrontational." The white mode, on the other hand, is relatively "low-keyed: dispassionate, impersonal, and non-challenging."[14] To translate Kochman's statements into plain terms, whereas black students are more likely to take a personal approach to social issues, their white counterparts tend to take a detached and "cool" stand on those issues. Given these differences in learning styles, I find it necessary to develop effective ways to make larger social issues relevant to students' personal lives and help them move beyond mere intellectual engagement.

Among several pedagogical tools I have used, video diaries have been one of the most effective. As a regular ongoing assignment, students in my class— most of whom are liberal arts majors—are required to film and share their personal and family stories in the form of home videos. Each student chooses three or four episodes to show in class throughout the semester. For the majority of students, these diaries become not only a means of self-expression but also a way to reach out to the community. Not surprisingly, these personal video diaries have documented various aspects of minority life in Fort Collins, the state of Colorado, and the nation as a whole: from hate crimes to grassroots activism. As an added benefit, students in the film-based class are much more enthusiastic about and committed to the learning experience than those in a typical undergraduate class. They seem to take a vested interest in their participation in class because they can share personal and political concerns with others.

Depending on student interests, service learning can also be an effective assignment. The simplicity of a camcorder and the cost-effectiveness of videotape allow them to do a film project as an alternative or complement to the video diary. The film project often sends students back into their communities.[15] More than a simple "shoot and show" technique, students are supposed to develop their technological skills and acquire real-world experience with pressing social issues. This is not a film studio course and film techniques are not required for enrollment, so I make sure technical help is available for students who need it. Over the past few years, I have tried to bring a filmmaker into the class at the beginning of the semester. Steve Wong, for example, a Denver-based Chinese American filmmaker, has visited the class many times and given an inspiring lecture on his documentary productions, followed by demonstrations from his film *One, Two Man* (1995). I have found that guest speakers' expertise and experience are more important than their ethnic background. David Foxhoven and Irene Rawlings, two Euro-American independent filmmakers, spoke about their work on the Amache camp—the World War II U.S.-style concentration camp for Japanese Americans in southeastern Colorado.

They not only helped students gain technical knowledge of filmmaking but also initiated contacts for them with several former Japanese American internees.

Taken together, these strategies have helped my students achieve a sense of immediacy between the topics revealed in a film and their concerns for social justice. Every community has civil rights issues an instructor can draw upon to make a film-based course more connected to students' personal lives. Each semester I am amazed at the range of topics covered in students' video presentations, as well as by students' enthusiasm about and commitment to their projects. Over the years I have built up a sizable collection of student videos. It is heartening to know that after the class is over, students continue to participate in various media-related projects, such as working in school media and becoming independent filmmakers.

VISUAL LITERACY

Although film aesthetics is not a primary concern in a class that focuses on ethnicity and race, creative artistry of film must be a part of our pedagogical vision. Since film is based on a certain level of literacy and we use films as primary texts, instructors of film-based courses need to tackle issues of sensibility, positioning, voice, and authority, as well as address the differences between the moving image and literary media. In most cases students step into a classroom with diverse educational experiences and different levels of preparation for film criticism, so helping them acquire a higher level of visual literacy should be integral to our pedagogical goals. Generally, visual literacy is defined as "a group of vision competencies" that "enable a visually literate person to discriminate and interpret the visible actions, objects, and/or symbols . . . that he encounters in his environment."[16] In teaching film, visual literacy can be defined as the ability to analyze the form and structure of the film medium and to be actively engaged in assessing the film's messages and less gullible to the film's manipulation.

With this goal in mind, I always introduce students to some major cinematic elements at the beginning of each class. I assign the chapter on visual language from John O'Connor's book *Image as Artifact*.[17] The reading offers students an introduction to filmic language and techniques, particularly the four primary film techniques: mise-en-scène, cinematography, editing or montage, and sound. After acquiring a basic vocabulary in film analysis, students are introduced to some of the critical concepts in media studies such as "image," "reality," and "objectivity." Those concepts are then elaborated in a set of key questions: What is the relationship between imagery and reality, especially in terms of the origins of racial and ethnic stereotypes; what constitutes the interaction between the images of others and self-images; and what is the nature of the relationship between societies or groups that produce films and the societies or groups represented in films?[18] In the next three sections I will describe how I have introduced to students three key concepts critical to visual literacy: film imagery, objectivity, and style.

Film Image

For years, much of the work on the cinematic representation of women and minorities has stressed the "positive" image as opposed to stereotypes. In discussions and public forums, the notion of creating a "positive" or "counter" image as an alternative to Hollywood stereotyping has often taken center stage. Only recently, scholars have begun to critique the concept of a "positive" image as a useful way of looking at ethnic representation in the media. For example, bell hooks has questioned the value of the "counter" image: "Often what is thought to be good is merely a reaction against representations created by white people that were blatantly stereotypical."[19] Similarly, Robert Stam and Louise Spence observed:

> Much of the work on racism in the media, like early work on the representation of women, has stressed the issue of the "positive image." This reductionism, though not wrong, is inadequate and fraught with methodological dangers. The exact nature of "positive," first of all, is somewhat relative; black incarnations of patience and gradualism, for example, have always been more pleasing to whites than to blacks.[20]

To help students understand the dynamics of representation and the potential forms of engaging it, I devote two class sessions to recent debates about positive image as a theoretical concept. To fully engage students, I have one group defend the concept and one group critique it during the first session. This pro-and-con format generates some highly creative responses. Eventually, the class agrees that the concept is both a reductionist idea and a misleading strategy. A crucial element is missing, however—what Stuart Hall calls the "politics of representation."[21]

In a follow-up session, to move the class beyond single-minded image analysis, I assign Carlos E. Cortés's essay "What Is Maria? What Is Juan? Dilemmas of Analyzing the Chicano Image in U.S. Feature Films." According to Cortés, the history of ethnic film images includes three main areas of research: content analysis—analysis of films as visual texts; control analysis—analysis of the film-making process; and impact analysis—analysis of the influence of films over the audience and vice versa.[22] By shifting the focus from image alone to questions of control and impact, students begin to realize the institutional dimension of media racism and its role in socially controlling society. Eugene Wong's book *On Visual Media Racism,* although somewhat dated, provides students with a powerful case study of how the film industry discriminated against Asian Americans in the past.[23] Wong argues that although the motion picture industry's racism toward Asians had definitive individual and cultural proponents, the institutionalized nature of the industry's racism was particularly humiliating.[24] Specifically, he identifies three industrywide racist practices: role segregation (yellow facing), role stratification, and role delimitation.

But it is Edward Said's theory of "Orientalism" that allows students to make the critical shift from the simplistic notion of imagery to representation in film as a means of political discourse. The concept of Orientalism has become a powerful analytical tool for my class in the study of racial, ethnic, and gender representation in visual media (especially with regard to Asians and North Africans).[25] It raises students' awareness of the relationship between media and power. The class also screens the recently released video of Said's interviews, *On Orientalism,* which contains clips from popular media about demonizing Islam.[26] The concept of Orientalism helps elevate class discussions about racism and colonialism to new intellectual levels, and as the course proceeds students acquire a more sophisticated understanding of the film image or, rather, of the system of representation.

Film and Objectivity

If understanding the dynamics of imagery poses a critical challenge for students in achieving greater visual literacy, the concept of "reality" or "objectivity" is no less complicated. In the so-called television era, most viewers, including students, intuitively believe the camera can never lie. Michael Isenberg, for example, has probed the "myth of the objective camera," which forces students "to take the camera eye as their eye, and [to realize that] the will of the filmmakers constantly impinges on their will."[27] Trinh T. Minh-Ha regards objectivity as the very foundation of representation. As she explains, "In a world where seeing is believing and where the real is equated with the visible (the all-too-visible, the more-visible-than-visible), the human eye and its perfected substitute, the mechanical eye, are at the center of the system of representation."[28]

To expose the facade of the "object-oriented camera," minority filmmakers—especially avant-garde artists—make special efforts to subvert some key elements of mainstream filmmaking (i.e., its "realism"), such as the symbolic order of time and space. They do this especially in documentaries, which allegedly possess a sense of objectivity because of "visible evidence," such as eyewitness interviews. My experience tells me that those avant-garde works probably provide the best means to help students see through the mechanical eye. I often showcase one or two avant-garde films by Asian American women, such as Trinh T. Minh-Ha's *Surname Viet Given Name Nam* (1989), Shu Lea Cheang's *Color Schemes* (1989), and *Memory/All Echo* (1991) based on the late Korean American writer Teresa Cha's influential book *Dictee.* To displace the notion of fixed time in film narrative, Trinh employs various experimental strategies. For example, she intercuts restaged interviews of five Vietnamese women with black-

and-white news footage and photographs that obviously belong to a different time period than the voice-over. Breaking up the spatial logic as it operates in screen and social space, *Color Schemes* is a parody of public space in the United States. Although the setting of the laundromat is "a racially mixed gallery," the wash motif inside the frame of the washing machines symbolizes limited social space for ethnic minorities. As Cheang said in an interview, "When you do a wash you separate whites and colors. The colors are always thrown in together with each other. . . . And that is the power structure that has us fighting each other. This is what the 'soak' cycle was to be about."[29] Both films are difficult and complex works for students to understand. At the first viewing, very few have any ideas about the films' challenges to realism and objectivity. After a screen-by-screen analysis, however, the class begins to understand the provocative issues the films raise about realism. Clearly, this is not the type of issue that would come up naturally in class discussions. I strongly recommend additional class time and more than one viewing of these films.

With careful guidance and attention to details, teachers can prepare students to "read" and evaluate a film's manipulative messages, which may not be obvious initially. Over time, students begin to understand that film is not an objective representation of reality but rather is a director's construct, informed by conscious decisions about the messages the director wants to convey and the emotions he or she wants to evoke in viewers. By the end of such a course, students will no longer innocently submit to the mesmeric power of the screen; they will see film as a text that must be "read" critically and carefully.

Film Style

Because I teach a film-based course in ethnic studies rather than an ethnic studies class that uses film as a visual aid, certain goals are accentuated. One that guides many pedagogical decisions is the emphasis on film style. Films are, after all, works of art, and artistry should be taken as seriously as content in the learning process. In other words, teaching and learning film must involve the study of concrete cinematic elements such as composition, rhythm, pacing, lighting, color, tempo, and symbolism. Film style bears special significance in view of the cultural misreading of minority cinema because a major mainstream critical practice regarding ethnic films is to discount their artistic merits. Ethnic films are generally viewed as history and sociology or as windows to exotic cultures. This culture/art divide trivializes minority artists, their works, and their cultures.[30]

As I am very conscious of legitimacy politics, I choose the films I show in class very carefully, paying equal attention to their thematic and artistic merits. Each film is judged for both its unique cultural and discursive practices, as well as for its complex dialectical relationship with Hollywood narratives and forms.

Based on student input, one of the best films I have shown is Wayne Wang's *Chan Is Missing* (1982). The film's plot is fairly simple. It is a story about two San Francisco Chinatown cabbies searching for Chan Hung, a missing partner who has $4,000 of theirs. Its style contrasts sharply with Hollywood's convention of glossy surface, continuity editing, and "visible style." The movie is noted for its discursive innovations. As a parody of Charlie Chan films, its narrative structure represents a distant departure from the Hollywood norm. Whereas the typical classical Hollywood detective drama is characterized by a relentless narrative acquisition of clues that eventually climax in the solution to the mystery, *Chan Is Missing* offers no solution to Chan Hung's whereabouts. Each clue only raises more questions in viewers' minds. The movie's ending is particularly symbolic. Jo, one of the cabbies, announces in a voice-over, "If this were a TV movie, an important clue would now pop up and clarify everything." No clue leads anywhere, and Chan is never found. Instead, Jo explains that even the search for neat coherence is a Western trait. For those who can "think Chinese," what is not there becomes as meaningful as what is there. Nothing means what it seems to mean. This open-ended plot seems to directly contradict the Charlie Chan mode, where the mystery is always solved. Director Wang put it beautifully: "Asians tend to have a much higher tolerance for ambiguity, and have always historically been able to deal with ambiguity a lot more than so-called Caucasian minds, or Western minds."[31]

Taught with a deliberate eye on style, different-genre films often lead to very different learning processes for students. For example, if my class discussions about *Chan Is Missing* go smoothly, I often encounter strong resistance from students—at least initially—toward experimental films. Used to watching Hollywood narrative dramas, some students find the experience of watching *Memory/All Echo,* for instance, irritating and perplexing, evoking frustration and even anger. It presents a nonlinear narrative and uses various provocative strategies. To begin with, the film form is difficult to define. Multimedia in format—with archival photos, historical narrative, calligraphy, lyrics, and poetry—the film blurs the conventions of genres. Another important technique the director employed involves the "multiplicity of voice," which entails switching constantly from perfect English to Pidgin English with a very strong accent. Its narrative structure is characterized by fragmentation. With its focus on mode of representation rather than a linear story, the narrator's family history is fully embedded in the struggle of decolonization. Even more challenging for students is the narration, with its multilingual references to Greek mythology, French grammar, and Chinese calligraphy. The Chinese characters, which thematically outline the film's plot—and are not translated into English— subvert students' normal reading and viewing experience. For the majority (occasionally, one or two students read Chinese), knowing just English is suddenly insufficient to comprehend the film's meaning. This can be disconcerting for some, in that they become "outsiders" for the first time in the classroom setting.

Indeed, the film poses a serious problem of acceptance. Some students, who are used to slick, action-packed Hollywood productions, easily dismiss this low-budget independent film as poor in quality. Others who have been articulate throughout the semester suddenly fall silent. To turn the discussion around, I ask students this critical question about positioning and power in representation: If we feel challenged by the screening situation, where does the discomfort come from? A lively and sophisticated discussion follows. An intriguing discovery can be made when students compare a chapter of the book *Dictee* with the film and realize there is a serious purpose behind the provocative techniques. Neither the writer nor the director is playing with the techniques for their own sake. Feminist, Marxist, and Postmodern in perspective, the film conveys important messages about colonialism, patriarchy, language, and a system of representation by using techniques that upset our expectations about what makes a good film.

In-depth discussions about cinematic tensions augment a film experience. These discussions often inspire students and transform the classroom into a rigorous and exciting learning environment for all involved. What is more, this attention to film style promotes students' critical thinking skills. Thus, with a little prodding, I believe students can be given the tools they need to confront critically the increasingly visual American culture.

NOTES

1. Barbara Abrash and Catherine Egan, eds., *Mediating History: The Map Guide to Independent Video by and About African American, Asian American, Latino, and Native American People* (New York: New York University Press, 1992), 3.

2. Ellen Summerfield, *Crossing Cultures Through Film* (Yarmouth, ME: Intercultural Press, 1993), 25.

3. Carlos E. Cortés, "Empowerment Through Media Literacy: A Multicultural Approach," in *Empowerment Through Multicultural Education,* ed. Christine E. Sleeter (Albany: State University of New York Press, 1991), 143–157.

4. Ibid., 147.

5. Paul S. Cowen, "A Social-Cognitive Approach to Ethnicity in Films," in *Unspeakable Images: Ethnicity and the American Cinema,* ed. Lester Friedman (Urbana: University of Illinois Press, 1991), 353.

6. Robert Stam, "Bakhtin, Polyphony, and Ethnic/Racial Representation," in *Unspeakable Images,* 251–276.

7. Ibid., 258.

8. Both tapes are available from Media Education Foundation, 26 Center Street, Northampton, MA 01060.

9. Beverly Daniel Tatum, "Talking About Race, Learning About Racism: The Application of Racial Identity Development Theory in the Class," *Harvard Educational Review* 62, 1 (1992): 5.

10. Haile Gerima, "Triangular Cinema, Breaking Toys, and Dinknesh vs. Lucy," in *Questions of Third Cinema,* ed. Jim Pines and Paul Willemen (London: British Film Institute, 1989), 65.

11. John Bodnar, "The Memory Debates: An Introduction," in his *Remaking America* (Princeton: Princeton University Press, 1992), 13–20.

12. Ibid., 14.

13. See "*Sa-I-Gu*'s Dai Sil Kim-Gibson and Elaine H. Kim," *International Documentary* 12, 8 (September 1993): 1.

14. Thomas Kochman, *Black and White Styles in Conflict* (Chicago: University of Chicago Press, 1981), 18.

15. See Inez A. Heath, "The Social Studies Video Project: A Holistic Approach for Teaching Linguistically and Culturally Diverse Students," *Social Studies* 87, 3 (May-June 1996): 106–112.

16. Quoted in Laverne Miller, "Teaching Visual Literacy With Films and Video, 'the Moving Image,'" *Educational Media International* 31, 1 (March 1994): 58.

17. John O'Connor, *Image as Artifact: The Historical Analysis of Film and Television* (Malabar, FL: Robert T. Krieger, 1990), 302–324.

18. I. C. Jarvie, *Movies and Society* (New York: Basic, 1970), 5.

19. bell hooks, *Black Looks: Race and Representation* (Boston: South End, 1992), 4.

20. Robert Stam and Louise Spence, "Colonialism, Racism, and Representation: An Introduction," in *Movies and Methods: An Anthology,* ed. Bill Nichols (Berkeley: University of California Press, 1976), 639.

21. Stuart Hall, "What Is This 'Black' in Black Popular Culture," in *Representing Blackness Issues in Film and Video,* ed. Valerie Smith (New Brunswick: Rutgers University Press, 1997), 131.

22. Carlos E. Cortés, "What Is Maria? What Is Juan? Dilemmas of Analyzing the Chicano Image in U.S. Feature Films," in *Chicano and Film: Essays on Chicano Representation and Resistance,* ed. Chon A. Noriega (New York: Garland, 1992), 83–104.

23. Eugene Wong, *On Visual Media Racism: Asians in American Motion Pictures* (New York: Arno, 1978).

24. Ibid., 1–55.

25. Edward Said, *Orientalism* (New York: Pantheon, 1978).

26. The video can be ordered from the Media Education Foundation, 26 Center Street, Northampton, MA 01060.

27. Michael Isenberg, "The Historian and the Myth of the 'Objective Camera': A Critique of Film Reality," *Teaching History* 1, 1 (spring 1976): 7.

28. Trinh T. Minh-Ha, *When the Moon Waxes Red: Representation, Gender and Cultural Politics* (New York: Routledge, 1991), 192.

29. Shu Lea Cheang, "Color Schemes: *CineVue* Interviews Video Artist Shu Lea Cheang," *CineVue* 4, 1 (March 1989): 5.

30. For details about legitimacy politics and cultural marginalization, see Jun Xing, "Marginal Cinema and White Criticism," in Xing's *Asian America Through the Lens: History, Representations and Identity* (Walnut Creek, CA: AltaMira, 1998), 175–198.

31. Diane Mei Lin Mark, "Interview With Wayne Wang," in her *Chan Is Missing* (Honolulu: Bamboo Ridge, 1984), 112.

PART II
REPRESENTING RACIALIZED COMMUNITIES

3

VIDEO CONSTRUCTIONS OF ASIAN AMERICA
Teaching *Monterey's Boat People*

MALCOLM COLLIER AND LANE RYO HIRABAYASHI

TOWARD AN ACTIVE APPROACH TO DOCUMENTARY VIDEOS

In our combined experience, which entails thirty-five years teaching Asian American and ethnic studies at the university level, we have found that many presenters' use of video documentaries is surprisingly casual. Rather than as-sume that an audience will "get what they need" by themselves out of a given program, which is passive pedagogy, instructors must think through what issues are important and develop relevant techniques to lead students into critical analysis of the production. This will both generate a more viable learning expe-rience from video documentaries and encourage and develop "visual literacy" as an integral part of visual media pedagogy.[1] To the extent that we are able to accomplish this, we will be providing an important intellectual service to our students and to other audiences.[2]

A version of this chapter originally appeared in *The Review of Education/Pedagogy/Cultural Studies,* vol. 21, no. 1 (1999 © Overseas Publishers Association, N.V.) and is reprinted with permission from Gordon and Breach Publishers.

This chapter offers ideas concerning uses of video and film in undergraduate courses in Asian American studies. We focus on the 1982 production *Monterey's Boat People* by Spencer Nakasako and Vincent DiGirolamo, although the basic approach we outline here could be extended to a host of similar productions.[3] Using this example thus helps to illustrate our general approach: (1) finding, accessing, previewing, and studying suitable audiovisual programs; (2) carefully assessing the relative strengths and weaknesses of these programs; and (3) conceptualizing how a given program fits into the curriculum—especially in terms of how it could contribute to the development of students' critical thinking skills.[4]

TEACHING ASIAN AMERICAN STUDIES

We believe passionately in the importance of teaching students and members of the larger public the essential patterns of Asian American history and contemporary experience. Not only do most students lack both historical perspective and any coherent grasp of present-day realities, but generally speaking, they are rarely exposed to even the most basic facts regarding Asians in the continental United States, Hawaii, and Alaska—let alone in the global diaspora, past or present.

We have found, however, that, although students may be greatly impressed by this "new" knowledge, it is not always easy to define instructional means to ensure that they actually gain and retain a reasonable understanding of Asian American experiences and issues, people and places, events and patterns. We see visual media as one means to help generate initial interest and obtain a fuller understanding and retention of the material we present to our students. Moreover, good visual media bring course content out of the realm of words and abstractions and into the arena of real people through whom students can make more personalized intellectual and emotional connections to course material. We have found that course content becomes more interesting to students when we link it to their own lives. The more effective this linkage, the more relevant the course is to them and the stronger their investment is in the class.

MONTEREY'S BOAT PEOPLE

Our discussion is framed around *Monterey's Boat People* because, although it is a fairly old production, it covers both historical and contemporary periods and encompasses the experience of several Asian American groups. (It is also easier to find a wider range of published resources to supplement an "older" production, which is important pedagogically, as we will illustrate later.) We will first synopsize the program and then outline some specific purposes and goals in utilizing this program in our courses. We also present some insights that, once considered, make the presentation of this video program in Asian American and ethnic studies courses more useful and the details of its usage applicable to other visual media productions.

From *Monterey's Boat People* by Spencer Nakasako and Vincent DiGirolamo

The film/video *Monterey's Boat People* was released in 1982. It is thirty minutes long, an ideal length for classroom use. It was co-produced by the Japanese American filmmaker Spencer Nakasako and Vincent DiGirolamo, then a Ph.D. candidate in American history at Princeton University. Both men were born and raised in Monterey, a fact that enhances the quality of the film. The film was well received upon its release, winning a Red Ribbon at the American Film Festival and a "finalist" status at the U.S. Film and Video Festival. The program is distributed on video and has been purchased by many university-level media services units across the United States.[5]

The focus of the program is the conflict between established Euro-American fishermen and entrepreneurs, who control the fishing industries in Monterey Bay, and Vietnamese refugees who are trying to enter and survive in this competitive field. The natural beauty of the bay and the surrounding region contrasts with the harsh criticism and violence the Vietnamese must endure to compete and survive. We hear from the beginning of the film the various complaints of the Euro-American fishermen: that because the Vietnamese do not speak good English and are seen as not knowing the system (i.e., the proper rules and fishing etiquette), they are unwanted and unwelcome; that the gill nets the Vietnamese fishermen use indiscriminately destroy the local marine life; that Vietnamese are overfishing the area generally, thus ruining the fishery for other folks who have been there for generations. We are also shown that because the wholesaling of fish is tightly controlled, the Vietnamese fishermen have difficulty selling their catch and at times encounter restrictions in unloading their boats.[6]

Beyond this, the film is especially significant and useful because of its historical contextualization of this contemporary confrontation. Nakasako and DiGirolamo utilize a combination of historical photographs, interviews with participants and specialists on the regional history of the bay, and narrative to establish, first, that Asians have long been involved in the bay's fishing industry and, second, that Asians endured discriminatory treatment as early as the nineteenth century as other fishermen in Monterey tried to force them out of business.

Nakasako and DiGirolamo draw from Sandy Lydon's research to document Chinese immigrants' establishment of a number of innovative and lucrative pursuits in the region, including what was to become a thriving fishing industry. Specifically, the Chinese pioneers fished a range of species not previously commercially exploited. They sold locally but also dried and shipped products back to China.[7] The film also examines the arrival of Japanese pioneers, who played a major role in California's fishing industry and made many innovative contributions, which in the Monterey area included abalone diving.

The film specifically documents the prejudice and discrimination that first the Chinese and then the Japanese suffered in Monterey. Multiple laws were passed to block open participation by both Asian groups in the fishing and processing industries, including an "anti-alien" restriction that granted fishing rights only to U.S. citizens (and those "eligible for naturalization"). Legislation prohibited certain fishing techniques, certain kinds and sizes of boats, and so forth. Eventually, both Chinese and Japanese were driven from the fishing professions in the area.

USES OF *MONTEREY'S BOAT PEOPLE*

Monterey's Boat People appeals to many of our students. Although sometimes bothered by the on location rather than studio sound quality of the film and despite the fact that the historical and more recent conflicts the film portrays are cruel, if not brutal, students still respond positively on a variety of levels. Some students are intrigued because they have visited the Monterey Bay region. Many are surprised to learn that some early Chinese families came intact on boats across the Pacific, thus complicating easy and conventional images of a universal "bachelor" society. Students are also interested to discover that a sizable Chinese fishing community lived practically on the site of one of the area's main contemporary attractions—the Monterey Aquarium.[8] This piece of history is all the more important because, as in most locales where Chinese ingenuity and labor were critical to the development of the economy, no visible reminder is seen at that site today of a Chinese presence or of Chinese immigrant contributions. Sometimes we ask students to ponder why this is the case, as well as what the implications for "race relations" might be if such information were readily available in schools or at the sites in question. In short, we consciously draw upon these kinds of initial interests and perceptions in stimulating classroom discussions.

Our experience indicates that a viewing/study guide handed out the session before showing the film can be very useful. A well-prepared guide will serve as an introduction to the program and provide students with an indication of what they should be looking for. Since most documentary films are multifaceted and complex, a single viewing does not normally allow students to catch all of the details. If time permits, we break students into discussion groups after the screening so they can share information and compare notes.

Questions we have posed in study guides for *Monterey's Boat People* include:

1. Why do many Vietnamese fishermen use the size boat and fishing techniques they do? How does this affect their efforts to make a decent living?
2. How do these fishermen raise the money to purchase a boat?
3. What is the Vietnamese fishermen's primary "catch" in the Monterey Bay, and why?
4. What can we say about how these fishermen sell their catch, including what they must often do to transport and market it?

5. Is anything mentioned about the role of women in the Vietnamese fishermen's families' domestic economies?
6. Why are some of the Euro-American fishermen shown in the film so critical of the Vietnamese fishermen?
7. Why do other Euro-Americans defend the Vietnamese?
8. To what extent do the Vietnamese fishermen seem to resist oppression by organizing themselves and fighting for their rights?

Beyond generating viable answers to these specific questions, however, a number of historical and contextual points need to be covered to make the best possible use of this film in the classroom. Although these points may complicate the use of the production, we suggest that it is important for students to learn that reality is not always simple.

From time to time expert fishermen or environmentally informed students may raise questions about the monofilament gill nets the Vietnamese fishermen utilize. Sometimes they agree with those in the film who censure the environmental impact of these nets. It is advisable to approach this issue with caution. In point of fact, these nets can be very destructive to marine life. We have found it useful to make several points regarding this question.

First, despite the impression given in the film, the use of gill nets on the California coast long predates the arrival of the Vietnamese. Gillnetting is a very old and widespread form of fishing limited historically by the use of natural fibers to make the nets. These fibers made the nets relatively expensive to make and maintain and also fairly bulky, thereby limiting the size of nets. The modern invention of cheap, mass-produced nylon nets changed this situation, making it possible for large nets to be set from fairly small vessels. The Vietnamese started fishing in Monterey Bay at a time when people were just beginning to recognize the ramifications of this technological change.

Second, students need to clearly recognize that the Vietnamese used gill nets because of their economic and social circumstances. They were restricted to small vessels by law because they were not yet citizens.[9] Moreover, as refugees they had very little capital, again limiting them to small vessels and low-cost technology. Finally, most other types of commercial fishing—all of which require more capital and larger vessels—were fully exploited by Euro-American fishermen, providing few alternatives to the Vietnamese who wished to apply skills brought from Vietnam to their efforts to survive in the United States. These points are raised in the film, so questions posed to the class can allow students to bring these factors up in discussion.

It is also important to point out that Euro-American fishermen have also used gill nets and that other destructive fishing techniques have not been subject to the same hostile criticism. For example, the use of trawls—another type of net that is dragged along the ocean floor, destroying much of what lies in its path—was common in the region. This technology, which required larger vessels and was strictly in the domain of Euro-American fisherman, is not criticized by those in the film who accuse the Vietnamese of environmental destruction. Likewise, the film mentions the destruction of the anchovy fishery in Monterey Bay by Italian American fishermen. This collapse of an entire fish species was the result of overfishing made possible by the development of a particular type of net. Yet Italian American fishermen were never targeted as a group for being environmentally destructive. Students can be asked to explore whether the hostility facing Vietnamese fishermen involved their techniques alone or evolved from "racialized" attitudes and discourse.[10]

A related point the instructor can raise involves climatic and environmental changes. Unbeknownst to the fishermen or the filmmakers at the time of this production, the Pacific was entering a period of shifts in temperatures, currents, and other factors. This phenomenon of weather and other natural occurrences came to be commonly referred to as *El Niño*. By itself, El Niño is now known to have dramatically impacted marine life in the eastern Pacific during the time the film covers. Indeed, shortly after the period depicted in the film, the squid catch in Monterey Bay was virtually depleted. Other environmental changes, including pollution and reduced water flows brought on by water diversions, have affected the California marine environment in ways still not fully understood. Set within the context of this new information, the comments of one fisherman in *Monterey's Boat People*, who complains about the drop in his crab catch and angrily blames the Vietnamese for "overexploiting" the fisheries and ruining the industry, appear in a new light. Of course, "scapegoating" is unfortunately an old theme in Asian American history. Using *Monterey's Boat People*, we can encourage students to consider the overall dynamic between ethnic and racial scapegoating during periods of local and national economic crisis and the social solidarity anti-Asian sentiments and activities have generated among members of the dominant society in the past.[11]

In addition, we have had success with library-based assignments related to this production. For example, students can tap into a range of interesting secondary sources to get a broader sense of Chinese pioneers' contributions to the Monterey Bay and other California fisheries.[12] This can be supplemented by research on Chinese fishing in other areas and on Japanese and Filipino contributions to the fishing industry both generally and regionally, as well as in terms of niches (tuna, for example, on the part of Japanese), techniques (live bait chumming, pole fishing), and the division of domestic labor (extended fishing voyages for Issei men, canning work for Issei women), and so forth.[13]

Another useful assignment involves drawing from local California newspapers to document racist harassment during the 1980s. Vietnamese fishermen from Moss Landing on the Monterey Bay were shot at, for example, and others' boats were sabotaged and even sunk.[14] Students can research how fishing violations by different groups are reported in the press and determine if any pattern exists in the way news reports label people racially or in ethnic terms.[15]

If nationally representative newspapers are available on microfilm, students can also find comparative information about the harassment of Vietnamese fishermen in other states, such as Texas and Florida, and the interethnic conflicts that sometimes exploded into violence in places such as Seadrift or Galveston Bay, Texas. Students may also use the library and other sources to determine what happened regarding Vietnamese fishermen and gill netting subsequent to the time of the film. This research could involve examination of newspapers, magazines, and, in California, state documents and legislative records.[16]

Students can do research on resistance by Vietnamese fishermen, particularly since this topic is not fully addressed in the film because key incidences of resistance did not emerge until some years after *Monterey's Boat People* was released. At one level this resistance took the form of formal associations such as the Vietnamese Fishermen's Association of America, which was organized to monitor and defend fishermen's rights. Resistance also involved lawsuits such as the Vietnamese fishermen's complaint about the U.S. Coast Guard's selective enforcement of the Jones Act—legislation that dated back to the late 1700s.[17]

Students may also be interested in researching the case in Seadrift, Texas, in which a local Vietnamese fishing association, along with some independent fishermen, attempted to sue the local Ku Klux Klan to get the group to stop its harassment.[18] Also notable is the fact that the Asian American Law Caucus took up the cause and helped the Vietnamese fishermen in California win media attention and educate the public about racial discrimination while also providing them with formal legal counsel. In addition, the point should be made that resistance is a key (and somewhat neglected) theme that runs through the history of Asians in America. Certainly, Chinese and Japanese fishermen resisted during the nineteenth and early twentieth centuries, but their ability to do so was limited because they were "aliens ineligible for U.S. citizenship," and their resources were fairly limited. The Vietnamese, by contrast, have had more legal options, predicated by their right to naturalization—a right not universally available to other Asian immigrants until 1952.

FURTHER CONSIDERATIONS

Beyond addressing the specific questions the study guide raises, this production works so well in the classroom because clear continuities exist among the experiences of the three racial groups—Chinese, Japanese, and Vietnamese—despite the clear differences in cultural origins, times of arrival in the United States, and the fact that they explored somewhat different niches within the fishing industry. This is one of the essential broad messages students in Asian American courses should receive and ponder.

These continuities are especially useful in engaging Southeast Asian students when covering Asian American history. They may commonly feel a lack of direct connection to earlier periods of Asian American history. And if the course does not include substantial coverage of the post-1975 period, they may feel completely left out. One of the beautiful aspects of *Monterey's Boat People* is that it makes an explicit and undeniable link between the experiences of two key pre–World War II immigrant groups, who made their living on boats in the Monterey Bay, and post-1975 Southeast Asian refugee fishermen, who often made their precarious escape by boat and who now struggle to make a living in the United States fishing off small boats in the same bay. Southeast Asian students can better conceptualize through their compatriots depicted in the program how aspects of the Southeast Asian experience in the United States fit directly into larger patterns of oppression pertaining to Asian American and American history.

Through additional questions or open-ended discussions, students can also be asked to define the economic strategies followed successively by Chinese, Japanese, and Vietnamese American fishermen, thus providing a starting point for discussion of the widespread development of economic niches by Asian Americans in the past and present as a means for economic survival. Another socioeconomic discussion the film can elicit concerns the transferability of skills in the immigrant experience. The film provides evidence of how three different groups of Asian American immigrants have attempted to apply prior knowledge and skills toward the struggle for economic survival in their new surroundings. These cases can be the basis for students providing other examples of how people have or have not been able to use prior skills and what factors have encouraged or limited their ability to do so. This is a crucial aspect of immigrant experience, past and present. This discussion may be expanded to include the role of families and communities as economic bases, the importance and limitations of ethnic enclave economies, the impact of lack of capital and English-language skills on economic options, and the economic, social, and emotional benefits, costs, and limitations of all of these factors for individuals and communities.

The film also explicitly examines the hostile, racialized reactions that may be encountered when Asian Americans begin to successfully develop an economic niche. The film thus provides an opportunity to introduce concepts such as "institutional racism," especially as it impacts Vietnamese refugees' economic and occupational pursuits today. Most significant, by the end of the film and discussion, most students have formulated a clear picture of the larger historical situation: that the Asians, past and present, who have attempted to make a living fishing in the Monterey Bay have been systematically prevented from engaging in fair and open competition; that racialization and discriminatory legislation have been key mechanisms Euro-Americans have utilized to block competitors; that in this sense the Vietnamese fishermen face a pattern whose features were established in the late nineteenth century and that has continued, in one form or another, to the present. Furthermore, although conditions have greatly changed, a deeper understanding of the Vietnamese fishermen's aspirations, conditions, and struggles is reached by learning about the Asian groups who preceded them into the area and the industry.

With some preparation, students can examine the film and associated materials or assignments for differences in the experiences of the three groups. In this way the film can serve simultaneously as a vehicle for the exploration of both continuity and distinctiveness. In this chapter, however, we concentrate on the larger patterns because the film provides such a strong basis for that discussion.

CONCLUSION

We emphasize again that to be most effective, instructors and presenters need to fully conceptualize why and how to use audiovisual programs in curricula. We are convinced that this is a far better pedagogical approach than merely allowing students to view a film or video passively, letting them come to their own conclusions—which we may also falsely assume will be the same as ours. If used conscientiously in the classroom, audiovisual materials can and should be a vehicle for promoting visual literacy and critical thinking for students and instructors alike.

We do not pretend, however, that this is all there is to "teach" from Nakasako and DiGirolamo's production. Many interesting economic patterns in the film are evident enough to be glossed by the instructor or researched by students if time and interest permit.[19]

We also have no problem with the point that, like any other documentary production, *Monterey's Boat People* is a construct and can be "deconstructed" as such. In fact, much discussion could focus on how and why Nakasako and DiGirolamo have selected and framed things as they have, as well as whether these are the "best" choices that could have been made methodologically, historically, aesthetically, or otherwise. With more advanced students we might even raise the more significant issue of what is possibly lost versus what is possibly gained when we, as advocates of Asian American and ethnic studies, construct a perspective on *Monterey's Boat People* that does in fact emphasize the commonalities and continuities among the Chinese, Japanese, and Vietnamese American experiences in Monterey. This is an important issue to consider, since our commitment to such a construction of "commonalities" may blind us to the discontinuities and significant disjunctures that also need to be seriously considered from both intellectual and political standpoints.[20]

In the final analysis, we think such exploration is integral to the continued growth of the field of Asian American studies. We also think it would be valuable to have an ongoing forum in which instructors could contribute to a body of pedagogically oriented work so that we can systematically explore the use of media to strengthen our efforts to teach effectively about the Asian American experience and thus about the American experience, whether in their historical or contemporary manifestations.

NOTES

1. For information about "visual literacy," see Martha Day, "Promoting Visual Literacy: The Forgotten Art of Critical Viewing," in *Proceedings of the Consortium of College and University Media Centers* from the 1993 spring conference "Catch the Edge," April 16–18, 1993, Boulder, Colorado. Many critics have examined popular media images and stereotypes of Asian Americans, including Eugene R. Wong, *On Visual Media Racism: Asians in the American Motion Pictures* (New York: Arno, 1977); many contributors to an anthology edited by Russell Leong, *Moving the Image: Independent Asian Pacific Media Arts* (Los Angeles: Asian American Studies Center and Visual Communications, Southern California Asian American Studies Center, 1991); and Thomas K. Nakayama, "Show/Down Time: Race, Gender, Sexuality, and Popular Culture," *Critical Studies in Mass Communications* 11 (1994): 162–179.

2. In this context we hope to promote more research into the pedagogical use of media in Asian American studies courses; at the same time, we recommend a critical self-consciousness concerning our motives as we do so. Contributions to an anthology edited by Elizabeth Ellsworth and Marianne H. Whatley, *The Ideology of Images in Educational Media: Hidden Curriculums in the Classroom* (New York: Teachers College Press, 1990), are worth considering in this regard, especially the chapter by Barbara Erdman, "The Closely Guided Viewer: Form, Style, and Teaching in the Educational Film," 27–43.

3. Surprisingly little literature is available on the pedagogical uses of documentary programs in Asian American studies classes. One publication, Renee Tajima, ed., *The Anthology of Asian Pacific American Film and Video* (New York: Third World Newsreel, n.d., circa 1984), 20, offers brief suggestions for showing such programs to community-based organizations.

4. Many of these ideas emerged during discussions the authors had at San Francisco State University while teaching Asian American Studies 200, "Introduction to Asian American History," and Ethnic Studies 220, "Asians in America," two lower-division survey courses on Asian American history and contemporary circumstances, respectively. The department typically offered multiple sections of these courses as part of a larger number of course offerings in any given term. In this setting instructors had to become more conscious of the use of films and videos because many students might have seen particular productions before in other classes. This concern became sufficiently serious that it was raised for discussion at faculty meetings. The general consensus was that it was not necessarily "bad" for students to see a given program two or three times across the overall curriculum as long as (1) instructors made it clear how the production connected to the particular concerns of each course, and (2) instructors provided the students with viewing directions that would address that particular focus.

5. *Monterey's Boat People* is available for rental or purchase from the National Asian American Telecommunications Association, 346 Ninth Street, Second Floor, San Francisco, CA 94103, (415) 863-0814.

6. Further information is available in the U.S. Commission on Civil Rights report, *Recent Activities Against Citizens and Residents of Asian Descent,* Clearinghouse Publication 88 (Washington, DC: U.S. Government Printing Office, 1987), 52. The publication includes details about the fact that eventually, because the Vietnamese fishermen at Moss Landing could not obtain access to extant facilities, they petitioned for construction of an additional public off-loading facility.

7. Much of this is discussed in the film. Additional information can be found in the award-winning book by Sandy Lydon, *Chinese Gold: The Chinese in the Monterey Bay Region* (Capitola, CA: Capitola, 1985). Of special interest, a documentary film by Geoffrey Dunn and Mark Schwartz was developed in part on the basis of Lydon's research; it is also titled *Chinese Gold.*

8. Potential users of this film may need to make sure their students do not confuse the town of Monterey on Monterey Bay (on the central California coast) with the incorporated (and heavily Chinese American) suburb east of downtown Los Angeles known as Monterey Park.

9. This law, which dates back to the 1790s, was apparently enforced differentially by the U.S. Coast Guard. See the U.S. Commission on Civil Rights account, *Civil Rights Issues Facing Asian Americans in the 1990s: A Report of the United States Commission on Civil Rights* (Washington, DC: U.S. Government Printing Office, 1992), 40. Refer also to note 27 in that volume.

10. For an outstanding statement on the dynamics of racialization, see Michael Omi and Howard Winant, *Racial Formation in the United States: From the 1960s to the 1980s* (New York: Routledge and Kegan Paul, 1986).

11. The classic study of such scapegoating is Alexander Saxton, *The Indispensable Enemy: Labor and the Anti-Chinese Movement in California* (Berkeley: University of California Press, 1971).

12. See Thomas W. Chinn and H. Mark Lai, *A History of the Chinese in California: A Syllabus* (San Francisco: Chinese Historical Society of America, 1969); H. Mark Lai and Philip P. Choy, *Outlines: History of the Chinese in America* (San Francisco: Chinese American Studies Planning Group, 1972); and L. Eve Armentrout Ma, "Chinese in California's Fishing Industry, 1850–1941," *California History* 60 (1981): 142–157.

13. For example, see L. Eve Armentrout Ma, "Chinese in Marin County, 1850–1950: A Century of Growth and Decline," *Chinese America: History and Perspectives* (1991): 25–48; Kanishi Stanley Yamashita, "Terminal Island: Ethnography of an Ethnic Community: Its Dissolution and Reorganization to a Non-Spatial Community" (Ph.D. dissertation, Comparative Culture Program, University of California, Irvine, 1985); and the film *Wataridori: Birds of Passage* (1976) distributed by National Asian American Telecommunications Association (includes additional material on Japanese Americans in the California fishing industry, including footage of tuna fishing). Filipino American contributions are surveyed in Fred Cordova, *Filipinos: Forgotten Asian Americans* (Seattle: n.p., 1983), 56–81; also see Chris Friday, *Organizing Asian American Labor: The Pacific Coast Canned-Salmon Industry, 1870–1942* (Philadelphia: Temple University Press, 1994).

14. See Paul D. Starr, "Troubled Waters: Vietnamese Fisherfolk on America's Gulf Coast," *International Migration Review* 15 (1981): 226–227.

15. In fact, reporting was racialized. Arrests of Vietnamese for fishing violations often included headlines about "Vietnamese Fishermen," whereas, for example, a major bust of

men engaged in illegal striped bass fishing (which, incidentally, involved gill nets), in which all the names of the accused were Italian, generated no reference to Italians in either the headline or body of the news article.

16. Gill netting is now banned off much of the California coast, as are certain types of trawling. The number of Vietnamese fishing on Monterey Bay is now about half that at the time the film was made (Prof. C. Chung, Asian American Studies program, San Francisco State University, personal communication, September 1994).

17. See Susan Freinkel, "Livelihoods on the Line: 200-Year-Old Law Unconstitutional, Viet Fishermen Say," *Recorder,* 28 September 1989; for additional details, see the reference cited in note 10.

18. See the U.S. Commission on Civil Rights report cited in note 9, 40–41; notes 130, 131, 134.

19. For example, one colleague, Prof. Ben Kobashigawa, who teaches a similar course at San Francisco State University, has designed an interesting assignment that encourages students to develop and apply an economic/class perspective to the evolving Vietnamese participation in the fishing industry as shown in *Monterey's Boat People.* In one instance Kobashigawa adapts and extends Barrera's model of Chicano labor segmentation by race and class in the Southwest to help students contemplate this dimension of the Vietnamese American fishing industry in Monterey. For Barrera's model, see Mario Barrera, *Race and Class in the Southwest: A Theory of Racial Inequality* (Notre Dame: University of Notre Dame Press, 1979), 212–219.

20. We acknowledge Professors Lon Kurashige and Hien Duc Do, as well as other participants, for their participation in the open-ended panel discussion session, "Teaching Asian American History," at the 11th National Association for Asian American Studies Conference at the University of Michigan, Ann Arbor, 7 April 1994, specifically for raising a similar question in a debate over whether a "pre–World War II/post–World War II" dichotomy is useful in thinking about and teaching Asian American history.

From *Dances With Wolves*, MGM/UA Studios, 1990

4

AMERICAN INDIANS IN FILM
Thematic Contours of Cinematic Colonization

WARD CHURCHILL

in memory of Leah Renae Kelly,
February 19, 1970–June 1, 2000,
film student extraordinaire

Politics is the ability to define a phenomenon and cause it to act in a desired manner.

—Huey P. Newton (1967)

The peoples indigenous to North America have occupied a position of centrality in North American cinema since its inception. This was certainly true of two of the first experimental flickers—*Buck Dancer* and *Serving Rations to the Indian*—in 1898 and no less so of the first significant narrative film crafted by a Euro-American, D. W. Griffith's *The Battle of Elderbush Gulch*, in 1913.[1] As well, it was true of the first docudrama, an epic entitled *The Indian Wars Refought*, produced by the Colonel W. F. (Buffalo Bill) Cody Historical Motion Picture Company a year later.[2] All told, the North American film industry—usually and rather inaccurately referred to as "Hollywood"—has ground out more than 2,000 movies and as many as 10,000 television segments on Indians and Indian themes during the past century.[3]

To be sure, the sheer vastness of output bespeaks the extent to which both the industry and its audience(s) appreciate, whether at a conscious level or more subliminally, the elemental nature of their relationship with/to the first peoples of this land.[4] Nothing, after all, is or could be more foundationally important to all that is now pronounced "American" than the verity that every square centimeter of territory from which "America" has been constructed and

From *The Battle of Elderbush Gulch*, Warner Bros. Studios, 1914

every nickel's worth of the "domestic" resources upon which it subsists have been extracted directly from us.[5] How this came to be, and how we ourselves came to "vanish" in the process, are pivotal questions, the answers to which are definitive of the American Story and thence the American Character.

Unfortunately for those whose task it is to tell it, the story is one a federal judge, when confronted with a fragment of the factual record, proclaimed sufficient to prompt persons of average sensibility to "wretch at the recollection."[6] The implications of this truth for the country's image, self-concept, and self-esteem are so obviously negative, at least from the perspective of those benefiting most tangibly from its creation and consolidation, that it must be veiled, deformed beyond recognition—better yet, completely expunged—through all available means. As Cherokee analyst Jimmie Durham has remarked, "The relationship between Americans and American Indians [is therefore] the most invisible and lied about" of any on the continent.[7]

From *The Battle of Elderbush Gulch,* Warner Bros. Studios, 1914

In this endeavor, literature, the press, and institutions of "responsible scholarship" have all played hefty roles.[8] Given the extraordinary and much-remarked potency of cinema/television in shaping consciousness,[9] however, it was perhaps predictable that moving pictures would serve as a disinformational workhorse beginning by some point in the mid-1930s.[10] Indeed no overstatement is embodied in observations that film and video have long since become the key media for articulating the Master Narrative by which North America's elites "explain" their history—and thus themselves—to the world.[11]

It comes as no surprise, then, to discover that virtually without exception Hollywood's massive spew of "Cowboy and Indian" movies has misrepresented the actualities of native cultures, as well as those of the emphatically Euro-derivative settler societies that have taken root and flourished here over the past several centuries, continuously rationalizing, sanitizing, inverting—in other words, systematically falsifying—the nature of the process by which the latter have come to all but completely decimate, dispossess, and dominate the former.[12] Such sins of commission are, moreover, compounded by and completed through the omissions embedded in hundreds—perhaps thousands—of additional films in which Indians are simply deleted from contexts and settings to which we rightly belong.[13] As Durham put it:

> A false history is [thus] supplied as an alibi to cover up the truth, and this alibi in turn informs [American] culture in ways that serve to reinforce its control. . . . The lies are not simply a denial; they constitute a new world, the world in which American culture is located. . . . By invasion, murder, theft, complex denial, alibi, and insignification, American culture gains tremendous (if pathological) psychological power and energy, which draw their strength almost exclusively from their own falseness.[14]

The hegemonic function served by Tinseltown's celluloid fabrications is unmistakable.[15] The dominant society—that is to say, that of the Euro-American settlers—is thereby led to believe, as it desires to do anyway, that realization of its self-anointed "Manifest Destiny" to subjugate all it encounters was/is not only natural, inevitable, and therefore right but, by easy extension, heroic, even noble.[16] In this triumphalist script, native people, who by virtue of our very existence stood in the way of the settlers' mythic evocations of "progress" and "civilization," can only be construed as obstacles, inferior beings consigned by the savagery—or, with more supposed charity, the "tragedy"—of our inherent "backwardness" to the fate of being supplanted and ultimately extinguished by our Euro-derivative "betters."[17]

Consequently, few signs of diseased conscience are evident among those who have always chosen to believe themselves entitled to replace us on our lands; no more need to mourn our "passing" than to regret the draining of a malarial swamp in making way for another golfing community in the south of Florida. To the contrary, such "developments" are typically couched—when they are discussed at all—as a cause for smugness, sanctimony, and celebration.[18] In a still more refined iteration, reality is reshaped, repackaged, and re-presented to the "viewing"—or "reading" or "voting"—public as if neither we nor the swamp had ever "truly" been here in the first place.[19] That which never really was, of course, need never be accounted for, either psychically or materially.

Freed almost entirely by this construction from the potential for instability-inducing cognitive dissonance any candid acknowledgment of historical factuality might unleash within the body politic, elite sectors of the settler populace—and this, to be sure, includes the upper echelons of the conglomerates producing the great bulk of North America's cinematic fare—have positioned themselves to pursue their peculiarly expansionist vision in an especially efficient and all-encompassing manner.[20] Of this there can be little better testimony than the fact that over the past century their presumed dominion has transcended first the continent, then the hemisphere—by now becoming unabashedly planetary.[21]

REVERSING THE LENS

Proceeding from the premises that the juxtaposition of Euro- to Native North America comprises the bedrock sociopolitical and economic relationship(s) of the continent and that movies and television have become the ingredient most indispensable to masking or denying the character of those relations,[22] it stands to reason that certain modes of cinematic analysis offer unparalleled opportunities to forge a genuinely counterhegemonic discourse and resultant liberatory consciousness. It is in fact possible at this juncture to craft an entire pedagogy in which film critique forms the curricular core.[23]

By this I do not mean an orthodox film studies approach, devoted to instilling "visual literacy" and exploring cinemagraphic technique—although such things are undeniably interesting and can at times be useful in their own right—but rather the kinds of interrogation and (re)interpretation of factual and thematic content increasingly evident over the past twenty years or so by bell hooks, Jun Xing, S. Elizabeth Bird, Ed Guerrero, Gina Marchette, Ella Shohat, Robert Stam, Jacqueline Kilpatrick, Ralph and Natasha Friar, Jimmie Durham, Richard Slotkin, and others.[24] The objective of such scholarship remains what it has been since its inception: a reversal of the lens, scrutinizing and unraveling the codes of disunderstanding embedded in simulations of sign and signifier in such ways as to transform them from "reel to real."[25]

For this to happen—with respect to portrayals of Native North America no less than of other Others[26]—the films selected for viewing must be subjected to a process of immanent critique. That is, as Max Horkheimer once put it, "to confront the existent, in its historical context, with the claim of its historical principles, in order to realize the relationship between the two and transcend them."[27] Taking the films viewed as "the existent" and "the claim [of their] historical principles" as explication of the phenomena depicted, apprehension of "historical context" can be seen as the methodological crux upon which attainment of transcendent (liberatory) understanding (consciousness) is contingent.[28]

Initially, the questions posed must concern the degree to which a given depiction embodies an accurate historicization of its subject matter and, to the degree that it may be discernibly inaccurate, the nature of the inaccuracies involved. The latter aspect must be approached comprehensively and with great precision, thereby forming a basis for the question of what interests are served by presentation of specific factual misrepresentations in the film(s). This in turn sets the stage for the question of whether the treatment(s) under consideration are in some sense anomalous or is/are instead emblematic of a broader stream of films incorporating similar or even identical distortions (as in, "How many anomalies are required to comprise a norm?").[29]

The more consistently the latter can be shown to be the case, the less plausible established apologetics about "inadvertency" and "literary license" begin to appear and the more acute the question about service of interest becomes.[30] The answer, ultimately and somewhat self-evidently, can emerge only from the kind of careful probing of the current socioeconomic-political order to which many people—especially but by no means exclusively those of "mainstream" (settler) background—are highly resistant in other contexts.[31] The perception of linkages between the historical and the topical is thereby facilitated at a highly concrete level of cognizance (i.e., the "reel" starts to become "real").

Such things cannot be accomplished, of course, simply by watching and discussing the technical or aesthetic merits of movies. The successful deconstruction of any hegemonic discourse demands a (re)construction among listeners, readers, and viewers of a knowledge base adequate to the purpose. As concerns assessment of the biases and inadequacies ingrained in Hollywood's Cowboy and Indian fantasy, those engaged in critique are thus required to be (or become) functionally conversant with the subject matters depicted. Considerable textual investigation of the historical events and personalities ostensibly portrayed on-screen is therefore essential.[32] The same can be said of related areas of inquiry—law, for example[33]—by which the relevant historical circumstances were and are informed. This is where some truly serious work comes in.

As students who have participated in my American Indians in Film classes will undoubtedly attest, it often takes a half-dozen hours or more to plow through the contextual material assigned in preparation for viewing a single movie. In addition, recommendations for still further reading are all but invariably generated by way of dispelling ongoing confusions and misperceptions revealed during postscreening discussion. Almost nothing I assign or recommend focuses on film per se. In my experience teaching the course mostly to undergraduates over the past decade, students, although frequently startled and occasionally disgruntled at the outset by my approach, usually end up finding it to have provided an overwhelmingly positive learning experience.[34]

ESTABLISHING AN ANALYTICAL FRAMEWORK

The sheer volume of primary material upon which one might base a course on American Indians in film seems in many respects daunting, even overwhelming. It would in principle be possible to teach it every semester for a century, screening a different work during every class session, without exhausting the presently available inventory of titles. This in itself can be used to advantage in framing the ongoing significance of native people to the American self-concept, both in terms of the gross emphasis that has so obviously been placed on us in the country's cinematic discourse and because the gigantic corpus of material all but inevitably subdivides itself into an array of overlapping but discrete thematic packages (stereotypes and tropes), ceaselessly reiterated.

The implications of this latter characteristic of the genre can be readily discerned in Nazi propaganda minister Josef Goebbels's famous observation that the more regularly a lie is repeated, the more plausible it is likely to appear.[35] On the other hand, as "postcolonial" theorist Homi Bhabha has noted, the very compulsiveness with which certain lies are repeated can reveal not only the degree of their falsity but the extent to which their authors understand them to be false.[36] According to analyst Bart Moore-Gilbert:

> "The Other Question" begins by observing the dependence of colonial
> discourse on concepts of "fixity" in its representation of the unchanging
> identity of subject peoples (as examples, the stereotypes of the "lustful Turk"
> or the "noble savage" . . . the "wily Oriental" or the "untrustworthy servant").
> However, for Bhabha there is a curiously contradictory effect in the economy
> of stereotype, insofar as what is supposedly already known must be endlessly
> reconfirmed through repetition. For Bhabha, this suggests that the "already
> known" is not as securely established as the currency and the rhetorical power
> of the stereotype might imply.[37]

Goebbels's and Bhabha's points alike are illustrated and confirmed by Hollywood's avalanche of Cowboy and Indian movies. In this it is entirely unnecessary—or undesirable, in that doing so opens one to accusations of setting up a straw man—to dwell upon the thousands of serials and otherwise indisputably shoddy epics with which most studio inventories are laden, although it is sometimes useful to screen a B movie or two as a means of exploring the ways in which the worst merely reflect the "best."[38] Selecting primarily—or only—the aesthetically finest fare the genre has to offer and grouping the films both chronologically and thematically, it is easily possible to demonstrate that, irrespective of the steadily evolving artistic and technical proficiency with which the films have been delivered, they are designed and intended to convey more or less precisely the same "messages" now that they were at the outset. The effect is to show that "the better they get" aesthetically, "the worse the movies become" in terms of their capacity to impart and sustain untruths of the most fundamental and calculated sort.

The question of intentionality bound up in the last sentence tends to generate considerable and at times vociferous debate among students. Here the focal points of controversy emerge as being whether much or even most of the disinformation at issue has not resulted from some majestic and essentially uniform "ignorance" among several generations of Euro-American filmmakers and, thus, whether the apparent thematic homogeneity of the films is not really a matter of "accident" rather than conscious design.[39] Once again, the movies themselves can be allowed to carry the weight in resolving such issues.

As concerns ignorance—here used for all practical intents and purposes as a synonym for "innocence"—there are a number of approaches to clarification. An obvious choice concerns elaboration of John Ford's long record of acknowledgments that he was fully aware that he was deforming both historical fact and popular impression by staging all of his "Indian" films in Monument Valley.[40] This couples well with King Vidor's admission during an interview conducted for the PBS series *Images of Indians* that he had deliberately distorted history in the making of *Northwest Passage* (1940).[41] Shifting to the current moment, there is the matter of the much-celebrated "exhaustive historical research" conducted by Bruce Beresford in the making of *Black Robe* (1991), a film that nonetheless perpetuates virtually every imaginable stereotype.[42] A capstone can, I have found, be placed upon the whole by juxtaposing Michael Apted's documentary *Incident at Oglala* (1992) to his commercial depiction of exactly the same subject matter in *Thunderheart* (1992). In the documentary, which was shot first but released belatedly and with the expectation that it would be viewed by a relatively restricted audience, he presents the facts fairly accurately;[43] in the commercial release, meant for mass viewership, he presents them in an altogether different fashion.

Usually, the idea of directorial ignorance—or innocence—has been thoroughly dispensed with by this point. Interestingly, the notion that the films' thematic unities result from accident or "coincidence" rather than conscious design is simultaneously abated, most often without direct discussion. To reinforce this newfound consensus of understanding among students, however, it is nonetheless helpful to briefly examine the economics and attendant management and oversight procedures entailed in studio production, with an emphasis on how little is actually left to chance in the corporatized mode of filmmaking that has increasingly prevailed since the early 1930s.[44]

As icing on the proverbial cake, the laws of probability can be deployed to devastatingly good effect: if mere happenstance explained anything with respect to the topic at hand, one could be confident to a mathematical certainty that at least one of the thousands of films on the Hollywood roster would have had to have reversed altogether the polarities of value imbedded in orthodox cinematic depictions of natives and settlers. The offer of an "A" for the course to any student who can find any such film has invariably proved sufficient to lay the matter to rest once and for all (there has yet to be a taker).[45]

Thus denied the convenience of dismissing—or even mitigating—the situation as something that in reality it is not, students instead have to decide whether they approve or disapprove of what in fact it is. Although I have personally encountered none prepared to attempt a defense on outright ideological grounds, a distinct minority have sought to evade the implications of their own conclusion(s) by resort to a line of argument—essentially a verbatim regurgitation of the studios' own tired prevarication on such matters—peculiarly circular in its logic. The first half of this contortion assigns a purely economic motive to the phenomenon, that "no one would want to watch" movies offering "alternative" interpretations of native-settler relations, thereby rendering them box office flops.[46] The second half holds that the studios produce what they do in response to popular demand because "that's what people want to see."

Asking which people—Indians, for example?—generally brings such polemics to abrupt pause. The question of how, since none have ever been placed in distribution, the studios—much less student polemicists—could possibly know whether "people" would pay to see genuinely alternative interpretations of American history is met with silence.[47] Equally unanswered go queries as to how "what the public wants" might have been determined, since "the public" has never really been offered the least choice in the matter. (It is one thing to note that Cowboy and Indian movies affirm the settler populace in what it already wishes to believe about itself and its Others, quite another to contend that it is unwilling to or incapable of entertaining other outlooks.[48])

This leaves things at the level of debates concerning those prerogatives supposedly attending an "artistic license" enjoyed by filmmakers. Here arguments typically devolve upon propositions that "everyone knows" movies are fictions—dramatic fantasies, to be precise—and that it is therefore "unfair" to assess films in the same sense that one assesses works of ostensible nonfiction.[49] The subtext to such contentions is, of course, that those taking cinema to be a conveyer of literal fact are at best "fools," themselves responsible for whatever misperceptions—or delusions—they incur.

Such premises begin to break down the moment someone introduces the fact that generations of children—none of whom might reasonably be expected to exercise the sort of critical discernment at issue—have grown up on movies and TV segments, much of it especially developed for their consumption.[50] This opens the door to examine how the tropes and stereotypes evident in "kiddie films" like Walt Disney's *Tonka* (1958) and *Pocahontas* (1995) parallel—or prefigure—those embodied in "adult" cinema, thus conditioning an insidious sort of receptivity to conflations of fact and fantasy among child viewers as and after they reach maturity.[51]

From there it is easy enough to demonstrate how Hollywood's fetishizing of "authenticity"—Bruce Beresford's going to extravagant lengths to ensure the exact correctitude of nail heads visible on the walls of a reconstructed French settlement appearing in the opening scenes of *Black Robe* presents a salient recent illustration[52]—is implicitly designed to consolidate such confusion among preconditioned adults. An even better example, at least to the extent that it is blatantly explicit, concerns director Elliot Silverstein's enlisting no less than the Smithsonian Institution—that quasi-official arbiter of all things historically and

From *A Man Called Horse,*
Paramount Studios, 1970

anthropologically "true" in the United States—to provide a scroll at the beginning of *A Man Called Horse* (1970) in which the film is pronounced "the most accurate and authentic ever made."[53]

Add to this the prideful declamations of numerous directors that they believe their work to have surpassed the traditional theatrical goal of leading audiences into a temporary "suspension of disbelief," instead imparting to viewers a lasting sense of having witnessed—or vicariously experienced—"history as it really was."[54] In substance, the "history" served up in the Cowboy and Indian movies is intended, expressly so, to be received as something vastly more "real" than history itself. Conversely, the objective—long since avowedly achieved—has been to convert popular conceptions of history into fantasy. Whichever way it is viewed, the magical line reputedly dividing art from its antithesis has been purposefully dissolved by the "artists" themselves, and with it has gone their pretensions to enjoy the license thereof.[55]

It follows as an unavoidable conclusion that Hollywood's filmmakers should in every respect be as much subject to the methods of assessment—and as accountable to concomitant standards of factuality—as are the historians, anthropologists, and other more "scholarly" types whose material they have so enthusiastically assimilated, reformulated, and to a noticeable extent supplanted in the public mind.[56] Arguing to the contrary under the circumstances described in this section—or brought out in corresponding class discussions—is to be actively complicit in a sophistry the film industry has been allowed to perpetrate for far too long.

THEMATIC CONTOURS

With the analytical underbrush thus cleared away, it is possible to proceed fairly rapidly in tracing the contours of the thematic packages in which Hollywood has consistently delivered its misrepresentations of American Indians to the settler population, thereby misrepresenting both the settlers and the countries they have crafted to the settlers themselves.[57] As with the number of available films, the range of potential emphases and orientations is far too broad to be encompassed within the constraints of a single course (or this chapter). Fortunately, focusing on only a handful of the major thematic elements has proven sufficient to achieve the desired results, allowing students time not only to delve into both the mechanics and the implications involved at an appreciable depth but to explore—and thereby, it is hoped, avoid—a few of the theoretical pitfalls that have lately resulted from "progressive" attempts to explain the meaning of it all.[58]

What follows is a sampling of the topics framed and investigated in my course—drawn mostly from the earlier-mentioned PBS series *Images of Indians,* which I use as a kickoff to each semester—and a synthesis of the perspectives elicited therefrom. In each case the films employed for illustrative purposes are specified, and the readings assigned or recommended are included in my annotation.

THOSE BLOODTHIRSTY HORDES

Probably the most enduring myth of Americana concerns attacks by "hordes" of "Bloodthirsty Savages" bent upon the "Massacre" of "Peaceful Settlers" (always white). Sometimes the savages succeed, albeit temporarily. In other variations "the Army" arrives at the last and most desperate moment to save the day. In still others the army is deployed as a substitute for the settlers, some portion of it being defeated—and thus, by definition, "massacred"—in the course of "Civilization's" final, inevitable, and triumphant victory over "Savagism," thereby allowing the beginning of a "New and Better Day for All Mankind."[59] Regardless of its particular construction, the unfolding plot invariably requires that the audience receive the deaths of settlers or their military surrogates with solemnity, a sense of loss, even grief, whereas the eventual vanquishment—"vanishment," really—of the savage "Red Men" is greeted with jubilation.[60]

The "historical" scenario is, to be sure, utterly dehistoricized. It is as if the settlers had always been here, struggling valiantly to "Tame" a "Vacant Wilderness," the natives brutally alien interlopers or a peculiarly vicious form of wildlife whose sole existential purpose is to obstruct "Progress"—that is, the settlers' attainment of "That Which Is Rightfully Theirs" (a phrase used to signify "all" and "everything")—in almost inconceivably horrific ways.[61] Thus constructed, the settlers' actions, no matter how extreme, are invariably justified and therefore heroic. Correspondingly, the fate of the natives, because of their innate and immutable "Cruelty" and "Aggression," is deserved; "They brought it on themselves," as the saying goes.[62] The Indians receiving their "Just Desserts" can—or must—be seen from this contrived viewpoint as cause if not to openly celebrate, then at least to experience a deep feeling of smug satisfaction that "Things Worked Out for the Best."[63]

Casting templates for cinematic iterations of this diametrical reversal of victim and victimizer appears to have been one of filmdom's first priorities, given that they materialize in both Griffith's *Battle of Elderbush Gulch* and the Cody Company's *Indian Wars Refought*. In *Elderbush Gulch* we find an archetype of the "Friendly Settler Family" besieged in their cabin by an equally archetypal band of mindless—or, in this case, seemingly drug-crazed[64]—savages, only to be saved at the last instant by the arrival of the third archetype, a troop of cavalry in full charge. To signal both the imminence and the magnitude of the peril settlers faced in the moments before the soldiers' timely appearance, Griffith also established another trope—"You Know What They Do to White Women, Don't You?" (discussed later)—by having the brother of heroine Lillian Gish prepare to use his last bullet to spare her "A Fate Worse Than Death" at the hands of their attackers.[65]

For its part, *Indian Wars*—which purported to be a literal reenactment of the 1890 "Battle" of Wounded Knee, where the 7th U.S. Cavalry Regiment used Hotchkiss machine guns and point-blank execution methods to slaughter around 350 defenseless Lakota prisoners: infants, children, women, and mostly elderly men[66]—portrayed the "Well-Intentioned" soldiers as attacked without provocation and nearly overwhelmed by an inexplicably but nonetheless homicidally enraged mass of howling "Warriors." To authenticate this putrid bilge—worthy of comparison to the worst material produced by Goebbels's propaganda ministry a generation later[67]—the Cody Company enlisted an endorsement of its accuracy from a much-acclaimed real-life "Indian Fighter," General Nelson A. Miles.[68]

There is no difficulty demonstrating an unbroken pattern of equally breathtaking historical distortions employed by Hollywood right up to the present, all of them plainly intended to valorize the settlers—especially soldiers—while demonizing their hopelessly outnumbered and outgunned victims.[69] Useful illustrations will be found in John Ford's classic "Cavalry Trilogy"—*Fort Apache* (1948), *She Wore a Yellow Ribbon* (1949) and *Rio Grande* (1950)—as when, in *She Wore a Yellow Ribbon*, "Hollywood's Old Master" invented a vast military alliance of literally every indigenous people of the Great Plains and Southwest regions to make the Indians seem properly "menacing," their executioners possessed of the requisite heroism.[70]

In many ways the crystallization of what Hollywood had so consistently in mind can be apprehended in its mythic treatment of Lt. Colonel George Armstrong Custer—a brevet major general who insisted subordinates address him by his honorary rather than his actual rank—described by his most reputable biographer as "a vainglorious . . . self-serving . . . unscrupulous . . . glory-seeking thug . . . all too willing to sacrifice his men, the truth or whatever else came to hand in furthering his own ambitions."[71] Although Custer's solitary significant "victory" over native people was the slaughter of a village full of noncombatant Cheyennes along the Washita River in November 1868[72] and his only claim to lasting fame came through a sensational blunder that cost him and 250 men under his command their lives at the Little Big Horn in June 1876,[73] Tinseltown unhesitatingly enshrined him as a "Cavalier in Buckskin."[74]

Although several earlier films were devoted to this purpose, the epitome was Rauol Walsh's *They Died With Their Boots On* (1941), starring the handsomely dashing Errol Flynn—angelically backlit in several scenes—as Custer (the real man, for all his posturing, was a big-nosed, balding, chinless wonder). Lending his hero a needed aura of moral fiber necessitated that the director deform history far more drastically than in mere cosmetics, of course. "The General" is presented as "a soldier's soldier," with no hint he was court-martialed and temporarily cashiered in 1867 for deserting his command in the field.[75] He is made out to be a champion of the Lakotas' treaty rights to the Black Hills, when he was in fact the officer most immediately responsible for violating those rights.[76] He is portrayed as trying desperately to prevent an "Indian War" in 1876, whereas the record plainly shows him to have been among its most eager advocates.[77]

Finally, Walsh depicts Custer—the war he had sought so strenuously to avoid nonetheless thrust upon him—nobly and knowingly sacrificing himself and his beloved troopers to save "the Frontier" from desolation at the hands of the usual bloodthirsty horde of savages. In actuality, Custer willfully disobeyed orders in a mad scramble to engage in what he erroneously believed would be a "turkey-shoot" sort of butchery akin to that in which he had indulged at the Washita. The motive underpinning his disastrous insubordination appears to have been sheer self-interest: a belief that another such "single-handed triumph" would propel him into the White House.[78]

Were *They Died With Their Boots On* the culmination of an early Hollywood trend or in any way anomalous, it might in itself be unworthy of the attention paid here. Dozens of movies subsequently, however, took the same tack. These were by no means confined to the 1940–1960 "Heyday of the Western."[79] Even Hollywood's so-called Protest Era during the late 1960s–early 1970s saw release of Richard Siodmak's big-budget extravaganza *Custer of the*

From *Little Big Man,* Paramount Studios, 1970

West (1967), a film adding up to little more than a poorly edited rehash of Walsh's quarter-century-old "classic." A 1991 made-for-TV production, *Son of the Morning Star,* constitutes Custerania's most recent cinematic representative.[80]

So central had the Custer figure become in cinematic efforts to nourish and sustain the thematic ingredients of *The Indian Wars Refought* that by 1970

From *Little Big Man*, Paramout Studios, 1970

the "revisionist" (or "protest") westerns making their initial appearance featured it with similar prominence. In these films—notably Arthur Penn's *Little Big Man* and Ralph Nelson's *Soldier Blue*—he was used to the same effect in an opposite fashion.[81] Whereas movies like Walsh's and Siodmak's were crudely celebratory of the processes their "Custers" were intended to represent, the traumatic effects on public consciousness of America's ongoing butchery in Southeast Asia—analogous in too many respects to the "Indian Wars"[82]—made it necessary for filmmakers like Penn and Nelson to utilize their own versions of "the General" to let everyone else off the figurative hook.

Consequently, in both *Little Big Man* and *Soldier Blue,* "Custer"[83] is portrayed in psychopathic terms—that is, as definitionally and decisively deviant from the sociopsychological norm—a manipulation allowing the norm itself to be represented as a stark contrast. The latter is accomplished through introduction of a "Good Settler"[84]—Dustin Hoffman's "Jack Crabbe" character in *Little Big Man,* Peter Strauss's "Honus Gant" and Candice Bergen's "Cresta Lee" in *Soldier Blue*—to symbolize the character of Euro-American society as a whole. In that manner, the ugliness of things that by the late 1960s could no longer be either denied or ennobled—My Lai, for instance, and the earlier massacres at places like the Washita (reenacted with considerable accuracy in *Little Big Man*) and Sand Creek (reenacted in *Soldier Blue*)[85]—is simultaneously acknowledged and assigned status as a phenomenon unreflective of Euro-America's "real" values and social mores.

In effect, "['explaining'] genocide by attributing it to the whims of a few unbalanced people, i.e., General Custer" exonerates the settler-state system of responsibility for the very processes on which its founding and expansion have been most absolutely dependent.[86] Concerning the "morale" of the settlers in a more individuated sense, they are led to feel righteously "appalled" by the carefully fragmented and thoroughly decontextualized glimpses of holocaustal reality appearing on-screen and thereby are absolved of it as well. After all, insofar as they "disapprove"—the sole requirement—they are empowered to imagine themselves signified by the "alternative" embodied in the equally imaginary Crabbe and Gant and Cresta Lee. This in itself positions them in their own minds to assume a place among "the Innocent" vis-à-vis what has occurred—and is thus *occurring*—even as they wallow in the benefits accruing from it.[87]

The thematic modifications pioneered in the revisionist flicks of thirty years ago have been steadily refined in such epics as Kevin Costner's *Dances With Wolves* (1990) and Michael Mann's subtly radical revamping of *Last of the Mohicans* (1992).[88] A still wider and more sustained audience has been attracted to television series such as *Dr. Quinn, Medicine Woman*—the top-rated TV program of the 1992–1993 season—advancing very much the same formulation.[89] By the time *Black Robe* was released, it had become possible to replace Errol Flynn's Custer with a missionary priest played by an equally appealing Lothaire Bluteau and for reviewers to resultingly adduce that, whatever its "wrongheadedness," the sweep of European conquest in North America was ultimately prompted by "love [of humanity], nothing else," adding up—of course—to "nothing less than sheer nobility."[90]

From *Dr. Quinn, Medicine Woman*, Twentieth Century Fox, 1993

The more things seem to change, the more the appearance sometimes merely disguises the fact that they have never changed at all. Lending just the right touch of symbological consistency to the movies throughout this somewhat protracted transformity in the codes of settler valorization have been those fabled hordes of howling savages, still as bloodthirsty today as they were a

From *Dances With Wolves*, MGM/UA Studios, 1990

hundred years ago: in *Dances With Wolves* there is the perpetually scowling Cherokee actor Wes Studi with his gaggle of mindlessly malevolent "Pawnees"; in *Last of the Mohicans* Studi returns, scowl and all, this time to head up a herd of demonic "Hurons"; *Black Robe* offers up an exquisitely sadistic—one is tempted to say "Inquisitional"—swarm of "Mohawk" torturers to imperil Bluteau's heroic Father LaForge.[91]

All told, it's enough—as it was always meant to be—to make even the most "wrongheaded" and otherwise flawed settlers seem, if not of uniform saintliness, then at least always "understandable" in contrast to the incomprehensibly merciless inhumanity of the Others they are compelled by circumstance to confront. In the end, the settlers have "no choice" but to "defend themselves"— sometimes, admittedly and regrettably, to the sort of "excess" born of their inherent "human frailties." Indians must thus be seen—as much now as through the lens of the Cody Company in 1914—to have precipitated our own fate(s), if not always by our actions, then surely by the inexcusable brutishness of our very "nature(s)."[92]

THE UNSPEAKABLE OTHER

As should be apparent, a simple substitution of victims for victimizers has been inadequate in itself to "explain" the near-total eradication of Native North Americans by 1890.[93] Pleas of "self-defense" hardly seem plausible when it comes to butchering babies, after all. It has therefore been essential that the indigenous victims of settler aggression be not only recast as aggressors—à la *The Indian Wars Refought*—but completely dehumanized in the bargain. Not infrequently, the process has been extended to the point of depicting Indians as a form of vermin or insect life—characterizations identical in every respect to SS potentate Heinrich Himmler's notorious comparison of the Nazis' extermination of Jews and Gypsies to "delousing."[94]

Most (in)famously, the Euro-American correlate to Himmler's pronouncement came on 28 November 1864 when Colonel John M. Chivington instructed his 3rd Colorado Volunteer Cavalry Regiment to systematically slaughter native infants at Sand Creek on the premise that "nits make lice."[95] The expression of such sentiments was anything but isolated, however, with comparable statements being recorded as far back as 1677[96] and attributable to many of the most distinguished "humanitarians" in American settler history.[97] Further, at one point or another it was the policy of every state among the U.S. "Lower 48" and the eastern provinces of Canada to pay a bounty similar to that offered on wolves and other "predatory beasts" for the scalps of American Indians of any age and either sex.[98]

For what are undoubtedly obvious reasons, Hollywood has encountered considerable difficulty finding a satisfactory method of visualizing native people at a sufficiently degraded level. One of the more effective solutions was that developed by John Ford for his benchmark western *Stagecoach* (1939), wherein "Apaches" are always lurking somewhere just over the horizon, never glimpsed until the final few minutes of the film. By carefully orchestrating settler dialogue and relying on viewers' imaginations to take over from there—filling in the visual blanks far more convincingly than his cameras ever could—Ford was able to inculcate an astonishing sense of dread among his audiences long before a darkly shadowed, grimly visaged, and altogether silent "Geronimo" finally makes his momentary appearance.[99]

Although often employed with respect to Indians, the technique has been most broadly applied by the makers of sci-fi and horror movies, in which the "monsters" are routinely withheld from view until very late and sometimes never seen at all.[100] At other times the "Indian-Monster" equation was established by the cruder expedient of simply casting a famous cinematic movie monster as an Indian: *Dracula*'s Bella Lugosi, for example, in the first version of *Last of the Mohicans* (1922) or *Frankenstein*'s Boris Karloff in Cecil B. DeMille's *The Unconquered* (1947).[101] "Wolfman" Lon Chaney was similarly cast for several B movies—most notably *The Long Rifle* (1964) as well as a late 1950s CBS-TV series called *Hawkeye and the Last of the Mohicans*.[102]

Probably the simultaneously most refined and concerted iteration of Hollywood's dehumanizing vernacular came in *The Stalking Moon* (1969), when director Robert Mulligan defined Indians in terms of a single "Apache" bestowed with the name "Salvaje"—literally "Savage" in Spanish—who, in keeping with Ford's *Stagecoach* formula, is withheld from view for almost the entire film. The requisite air of supernatural inhumanity is lent this unseen presence by tracing his route across Arizona and New Mexico—he is supposedly stalking the movie's stars, Gregory Peck and Eva Marie Sainte, the entire time—along the astonishingly large trail of corpses he single-handedly leaves in his wake. When the "killing machine" is at last "revealed," it is only—but repeatedly—as a shadowy, faceless shape cloaked in a bearskin, stunning in its relentless ferocity.[103]

At its most blatant, as in John Huston's *The Unforgiven* (1960), the recipe leads to descriptions of Indians—or, more accurately, Indian "blood"—as "filth." In such framing there is absolute clarity to the Manichean distinction drawn between "men" on the one hand and Indians—or "red niggers," as we are more often called in the Alan LeMay novel upon which Huston based his film[104]—on the other. This in turn imbues even the most frankly genocidal utterances of the movie's settler characters—for example, "I say to you, they must be cleansed from the face of this Earth! Where one drop of their blood is found, it must be destroyed! For that is man's most sacred trust, before Almighty God!"—with an aura of implicit reasonability.[105]

Although the implications attending the cinematic trope of Indians as "Unspeakable Others" tend in many ways to speak for themselves, it is nonetheless worthwhile to hammer home the point that they are by no means unique within settler consciousness. This can be accomplished in part by a brief survey of the dehumanizing and exterminatory thematics bound up in Anglophile literary depictions of Native North Americans since at least as early as John Smith's

1612 tract *A Map of Virginia*.[106] Further insight can be gleaned from examining instances where the sensibilities reflected in such material have "bled" into Euro-America's collective fantasies concerning an array of non-Indian racial Others.[107]

In this last connection it is often sufficient to focus on the contents and immense popularity of the "Yellow Peril" literature of the late nineteenth–early twentieth centuries, exemplified in Jack London's "The Unparalleled Invasion," a 1910 short story in which the author openly dreams of establishing an "Aryan utopia" by eradicating in its entirety the "swarming" population of China. The means selected to achieve this lofty goal consist of first introducing among them "scores of plagues . . . every infectious form of death," then summarily executing "all survivors . . . wherever found."[108] An interesting cinematic corollary will be found in D. W. Griffith's *The Flying Torpedo* (1916) in which futuristic weapons are used to destroy vast legions of "yellow men from the East." At this juncture there is usually no need to offer further comparisons to Nazi rhetoric and ideology.[109] Any lingering doubts as to whether a "Genocidal Mentality" is involved have been thoroughly retired.[110]

You Know What They Do to White Women, Don't You?

As mentioned earlier, one of the most dramatic moments in the seminal *Battle of Elderbush Gulch* occurred when Griffith directed that one of his celluloid settler-heroes prepare to put his last bullet through the head of the film's white heroine lest she fall alive into the hands of a group of Indians about to overrun the settlers' beleaguered cabin.[111] More than three decades later, John Ford used an identical plot device in the much-celebrated *Stagecoach*—indeed, it was virtually the same scene—to even more sensational effect. Fifteen years later still, in *Winchester '73* (1950), at a moment when the pair is surrounded by Indians and running short on ammunition, director Anthony Mann had his white heroine explain to the movie's settler-hero that she understood "about the last bullet."[112] In *Fort Massacre* (1958), the settler-hero's wife actually follows through, killing not only herself but her two children in the face of capture by the dread "Apaches."

The motive, although left delicately unstated in each of these films—and hundreds of others—was voiced in a question another trooper put to Honus Gant during the opening scenes of *Soldier Blue*: "You know what Indians do to women, don't you?" The matter is further clarified in *Chato's Land* (1972), when the movie's settler-hero restates the query: "Did you ever see what Indians do when they get a white woman?" Perchance anyone missed the point, Candice Bergen, playing Cresta Lee in *Soldier Blue,* informs a horrified Gant after they have been captured by "hostiles" that she will, as a consequence, be raped. Indeed, as a cavalry officer matter-of-factly explains in *The Gatling Gun* (1972), all any female settler taken captive by Indians has "to look forward to is rape and murder."[113]

From *Stagecoach,* Warner Studios, 1939

Punctuation to this "truth" was provided by director Robert Aldridge in *Ulzana's Raid* (1972) through portrayal of a white woman as having been raped into a state of drooling insanity by the usual horde of marauding "Apaches." Actually, the victim was "lucky," according to the movie's settler-hero, a veteran scout played by Burt Lancaster, because, he confides to the audience, such captives "are usually raped to death."[114] Given such circumstances, there can be little wonder why filmdom's gentle settler sex is forever putting a gun to its head—or having its stronger male counterparts do the deed for them[115]—whenever a random Indian man wanders near.

A model for the overwhelming traumatic effects supposedly suffered by fair-haired females subjected to "ravages by savages"[116] had been established by the inimitable John Ford in his Academy Award–nominated 1956 "masterpiece" *The Searchers,* perhaps the most grotesquely twisted depiction ever made of the psychosexual dynamics marking native-settler interaction. In this "landmark of the genre," Ford's settler-hero, played by John Wayne—who had also starred in *Stagecoach* and all three films of the Cavalry Trilogy—spends virtually his entire stint on-screen, a period ostensibly covering about fifteen years, re-

From *The Unforgiven*, MGM/UA Video, 1960

lentlessly tracking a band of Comanches who had abducted his niece (a child at the outset).[117]

After a while, as the little girl may be assumed to have reached maturity, Wayne's purpose has clearly evolved from simply wreaking vengeance on the Indians to also killing the niece, thus freeing her from the unutterable indignities she has suffered by being mated to "Red Vermin" (the effects of which are insinuated graphically during a scene in which he encounters a pair of female captives "recovered" by the U.S. Army; both have been driven to stark madness by their experience, prompting Wayne to proclaim them no longer "white").[118] At the last moment, however, the hero reveals the true depth of his nobility by sparing the young woman, "reclaiming" her despite her spoliation and thus, it is implied, empowering her to live happily ever after.[119]

65

From *The Unforgiven*, MGM/UA Video, 1960

The Searchers—both Ford's cinematic iteration and the Alan LeMay novel on which the film was based[120]—concern themselves with "reinterpreting" the famous case of Cynthia Ann Parker, a nine-year-old taken during an 1836 raid by Quahadi Comanches against encroaching settlers in west Texas. The real Cynthia Ann was

From *The Unforgiven*, MGM/UA Video, 1960

raised as a Comanche and eventually married Pina Nacona, a noted Quahadi leader, bearing him a daughter and two sons (including the major symbol of Comanche resistance known as Quannah Parker[121]). After being "freed" by a group of Texans, including her uncles, in 1860—Pina was killed in the process—she repeatedly ran away, seeking to rejoin the Quahadis. Finally, confined to her room to prevent further escape attempts, she "wasted away [and] died of a broken heart" (i.e., starved herself to death rather than live among settlers).[122]

The Parker example is in many respects emblematic of a much larger whole. No less than Benjamin Franklin is known to have lamented during the 1750s

From *The Searchers*, Warner Studios, 1956

that "when white persons of either sex have been taken prisoners by the Indians, and lived a while among them, tho' ransomed by their Friends, and treated with all imaginable tenderness to prevail with them to stay among the English, yet in a Short time they become disgusted with our manner of life . . . and take the first good Opportunity of escaping again into the Woods, from thence there is no reclaiming them."[123] Overall:

> Although most of the returned captives did not try to escape, the emotional torment caused by separation from their adopted families deeply impressed the colonists. . . . "Some, who could not make their escape, clung to their savage acquaintance at parting, and continued many days in bitter lamentations, even refusing sustenance." Children "cried as if they would die when they were presented to [their self-described 'rescuers']." With only small exaggeration an observer . . . could report that "every captive left the Indians with regret."[124]

The principle applied as much to adult females as to men and children. Even the more celebrated "captive narratives" produced by women such as

From *Blood on the Arrow*, Allied Artists Pictures Corporation, 1964

Mary Rowlandson (1682) flatly denied that their "chastity" had been threatened,[125] whereas less acclaimed tracts—that of Isabella McCoy (1747), for instance—went so far as to assert that the treatment accorded the authors by settler society was far worse than anything they had experienced at the hands of Indians.[126] Ultimately, as Richard Drinnon, Richard Slotkin, and others have noted, it was left for "Puritan Fathers" like Cotton Mather to invent the "violence pornography" of native rapists finalized during the mid-twentieth century by Hollywood "masculinists" of the Ford-Aldridge school[127] and subsequently adapted as an element of the "groundbreaking feminist scholarship" practiced by Susan Brownmiller.[128]

Tellingly, although a paucity of evidence suggests that rape was common among any Native North American people[129]—by all indications it was virtually nonexistent among the strikingly "prudish" Apaches[130]—there is a veritable mountain of documentation concerning settlers raping us as an ubiquitous historical reality.[131] Indeed, as was lately demonstrated in revelations of the endemic and sustained sexual predation suffered by the roughly half of all native children consigned to Canadian residential schools after 1900—and undoubtedly those lodged in U.S. facilities as well—the ugly pattern extended well into the 1980s.[132] Suffice it to observe that Hollywood has yet to release a single film devoted to the wholesale rape of native women captured by settlers, much less the institutionalized molestation of American Indian youngsters of both sexes as recently as twenty years ago.[133]

Nor, for that matter, have Brownmiller's mainstream—that is, "Western" or "Euro-"—feminist heirs offered appreciably better. To the contrary, following their mentor's astonishing conversion of Eldridge Cleaver's emphatic repudiation of the supposed liberatory signification embodied in transracial rape into an "advocacy" or "glorification" of it,[134] many Euro-feminists have embraced the mythic sexual aggression assigned men of color in the colonial master narrative as if it were a historical given.[135] Seizing upon the contemporary panorama of psychosexual dysfunctions inculcated among American Indians by such traumas as the residential school experience—rather than upon the nature and predictable effects of the experience itself[136]—they have consistently "read it back" in time as if such maladies had always been integral to native societies.[137] This in turn has positioned them to advance a theoretical foreclosure on the "nationalist" efforts of indigenous people to resume a self-determining existence on the basis that these would be inherently "phallocentric" and thus would "do violence to women."[138]

From there Euro-feminism, in subscribing to such notions, entitles itself to speak for the Others incarnated in its darker sisters by denouncing the "sexism" with which it imbues its simulations of traditional non-Western cultures,[139] its adherents thus replacing their masculinist counterparts in the reconstitution of a cornerstone rationalization of Euro-supremacism: the hallowed "civilizing" narrative of a "moral imperative" upon which basis, as Gayatri Spivak has described it, "white [wo]men [are forever] saving brown women from brown men."[140] This, to be sure, is but a short step from a final occlusion in which Euro-feminists substitute themselves for the oppressed altogether; that is, in imagining themselves as objects of the modes of rape delineated earlier, they reconfigure "herstory" in terms of their having been perpetual victims of the very racially and culturally Othered males most heavily damaged by processes of colonialism and racial subjugation in which white women are historically and currently complicit.[141]

The circle is thus both seamless and complete. The fervor with which settlers of every stripe cling to the fable of "Indians as Rapists" forces them into an overarching conceptual compact that dissolves the ideological divisions normally distinguishing those of the left from their right-wing opponents: anarchists from yuppies, say, or the Jerry Falwell–Pat Robertson school of reactionary clergymen from radical feminists like Robin Morgan. One is hard-pressed to account for this other than as a need, desperate to the point of neurosis and often deeply sublimated—manifested by those buying in to secure at least some semblance of justification for the prevailing socioeconomic and political order (i.e., "the Patriarchy," "the Hierarchy," or whatever else it might more fashionably be called).[142]

To the extent that this is so, the otherwise bizarre consensus can—indeed, must—be viewed as integral to what George Lipsitz has denominated "the possessive investment in whiteness," a process functioning both to the material advantage of investors and—in some ways far more decisively—affording them the delusional psychic luxury of believing themselves to be not only "part of the group in charge" but "naturally" entitled to such exalted standing.[143] For all the theoretical sophistry with which it has been recently adorned, the story is as old and as unsavory as Euro-supremacism—which is to say, European and Euro-derivative forms of imperial domination—itself.[144]

Still more explicitly, it can be seen—especially when combined with the tropes discussed in the previous subsections—as serving essentially the same purpose in contemporary North American settler society as did the myths of "Jewish Blood Rituals" and *The Protocols of the Elders of Zion* in Germany during the interwar period.[145] If a major functional distinction can be drawn, it is that the Nazis deployed their monstrous fiction(s) to engender acceptance of incipient genocide among Germans while the North American equivalents are peddled to quell potential qualms among a populace in whose name genocide has already been perpetrated. Subtextually, the messages are identical: the victims, by some especially egregious victimization of their victimizers, got—or are getting or will surely get—"what's coming to them," nothing more; so "under the circumstances" there is really "nothing to feel guilty about."[146]

In the Spirit of Gunga Din

With this groundwork laid, it would be possible to rapidly investigate several other constructions—characterizations of homosexuality within indigenous cultures, for instance,[147] or the Pocahontas-like attraction to white men all native women allegedly evince,[148] or the evils supposedly accruing through miscegenation[149]—clustered within the thematic package devolving upon questions of gender and sexuality. As mentioned earlier, however, time constraints tend to preclude thorough consideration of more than one construct per course, and so it is best that we move along to another topic.

A question always arising, often repetitively and long before analysis of the first three packages has been completed, is whether cinematic depictions of American Indians have really been so monolithically negative as our focus has made it appear. The answer is that they have not, but this in itself opens to scrutiny the elements from which a "Good Indian" is composed by Hollywood and the nature of the image implanted thereby in the public consciousness.

Here one might be tempted to simply repeat the (in)famous 1869 declaration of General Phil Sheridan to the effect that "the only good Indian is a dead one"[150] while pointing out that many scores of thousands of native people have been slaughtered on-screen over the years.[151] This in itself would be true enough, but the matter is a bit more complicated.

The template for another sort of Good Indian was established by novelist James Fenimore Cooper in his "Leatherstocking Tales"—*The Pioneers, The Last of the Mohicans, The Deerslayer, The Prairie,* and *The Pathfinder*—during the first half of the nineteenth century.[152] This took the form of a character dubbed "Chingachgook," supposedly the last surviving member of his people,[153] who, in the words of Cherokee analyst Rayna Green, "acts as a friend to the white man, offering . . . aid, rescue and spiritual and physical comfort even at the cost of his own life or status and comfort in his own [nation] to do so. He saves white men from 'bad' Indians and thus becomes a 'good' Indian."[154]

Or, to follow Canadian author Daniel Francis, Cooper's notion of a "good Indian is one who stands shoulder to shoulder" with whites in their "settlement" of North America, serving as "loyal friends and allies" to the invaders.[155] It was, concludes Robert S. Tilton, "their antiquated, stoic acceptance" of their own presumed inferiority to the settlers and, consequently, of "their individual fate and the ultimate demise of their people[s] that endeared these noble savages to whites."[156] In other words, the Cooperian concoction was/is designed to foster an emotionally satisfying sense among settlers that an indigenous seal of approval had been affixed upon the obliteration of Native North America.

So great has been the contemporary resonance of this formula that *The Last of the Mohicans* alone has been produced as a feature film on three occasions (precursors to the earlier-mentioned 1992 version were made in 1920 and 1936). *The Pathfinder* hit the big screen twice (1952 and 1996), and *The Deerslayer* has seen production both as a feature film (1957) and as a television series (1957–1958).[157] In addition, certain archetypal characters deployed in Cooper's novels—not only the Good Indian represented by Chingachgook but his settler "brother," the "Man Who Knows Indians" embodied in Natty Bumppo (otherwise known as "Hawkeye" to whites, "the Deerslayer" to native people)[158]—have been adapted to countless other skits on both big screen and small.

Undoubtedly, the figures most indelibly imprinted on the American consciousness in this respect remain the Lone Ranger and "Tonto, his faithful Indian companion" ("Tonto" is a Spanish word meaning "dunce," "fool," or "dolt"). Created in Zane Grey's best-selling 1915 novel *The Lone Ranger: A Romance of the Border,* the dynamic duo inhabited an extremely popular radio program broadcast weekly from 1933 onward. By 1938 they were also appearing regularly in movie theaters, as Hollywood serialized them in Saturday matinee fare. Their first feature film was released under the title *Hi-Ho Silver* in 1940 (remade in 1956), followed by such epics as *The Lone Ranger* (1956,

From *The Half-Breed*, RKO Radio Pictures, Inc., 1952

remade in 1981) and *The Lone Ranger and the City of Gold* (1958). Meanwhile, beginning in 1948 the concept had been developed into a long-running ABC-TV series.[159] There have been myriad mutations all along, the most recent variation found in the characters of Sully and Cloud Dancing in the pop-feminist CBS-TV series *Dr. Quinn, Medicine Woman.*[160]

At this point it is useful to hammer home the nature of Euro-America's Good Indian stereotype by setting it side by side with that found in the literature of classic colonialism. The best-known example to draw upon is probably that of "Gunga Din," an East Indian invented by Rudyard Kipling during the late nineteenth century in an epic poem of the same name.[161] In Hollywood's version, *Gunga Din* (1939), the subaltern "ennobles" himself by blowing a bugle at the crucial moment, thereby warning a company of British lancers who have "adopted" him that they are riding into a trap set by his kinsmen. In thus saving his lancer "friends" from their fate—that is, their defeat—Din sacrifices his own life along with those of his relatives, consigning his country to a century of British imperial rule. He therefore signifies not just goodness but "heroism" of a sort, not to his own people—they have every reason to consider him a traitor of the worst kind—but to those who subjugate them.[162]

From *They Rode West,* Columbia, 1954

"Good" is, of course, always and most dramatically defined not in terms of idealist affirmation but in opposition to "bad." Hence in establishing the presence of the Good Indian, who—whether embodied as Gunga Din, Chingachgook, Tonto, or Cloud Dancing or, for that matter, as Pocahontas or Sacajawea—is invariably constructed as an "exceptional" individual, colonialist mythmakers, both literary and cinematic, position themselves handily to amplify "the rule" against which such exceptions are posed. It follows that, as S. Elizabeth Bird has observed, "the brutal savage is still present" in the colonizers' Good Indian fables, most often "in the recurrent image of the renegade."[163] Bird continues:

> These ["bad"] Indians have not accepted White control, refuse to stay on the reservation, and use violent means to combat White people, raiding farms and destroying White property. Although occasional lip service is paid to the justness of their anger, the message is clear that these warriors are misguided. [Enlightened settlers] are frequently seen trying to persuade the friendly Indians to curb the ["Hostiles'"] excesses. The renegades are clearly defined as deviant, out of control, and a challenge to the [Good Indian] who suffers all

indignities with a stoic smile and acknowledgment that there are really many good, kind White people who wish this had never happened.[164]

As a consequence, the literary-cinematic contrivance of Good Indians must be seen mainly as an expedient in completing and consolidating the overwhelmingly negative characterization of native people more generally—and thus the goodness of settlers—as discussed in the preceding three sections (witness a recent episode of *Dr. Quinn* in which Cloud Dancing's son wins eternal Good Indian status by sacrificing himself to save a white female captive from being gang-raped by a group of renegade Cheyenne dog soldiers).

Students' understanding can be sharpened by asking them to consider the hypothetical question of how, had they been victorious in World War II, the Nazis might have been inclined to represent different factions among the peoples they had conquered: the collaborationist Vichy French, for instance, vis-à-vis the French Resistance.[165] Little controversy attends a prognosis that figures such as Vichy leader Pierre Laval would undoubtedly have been offered up as symbols of "the Good Frenchman" by postwar Nazi filmmakers while Charles DeGaul and his Free French forces, especially the Maquis ("Partisan") guerrillas, would with equal certainty have been depicted as "renegades," sinister, deviant, and violently "out of control." Thus would the polarities of French patriotism and treason have been completely reversed, not by the French themselves but by their German occupiers-colonizers (in reality, DeGaul was treated as a hero by the vast majority of his countrymen and elected president of the postwar French Republic, whereas the Vichy collaborators were deeply reviled, many of them executed or imprisoned).[166]

It can be, and sometimes is, argued that the comparison is misleading since it concerns the portrayal of actual historical personalities, whereas the Good Indians heretofore discussed, whether Kipling's or Cooper's, are fictional. The validity of the point can be readily conceded, if only as a basis upon which to pivot into an examination of the ways in which Hollywood has gone about characterizing certain real indigenous leaders as "good," others as "bad." In this connection a key will be found in Delmer Daves's much-acclaimed 1950 "sympathy" film *Broken Arrow.*[167] It takes no time to demonstrate how Cochise, a very significant figure in Chiricahua Apache history,[168] is first misrepresented as having been a veritable Tonto (or Gunga Din or Pierre Laval)—thus to render him appealing to settler audiences—in no small part by contrasting him with a viciously irrational "Geronimo" (symbolizing the already thoroughly demonized Apache resistance).[169] *Broken Arrow* was so well received that it was quickly developed into a highly rated TV series that lasted several seasons.

The same pattern can easily be shown to have prevailed as recently as the 1994 *Squanto,* the formula applied to even the most substantial pillars of native resistance. Probably the most glaring example of the latter comes with *The*

From *Broken Arrow,* Twentieth Century Fox, 1950

White Buffalo (1977), wherein none other than the legendary Oglala Lakota patriot, Crazy Horse,[170] is portrayed as teaming up with settler-hero Wild Bill Hickock to save humanity from the beast featured in the film's title. Since the white buffalo is actually a prime symbol of Lakota spirituality, the filmmaker's co-optive design is readily apparent: Crazy Horse (DeGaul) is shown as a man dedicated to nothing so much as subversion of his own tradition (Laval), thereby converting treason into a figuration of its opposite.

On the basis of all that has been digested up to now, it is appropriate to explore the implications of the fact that native as well as settler children are, and have long been, subject to continuous and increasing bombardment with the kinds of imagery and thematics we have discussed.[171] Since the impacts of such things on the formation of self-concept among American Indian youth are obviously no less germane than those pertaining to mainstream kids, the matter can be reframed: What kind of self-esteem is manifested when native youngsters burst into cheers whenever a cinematic bugle call signals that the cavalry will soon arrive on-screen to symbolically slaughter their own forebears?[172]

From *The Squaw Man,* Famous Players-Lasky Corporation, 1918

There is no need for abstraction in this connection. Suicide is presently the leading cause of death among Native North American teenagers, standing at about 1,400 percent the rate for the same age group among the general population.[173] In northern Manitoba, to offer but one exceedingly well-documented illustration, an estimated 70 percent of indigenous youngsters from six to sixteen habitually inhale gasoline and solvents in a desperate effort to utterly and in all too many cases permanently blot out their consciousness.[174] The grim toll could be recounted at far greater length, but there should be no need.

It would, to be sure, be grossly inaccurate to name cinema as the only culprit generating such ghastly results—apart from the conditions of material degradation that for generations have marked the quality of life in the great majority of native communities[175] there are myriad psychological instigators, ranging from a proliferation of demeaning "Indian" sports team mascots[176] to routine use of the word *squaw* in both official and popular settler discourse[177]—although it must, by virtue of its undisputed potency as an instrument of perceptual shaping, be regarded as a primary offender. The fact that any society could subject another to such ongoing misery by indulging in a subterfuge designed solely to enable its own constituents to nonetheless "feel good about themselves" reaffirms our earlier conclusion that a genocidal mentality is at work among North American settlers, although this time with respect to contemporary rather than merely historical circumstances.[178]

On Terra Nullius

By now it should be apparent that, however intricate the route, all roads lead to the same destination where Hollywood's portrayal of American Indians is concerned. Along the way it was perhaps inevitable—or at least far simpler—that, as people, we would be reduced largely to dehumanized caricatures, the magnificent sweep of our histories constrained to a brief interlude in which we do combat with or provide assistance to the settlers who are overrunning us. Possessed of neither pasts nor futures, we are imbued with meaning only by Them,[179] the rich diversity and complexity of our cultures confined to a single dimension of interchangeability: "Seen one Indian, seen 'em all," or so the saying goes. As Cherokee law professor–*cum*–media critic Rennard Strickland has noted:

> You'd think, if you relied on Indian films, there were no [indigenous peoples] east of the Mississippi, none but the Plains Indians [and Apaches], except possibly the Mohawks, and that the continent was unoccupied throughout the entire Great Lakes and Central region except for an occasional savage remnant, perhaps a stray Yaqui or two who wandered in from the Southwest. We almost never see a Chippewa or a Winnebago or a . . . Hopi or even a Navajo on screen.[180]

In "the early days"—that is, until well into the 1950s—almost all Cowboy and Indian flicks were filmed in southern California, a financial and logistical convenience convincing generations of children situated in other locales—myself included—that Kansas looked like Death Valley and utterly annihilating the concept that the least relationship might exist between the Plains cultures ostensibly depicted and the environments in which they actually evolved and flourished (by the 1930s, of course, John Ford had come along to "fix" all that by relocating his cinematic Cheyennes to Monument Valley[181]). The level of deformity in understanding conveyed was tantamount to representing life in Sicily by setting it in Sweden, but who cared? "Aesthetic" concerns were involved, and mere Indians were being misrepresented.

Even after U.S. geography teachers conspired to compel filmmakers to more or less clean up their act in topographical terms,[182] the cultural emulsification of native people continued unabated. The Smithsonian-vetted *A Man Called Horse,* to offer one of the sorrier illustrations, creates a visual hodgepodge of Crow, Mandan, Assiniboin, and Comanche attributes; intermixes a variety of nonexistent "customs"; and ladles the whole mess up as a representation of "the Sioux."[183] Equally egregious examples abound, from "Everglades-dwelling Seminoles wearing Plains feathered warbonnets and battling blue-coated cavalry on desert buttes" in *Seminole Uprising* (1955) to the eagle feather–wearing "half-Choctaw" played by Billy Bob Thornton in *Pushing Tin* (1999).[184]

One can only imagine the reaction among settlers were some studio to release a cinematic extravaganza—purportedly "the most accurate rendering ever" of ancient Greece or Rome—in which the actors were dressed in a combination of kilts and ballroom attire, conversed in "authentic Spanglish," worshipped Odin, dined mostly on spaghetti and sauerkraut (with or without truffles and chocolate malts), and seemed to spend the bulk of their time galloping wildly across the steppes before retiring each night to harem-filled Irish fishing villages where, backdropped by the Matterhorn, they performed perfect ritual impersonations of the Marquis de Sade. The scenario is no more absurd than that imposed upon American Indians as a matter of course.[185]

Ultimately, as critic Richard Maltby has acknowledged, "in the Hollywood western, there are no 'real' Indians, only Hollywood Indians with different names," props serving as the backdrop to unending tales of Noble White Men.[186] Making a transition from this stance to having whites supplant Indians altogether is a matter of only minor adjustment. Actually, in a literal sense there was no adjustment to make because filmmakers have insisted upon casting whites as Indians from the outset (one of the first was Mary Pickford as the title character in a 1912 ditty called *Iola's Promise*).[187] The results have often been sublime, as when Chuck Connors—a 6-foot 4-inch, blond-haired, blue-eyed Viking—was selected to play the 5-foot 3-inch, swarthy Geronimo in the 1962 film of the same title.[188] Meanwhile, native actors have been turned away in droves, usually on the pretext that they would be "unconvincing" if allowed to portray themselves on-screen.[189]

Figuratively and in many respects more insidiously, there is often a settler-hero who comes off as "more Indian than the Indians."[190] As has been observed with respect to *Dr. Quinn,* "Sully's role is to stand in for the Cheyenne, so that their culture is represented, while they as people can be pushed into the background. After all, he is a better Indian than the Cheyenne, as is made abundantly clear in the opening scene of one episode, when he beats Cloud Dancing in a tomahawk-throwing contest."[191] In this, Sully has everything in common with Cooper's Natty Bumppo, Walt Disney's *Davy Crockett, King of the Wild Frontier* (1955),[192] Robert Redford's title character in *Jeremiah Johnson* (1972), or any of a thousand other illusionary scouts and frontiersmen with which the silver screen has been set alight.

Although there are many contenders, probably the most preposterous characterizations of all are those in *A Man Called Horse* where it becomes necessary for a captive English aristocrat played by Richard Harris to teach "the Sioux" how to defend themselves against other Indians with bows and arrows, thereupon becoming their leader.[193] This absurd plot device was received so well by mainstream audiences that *The Return of a Man Called Horse,* a sequel to the original movie, was released in 1976 and a revision of the bow-and-arrow scene—this time using firearms—was included in the hugely popular *Dances With Wolves* as recently as 1990.

Even when things are not pushed to such extremes, the "Indian side of the story" is forever being told not by Indians but by some "sympathetic" settler character: Jimmie Stewart's "Tom Jeffords" in *Broken Arrow,* for instance, or the white schoolmarm John Ford has bouncing along in a buckboard beside the fleeing savages in *Cheyenne Autumn* (1964),[194] or Dustin Hoffman's character in *Little Big Man,* or Matt Damon's "Britton Davis" in the 1993 version of *Geronimo,*[195] or the gravel-voiced bartender in *Last of the Dogmen* (1995).[196] As Jimmie Durham has pointed out, no Indian—"neither Queequag in *Moby Dick,* nor Tonto, nor the Indian in Ken Kesey's *One Flew Over the Cuckoo's Nest*"—has ever really been allowed to portray himself or herself, less to articulate the perspective of his or her people, and still less to represent the voice of authority assigning the meaning to Indian-white interactions.[197]

With Native Americans effectively eclipsed by whites even in the most "Indian-oriented" movies, it has been possible for filmmakers to simply erase us from the landscape whenever we have not been useful as an element of set decor. "In the last great wave of Hollywood westerns—*Shane* [1953], *High Noon* [1952], et al.," Durham has observed, "the settlers are all by themselves on the endless prairies. They cannot remember when they last had to kill 'Indians.'"[198] The same might be said of such far more recent films as Clint Eastwood's Academy Award–winning *The Unforgiven* (1992), Lawrence Kasdan's *Wyatt Earp,* and George Cosmatos's *Tombstone* (both 1994), but the point remains unchanged: "At some point late at night by the campfire, presumably, the Lone Ranger ate Tonto. By the time Alan Ladd becomes the Lone Ranger in *Shane* he has consumed his Indian companion. Now the Lone Ranger is himself the stoic, silent, Noble Savage, so much neater and more satisfactory at the job."[199]

All appearances to the contrary notwithstanding, this final cinematic conjuring—that of a complete native absence—is not something innovative and new. Rather, it harkens back to the earliest European fantasies of the New World, the mythic claim that the Americas, or at least appreciable portions of them, were composed of *Terra Nullius* ("vacant land," that is, devoid of human inhabitants and therefore free for the taking by any Old World settler who wished to grab a chunk).[200] As we have seen, much of Hollywood's (re)presentation of North America's indigenous population has been designed to dehumanize us sufficiently as to make the notion of *Terra Nullius* resonate as symbolic truth, even today. How much "neater and more satisfactory," however, if the concept could be received as something closer to that which was—and thus remains—quite literally true.[201]

BLIND ALLEYS

Yet self-evidently, Indians were not only here when a lost Italian seaman "discovered" us by washing up on a Caribbean beach half a world away from where he thought he was—thus becoming known to posterity as "the Great Navigator"[202]—but after all the centuries of ensuing horror, we are still here. With equal certainty it can be asserted that as a whole—irrespective of the twists, turns, and convolutions by which they have sought and still seek to avoid coming to grips with the knowledge—the settler populace is quite aware of this.[203] They are, moreover, aware that we exist today as the poorest of the poor in North America—stripped at gunpoint of the bulk of our property, the residues of our homelands subordinated to settler-state control, disemployed, our remaining resources siphoned off to fuel the settler economy, even the pittance we are ostensibly paid in exchange impounded and often stolen by settler-state authorities.[204] As Sartre put it, "You begin by occupying the country, then you take the land and exploit the former owners at starvation rates. Then, with mechanization, this cheap labor is still too expensive; you finish up taking from the natives their very right to work. All that is left for [them] to do, in their own land, at a time of great prosperity, is to die of starvation."[205]

On this basis it can be stated without hesitancy or equivocation that we exhibit all the attributes of colonized nations.[206] That is, we are presently subjected to a political status prohibited under international law since the United Nations Charter was ratified in 1945 (whatever confusion attended the Charter's language was dispelled in 1960 with the passage of U.N. Resolution 1514, otherwise known as the Declaration on the Granting of Independence to Colonial Countries and Peoples).[207] Although the implications for both extant North American states are readily apparent—this is true of the United States in particular, given the pride it professes in being "a nation of laws, not men"[208]—the issue is customarily greeted with thundering silence within even the most purportedly progressive sectors of settler society.[209]

"If 'Indians' are not to be considered victims of colonial aggression," Jimmie Durham has asked, "how are we to be considered?" The question is so urgent given the dire conditions prevailing throughout Native North America that Durham pronounces himself "tempted to write the question twice, for emphasis." The first "implies a second question, however: why are we not considered as colonized? For any 'Indian' person, the questions are subjective and quotidian: 'How might I exist?'"[210] Or, following Sartre once again, the question might be reframed as "whether and for how long may I be permitted the option of existing at all."[211]

The crux of the all but monolithic refusal by Euro-Americans of all political postures to acknowledge the fundamental illegitimacy of the internal colonial structures prevailing in both the United States and Canada, Durham reflects, seems bound up in their awareness of the legal and moral obligation to decolonize that would attend any such admission and what this might mean in terms of a diminishment in the relatively privileged socioeconomic positions they are accustomed to occupying.[212] Durham continues:

> The state called "France" is connected to something like a country, also called "France." The state called "America" is connected to an independent settler colony. At the end of its "empire" Great Britain could return to that island in Europe. The economic power of the US is losing its grip in much of the world, but at the end, to where might it return? It is only a state, only a political entity [without a land base].[213]

"If someone imagines otherwise," Durham sums up, "at the end of America's 'external' empire it follows that there is a country called America. Would my country [the Cherokee Nation] become free of the US? If so, where is America?"[214] He recounts having explained "'American Indian' legal rights [to self-determination] and the consequent demands of the American Indian Movement" to a supposedly radical Euro-American scholar-activist employed by the staunchly anti-imperialist Institute for Policy Studies. His listener was aghast, sputtering in mortified astonishment that decolonization of Native North America "would mean the break up of the United States."[215]

Exactly so. And with it would go the system of White Skin Privilege upon which the vast majority of settlers, "radicals" no less than others, depend for the "quality of life" to which they believe themselves innately entitled.[216] Reactionaries like Allan Bloom and Arthur Schlesinger Jr. have been reasonably straightforward in their defense of the status quo,[217] but their opponents can hardly afford to be. Hence the latter have increasingly resorted to theoretical obfuscation and deception as methods of protecting their standing as "oppositionists" even as they endeavor to preclude emergence of the sort of consciousness requisite to seriously disrupting the colonial order.[218]

One such "ludic" subterfuge, found in Euro-feminism's clever substitution of white women for black and other men of color as a historically oppressed group, has been to some extent addressed.[219] The feminist example is by no means unique. A comparable but much older scam will be apprehended in Marxism's insistent subsuming of racial, ethnic, and national distinctions under the rubric of a totalizing kind of "democratic class solidarity" in which white workers inevitably end up the largest component, thereby ensuring that "liberation" will be defined more-or-less exclusively in terms of a "redistribution of social product" derived from the preservation rather than the dissolution of existing state territorialities.[220]

Moreover, Karl Marx himself—in common with the worst of Europe's nineteenth-century imperialists—openly advocated colonialism as exerting a "civilizing influence" on non-Western peoples.[221] Attitudes have changed little among Euro-Marxists during the century and a half since Marx's death. Indeed, "Sartre was the first (and last) European Marxist theorist to develop a theory of history in which colonialism, and the endemic violence of the colonial regime, was a major component, and which gave a significant role to anti-colonialist resistance."[222] In point of fact, however, there seem to be substantial questions among Marxists, Euro- and otherwise, as to whether Sartre can rightly be categorized as such.

A far slipperier innovation will be found in the recent emergence of "postcolonial theory," a concoction assigning primacy to many of the destructive effects of colonialism Euro-Marxism denies but—as its name implies—that does so by way of placing it arbitrarily in the "bad old days" of the past tense.[223] As Anne McClintock has noted, having embraced a set of assumptions "organized around a binary axis of time rather than power," proponents are guilty of "obscuring the continuities . . . of colonial and imperial power."[224] She continues:

> The term "post-colonial" is, in many cases, prematurely celebratory. Ireland may, at a pinch, be "post-colonial," but for the inhabitants of British-occupied Northern Ireland, not to mention the Palestinian occupants of the Israeli Occupied Territories and the West Bank, there [is] nothing "post" about colonialism at all. Is [New Zealand] "post-colonial"? [Canada?] Australia? By what historical amnesia can the United States of America, in particular, qualify as "post-colonial"—a term which can only be a monumental affront to the Native peoples currently [encapsulated therein]?[225]

The question of whether Canada—and, by extension, New Zealand, Australia, and the United States—are to be considered "postcolonial" has been answered in the affirmative, emphatically so, by such Euro-Canadian academics as Diana Brydon, who has written that anyone "truly interested in postcolonial . . . perspectives will come to us."[226] By "us" she means North America's settler population, which has assumed independent or "Commonwealth" status vis-à-vis the old British imperial center (as have those resident to Australia and New Zealand).[227] Thus do colonizers substitute themselves for colonized in the "postcolonial" equation, a sleight of hand entirely reminiscent of—but far more sweeping than—that earlier performed by Euro-feminism.[228] In any event, postcolonialism's obscuring of native circumstance—even of native existence—is as thoroughgoing as anything ever dreamed up by Hollywood.

Beyond the domain of "postcoloniality," one encounters the more rarefied dominions of "poststructuralism" and "postmodernity"—one expects, upon entering this preciously avant-garde netherworld, to be confronted at any moment with the ascendancy of Post Toasties as a "predominating mode of discourse"[229]—preoccupied with the supposedly "ahistorical operation of signs and tropes."[230] Devoted to "deconstructing" what they see as the "totalization" inherent to all "universalizing narratives"[231]—especially those harnessed to "hierarchy" (a term proponents often appear to confuse, alternately, with "structural oppression" and "elitism"[232]), "essentialism" (by which they seem to mean, alternately, "reification" and "meaning" itself),[233] "teleology" (frequently conflated with "sense of purpose"),[234] and "rationality" (that is, all claims that there is, or even could be, an inherent order to the universe)[235]—postmodernists posit as an alternative the conception of an infinite "plurality" of "decentered selves," each exercising the "free agency" of defining its own "identity" within a "permeable" arena subsisting upon equal quantities of "irony" and "contingency."[236]

At their most ludic—or "spectral," to borrow a term from Christopher Lasch[237]—postmodernists like Jean Baudrillard have argued that "history [is to be] had right now, in culture, discourse, sex and shopping mall, in the mobility of the contemporary subject or the multiplicities of social life," thereby offering "a false utopianism [that] projects the future into the present, thus selling the future short and imprisoning the present within itself."[238] All that is left to those discontented with this strange new best of all possible worlds are vacuous acts of "mimicry" or "trickster-like forms of parody."[239]

Even at its most constructively engaged, the individuation—sociopolitical atomization, really—inherent to the postmodernist vision precludes any possibility of a viable transformative politics, reducing both "opposition" and "resistance" to purely textual pursuits.[240] Indeed, having first adopted Foucault's premise that "the relations of discourse are of the nature of warfare,"[241] the highly influential theorist Homi Bhabha—an eclectic thinker whose work dissolves many of the boundaries separating postcoloniality from postmodernism[242]—has delighted in an "exorbitation of discourse,"[243] consciously "inflat[ing] the critic's role at the expense of the obviously much more critical role played by both armed resistance and conventional forms of political organization in ending the system of formal imperialism and challenging the current system of neocolonialism."[244]

For all its pontifications on its own "extremity," then, postmodernism "has the look of a sheepish liberalism in wolf's clothing," the "privileged view" of a subset within the settler intelligentsia—and among its compradors—whose function is diversionary; it is carefully designed to appear "politically oppositional" even as it functions in a manner "economically [and otherwise] complicit" with the status quo.[245] Taken as a whole:

> [Postmodernism] is just another depressing instance of the way that much radical academia in the United States has managed to translate urgent political issues into its own blandly professional terms, so that conflicts beyond the campuses become transposed in unseemly fashion into tussles over defending academic patches, fighting off radical competitors in the academic marketplace, securing funds for this or that avant-garde enterprise.[246]

This is not to say that nothing useful can be learned either from the "discourses of post-ality" or from their (neo)Marxist-feminist counterparts.[247] Whatever utility they may yield is, however, entirely contingent upon recognizing from the outset the ultimate vestiture of their interest(s) in preserving the hegemony of Euro-supremacism.[248] Adopting any or some combination of the "posts" as an analytical paradigm can therefore lead only to a disjunctural blind alley in terms of apprehending either the existence or the significance of the realms of factuality revealed in this chapter. Instead, educators will unerringly place themselves, intentionally or not, in the position of legitimating many—or all—of the interrelated streams of distortion and denial explored here.[249]

TO SEE THINGS CLEARLY

What is needed is a theoretical-analytical framework such as that employed here, harnessed to and equipped first and foremost for the nomenclatural task of assigning things their right names, hedging no bets in the process. Colonialism remains colonialism in this schema—not an ambiguous something qualified through addition of the prefix "neo"[250] or foreclosed by the addition of "post"—and, as Sartre observed rather famously in 1968, is directly equatable to genocide.[251] Viewed with this precision, no room obtains for the usual sorts of equivocation: there are no "good colonizers" to be counterpoised against "bad colonizers" (no more than there could be good Nazis); there are only those whose first commitment is to destroy colonialism, root and branch, and those whose sense of self-interest and entitlement dictates its preservation (whether by their direct and knowing participation in its imposition or through the more mealymouthed acceptance embodied in their ignoring, discounting, relativizing, or trying to explain away its genocidal effects).[252]

Such explication compels all concerned to undertake an often painfully subjective process of personal values clarification—Ngugi Wa Thiongo has described it as being one of "decolonizing the mind"[253]—determining the side on which they wish to stand.[254] From there, *pace* postmodernist contends, it is not only possible but desirable to attain a truly centered sense of self in which agency is manifested not simply by rejection of the existing master narrative(s) but through an embrace of counternarratives both redefining history and revealing its liberatory potentials for the future.[255] This in turn—and alone—forms the basis for (the resumption of) exactly the sort of effective transformative politics proponents of postality have renounced.

To be sure, precedents exist for the conceptualization at issue, most deriving from the period when imperialism was still called imperialism rather than "globalization."[256] These can be located to some extent in the explicitly anti-imperialist conception of "consciencism" propounded by Kwame Nkrumah and refined by Amilcar Cabral, among others,[257] reaching what was probably its greatest degree of fulfillment in the works of Frantz Fanon and Albert Memmi.[258]

Overall, the perspective was once known as "Third Worldism,"[259] although it has subsequently undergone profound challenges and revisions because of its failure to accommodate the reality and rights of an underlying "Fourth World" composed of indigenous peoples.[260] The resulting reconfiguration is sometimes referred to as "indigenism."[261]

In any event, resuming our focus on North America, it can be observed that the explicitly anti-imperialist gaze of consciencism is most appropriate to apprehend the racially constructed internal colonization not only of indigenous people but of African Americans,[262] Latinos,[263] and even sectors of the settler underclass itself.[264] Freed of absurdist allegations of such sins as "inherent phallocentrism,"[265] "reverse racism,"[266] and "totalization,"[267] a revitalization of the Third Worldist orientation—albeit in a much evolved form[268]—establishes the foundation on which a "Fanonist pedagogy" leading to a genuinely "revolutionary multiculturalism" can be achieved.[269]

In this way and perhaps only in this way can we at last move "beyond pedagogies of protest [developing] a praxis that gives encouragement to those who, instead of being content with visiting history as curators or custodians of memory, choose to live in the furnace of history where memory is molten and can be bent into the contours of a dream and perhaps even acquire the force of a vision."[270] The point of any such exercise is, paraphrasing Marx, to empower students not only to interpret the world more accurately but to change it.[271] The fact that both the vision and the change must center upon repealing the colonization of Native North America—and, as a concomitant, the structural oppression of others made possible by the colonial arrangement on this continent—should at this point seem utterly unremarkable. In the alternative, we seem fated to live out Hollywood's dreams of genocide in grotesque and endless repetition.[272] Surely, we owe ourselves—and more, our posterity—something infinitely better.

NOTES

1. Scott Simmon, *The Films of D. W. Griffith* (Cambridge: Cambridge University Press, 1993), 9. Although it is often credited as such, *Elderbush Gulch* was not the first piece of coherent narrative cinema created by a Euro-American. It was preceded by such otherwise unremarkable fare as *Apache Gold* (1910), *The Curse of the Red Man* (1911), *On the Warpath* (1912), and *A Prisoner of the Apaches* (1913).

2. Rennard Strickland, "Tonto's Revenge, or, Who Is That Seminole in the Warbonnet?" in his *Tonto's Revenge: Reflections on American Indian Culture and Policy* (Albuquerque: University of New Mexico Press, 1997), 33.

3. The numbers accrue from *Images of Indians,* a five-part PBS series produced by Phil Lucas and narrated by Creek actor Will Sampson in 1981. For the best filmographies, neither of them complete, see Michael Hilger, *The American Indian in Film* (Metuchen, NJ: Scarecrow, 1986); Elizabeth Weatherford and Emelia Seubert, eds., *Native Americans in Film and Video,* 2 vols. (New York: Museum of the American Indian, 1981, 1988).

4. See Vine Deloria Jr., "Foreword: American Fantasy," in *The Pretend Indians: Images of Native Americans in Film*, ed. Gretchen Bataille and Charles L.P. Silet (Ames: Iowa State University Press, 1981), xv–xvi.

5. A good overview is provided in Imre Sutton, ed., *Irredeemable America: The Indians' Estate and Land Tenure* (Albuquerque: University of New Mexico Press, 1985). Also see my *Struggle for the Land: Native North American Resistance to Genocide, Ecocide and Colonization*, 2d ed. (Winnipeg: Arbeiter Ring, 1999).

6. Judge Warren Urbom, *U.S. v. Consolidated Wounded Knee Cases*, 389 F. Supp. 235 (1974), 238–239.

7. Jimmie Durham, "This Ground Has Been Covered," in his *A Certain Lack of Coherence: Writings on Art and Cultural Politics* (London: Kala, 1993), 138.

8. For penetrating structural analyses, albeit deployed in analogous contexts rather than that specifically at hand, see Jacques Ellul, *Propaganda: The Formation of Men's Attitudes* (New York: Alfred A. Knopf, 1965); Noam Chomsky, *Necessary Illusions: Thought Control in Democratic Societies* (Boston: South End, 1989). More targeted readings with respect to literature are found in Robert F. Berkhofer, *The White Man's Indian: Images of the Indian From Columbus to the Present* (New York: Alfred A. Knopf, 1978); Raymond William Stedman, *Shadows of the Indian: Stereotypes in American Culture* (Norman: University of Oklahoma Press, 1982); Richard Slotkin, *Regeneration Through Violence: The Mythology of the American Frontier* (Middletown, CT: Wesleyan University Press, 1990). On academia, see, e.g., David Hurst Thomas, *Skull Wars: Kennewick Man, Archaeology, and the Battle for Native American Identity* (New York: Basic, 2000). An excellent historical survey of press performance is contained in David Svaldi, *Sand Creek and the Rhetoric of Extermination: A Case Study in Indian-White Relations* (Lanham: University Press of America, 1989).

9. The benchmark work in this connection remains, in my estimation, Marshall McLuhan, *Understanding Media* (New York: McGraw-Hill, 1964). Also see Andrew Tudor, *Image and Influence: Studies in the Sociology of Film* (New York: St. Martin's, 1975).

10. This point was made early and well by Ralph and Natasha A. Friar in *"The Only Good Indian . . .": The Hollywood Gospel* (New York: Drama Books, 1972).

11. On the concept of "Master Narratives"—also known as "Great" or "Grand" Narratives, as well as "metanarratives"—see Fredric Jameson, *Political Unconscious: Narrative as Socially Symbolic Act* (Ithaca: Cornell University Press, 1981). As applied specifically to American Indians, see Jimmie Durham, "Cowboys and . . ." in *Lack of Coherence*, esp. 173–175.

12. For an exhaustive discussion, see Richard Slotkin, *Gunfighter Nation: The Myth of the Frontier in Twentieth-Century America*, 2d ed. (Norman: University of Oklahoma Press, 1998).

13. I cover this in the title essay of my *Fantasies of the Master Race: Literature, Cinema and the Colonization of American Indians*, 2d ed. (San Francisco: City Lights, 1998), 168–172. Also see Durham, "Cowboys" in *Lack of Coherence*, 176.

14. Durham, "This Ground Has Been Covered" in *Lack of Coherence*, 138.

15. For explication of the term in the sense intended here, see Walter L. Adamson, *Hegemony and Revolution: A Study of Antonio Gramsci's Political and Cultural Theory* (Berkeley: University of California Press, 1980), 170–179.

16. See Frederick Merk, *Manifest Destiny and Mission in American History: A Reinterpretation* (New York: Alfred A. Knopf, 1963); Rita Parks, *The Western Hero in Film and*

Television: Mass Media Mythology (Ann Arbor: University of Michigan Research Press, 1982); Slotkin, *Gunfighter Nation.*

17. Superb tracings of this thematic cluster are found in Roy Harvey Pearce, *Savagism and Civilization: A Study of the American Indian in the American Mind* (Baltimore: Johns Hopkins University Press, 1953); Richard Drinnon, *Facing West: The Metaphysics of Indian-Hating and Empire-Building* (Minneapolis: University of Minnesota Press, 1980); Reginald Horsman, *Race and Manifest Destiny: The Origins of American Racial Anglo-Saxonism* (Cambridge: Harvard University Press, 1981). More broadly, see Robert Young, *White Mythologies: Writing, History and the West* (New York: Routledge, 1990), and the essays collected in Mick Gidley, ed., *Representing Others: White Views of Indigenous Peoples* (Exeter: Exeter University Press, 1994).

18. Worthwhile readings on the topic are collected in John Ewell, Chris Dodge, and Jan DeSirey, eds., *Confronting Columbus: An Anthology* (Jefferson, NC: McFarland, 1992).

19. A classic illustration of this mentality at work is found in Allan van Gestel, "When Fictions Take Hostages," in *The Invented Indian: Cultural Fictions and Government Policies,* ed. James A. Clifton (New Brunswick: Transaction, 1990), 291–312.

20. Chomsky, *Necessary Illusions.* Also see Edward S. Herman and Noam Chomsky, *Manufacturing Consent: The Political Economy of the Mass Media* (New York: Pantheon, 1988).

21. A good tracing of the trajectory is found in Noam Chomsky, *Year 501: The Conquest Continues* (Boston: South End, 1993). Also see Frank Furedi, *The New Ideology of Imperialism: Renewing the Moral Imperative* (London: Pluto, 1994).

22. This is as true within the classroom as without; see, e.g., the essays collected in Elizabeth Ellsworth and Marianne H. Whatley, eds., *The Ideology of Images in Educational Media: Hidden Curriculums in the Classroom* (New York: Teachers College Press, 1990). Also see David Trend, "Nationalities, Pedagogies, and the Media," in *Between Borders: Pedagogy and the Politics of Cultural Studies,* ed. Henry A. Giroux and David McLaren (New York: Routledge, 1994), 225–241.

23. For the broad outlines of what I have in mind, see bell hooks, *Teaching to Transgress: Education as the Practice of Freedom* (New York: Routledge, 1994) and *Outlaw Culture: Resisting Representation* (New York: Routledge, 1994). At a more rarefied level, better suited to graduate students, see Gayatri Chakravorty Spivak, *Outside in the Teaching Machine* (New York: Routledge, 1993).

24. Exemplars of the scholarship at issue include bell hooks, *Black Looks: Race and Representation* (Boston: South End, 1994); Jun Xing, *Asian America Through the Lens: History, Representations and Reality* (Walnut Creek, CA: AltaMira, 1995); S. Elizabeth Bird, ed., *Dressing in Feathers: The Construction of the American Indian in Popular Culture* (Boulder: Westview, 1996); Ed Guerrero, *Framing Blackness: The African American Image in Film* (Philadelphia: Temple University Press, 1993); Gina Marchette, *Romance and the Yellow Peril: Race, Sex and Discursive Strategies in Hollywood Fiction* (Berkeley: University of California Press, 1991); Ella Shohat and Robert Stam, *Unthinking Eurocentrism: Multiculturalism and the Media* (New York: Routledge, 1994); Jacqueline Kilpatrick, *Celluloid Indians: Native Americans and Film* (Lincoln: University of Nebraska Press, 1999). Also see Friar and Friar, "*The Only Good Indian . . .*"; Durham, *Lack of Coherence*; Slotkin, *Gunfighter Nation*; Churchill, *Fantasies.*

25. bell hooks, *Reel to Real: Race, Sex and Class at the Movies* (New York: Routledge, 1996).

26. The distinction between "other" and "Other" intended here follows that delineated by Homi K. Bhabha in "The Other Question: Stereotype, Discrimination and Colonial Discourse," in his *The Location of Culture* (New York: Routledge, 1990), 66–84. Also see Tzvetan Todorov, *The Conquest of America: The Question of the Other* (New York: Harper and Row, 1984).

27. Max Horkheimer, *The Eclipse of Reason,* quoted in Paul Z. Simmons, "Afterword: Commentary on Form and Content in *Elements of Refusal*," in *Elements of Refusal,* 2d ed., ed. John Zerzan (New York: C.A.L. Press/Paleo ed., 1999), 266.

28. This conforms generally to the approach advocated in other analytical arenas by Linda Tuhiwai Smith in *Decolonizing Methodologies: Research and Indigenous Peoples* (London and Dunedin: Zed and University of Otago Press, 1999).

29. Overall, the strategy is not dissimilar to that described by Paulo Freire in *Education for Critical Consciousness* (New York: Continuum, 1982). Also see Barbie Zelzier, "Reading the Past Against the Grain: The Shape of Memory Studies," *Critical Studies in Mass Communications* (1995): 214–239.

30. For transparent iterations of such apologetics with regard to the handling of American Indians in commercial cinema, see Jack Nachbar, *Focus on the Western* (New York: Prentice-Hall, 1974); John H. Lenihan, *Showdown: Confronting Modern America in the Western Film* (Urbana: University of Illinois Press, 1980). As one astute analyst has summarized the Lenihan tract, "A book such as Lenihan's, which was considered sufficiently well-researched to earn a Ph.D. . . . actually does little more than extend the propaganda contained in the films themselves"; John Tuska, *The American West in Film: Critical Approaches to the Western* (Lincoln: University of Nebraska Press, 1988), 251.

31. The resistance to probing such things is formed quite differently within the two groups involved. Concerning so-called mainstreamers, see Stuart Hall, "The West and the Rest: Discourse and Power," in his and Bram Gieben's coedited volume, *The Formations of Modernity* (Oxford: Polity and Open University, 1992), 276–320. On those of other than mainstream backgrounds, see Ashis Nandy, *The Intimate Enemy: The Loss and Recovery of Self Under Colonialism* (New York: Oxford University Press, 1989).

32. Again I am following Freire, this time his *Literacy: Reading the Word and the World* (London: Routledge and Kegan Paul, 1987), as well as *Education for Critical Consciousness.*

33. See, e.g., John Denvir, ed., *Legal Reelism: Movies as Legal Texts* (Urbana: University of Illinois Press, 1996).

34. This is true at least insofar as students' anonymous end-of-semester evaluations are concerned, "American Indians in Film" never having received an aggregate rating lower than the top tenth percentile of all courses offered on campus during the semesters it has been taught.

35. Quoted in Ellul, *Propaganda,* 139.

36. Bhabha, "The Other Question" in his *Location of Culture,* esp. 69.

37. Bart Moore-Gilbert, *Postcolonial Theory: Contexts, Practices, Politics* (London: Verso, 1997), 117.

38. It is useful, however—if only to illustrate the scope and sustained nature of the effort to condition public sensibilities involved—to provide students with lists of lesser films represented in terms of message by the "classics" screened and analyzed more directly. The Friars provided an invaluable service in compiling such a thematic itemization at the

back of *"The Only Good Indian . . ."* (minor updating is required). This, among other things, empowers skeptics to make a trip to their local video rental outlet and "see for themselves."

39. This is a variation on the charade of "American Innocence" dissected well by Stewart Creighton Miller in *"Benevolent Assimilation": The American Conquest of the Philippines, 1899–1903* (New Haven: Yale University Press, 1982), 1–2, 253–267.

40. See, e.g., Richard Maltby, "A Better Sense of History: John Ford and the Indians," in *The Book of Westerns,* ed. Ian Cameron and Douglas Pye (New York: Continuum, 1996), 34–49.

41. The interview is contained in Part 3 of the five-part PBS series *Images of Indians.*

42. See my "And They Did It Like Dogs in the Dirt: An Indigenist Analysis of *Black Robe,*" in *Fantasies,* 225–242. It should be noted, however, that *Black Robe,* having been made in Canada by an Australian director, is not in the conventional sense a "Hollywood" movie.

43. Apted seems to have shot the documentary mainly to attain acceptance by, credibility among, and thence cooperation from Oglala Lakotas resident to the Pine Ridge Reservation, where the events portrayed in *Thunderheart* had recently occurred. This enabled him to market the "authenticity" of his having set his distortive fiction in the actual locations where the events transpired, even including in some scenes a sampling of the personalities involved. Overall, it strongly appears that he never really planned to complete the documentary, doing so only after several of the Indians he had conned threatened to undo much of his effort at authentication by venting their sense of betrayal in a very public fashion.

44. For what, despite its rather unfortunate subtitle, proves to be a very insightful study of the development, politics, and priorities inherent to the studio system, see Neal Gabler, *An Empire of Their Own: How the Jews Invented Hollywood* (New York: Anchor, 1989).

45. Actually, there are a few in my opinion, albeit all of them are Canadian and therefore do not technically qualify as "Hollywood" productions. Notably, they include Donald Shabib's *Fish Hawk* (1980), with Will Sampson in the title role; Richard Bugajski's *Clearcut* (1991), featuring the Oneida actor Graham Green; and Jim Jarmusch's 1996 *Dead Man,* costarring Gary Farmer (Cayuga). See Leah Renae Kelly, "A Waltz of Violence and Counterviolence: Reflections on *Clearcut,*" in her *In My Own Voice: Explorations in the Sociopolitical Context of Art and Cinema* (Winnipeg: Arbeiter Ring, 2001), 119–122; Jonathan Rosenbaum, "A Gun Up Your Ass: An Interview With Jim Jarmusch," *Cineast* 22, 2 (1996); Kilpatrick, *Celluloid Indians,* 169–176.

46. This is simply false, as is readily demonstrated by the spectacular success garnered by films like *Little Big Man* and *Soldier Blue*—or, for that matter, *Easy Rider*—explicitly if rather misleadingly marketed as "alternative" fare during the early 1970s. See, e.g., Margo Kasdan and Susan Tavernetti, "Native Americans in a Revisionist Western: *Little Big Man,*" in *Hollywood's Indian: The Portrayal of Native Americans in Film,* ed. Peter C. Rollins and John E. O'Connor (Lexington: University Press of Kentucky, 1998), 121–136.

47. Again, the argument is dubious on its face. Although until recently it was advanced in almost identical terms as a rebuttal to demands for a relatively autonomous black cinema, the subsequently successful career of African American director Spike Lee alone offers ample testimony to the dimension of its falsity.

48. Herman and Chomsky offer a magnificent explication of this point in *Manufacturing Consent*.

49. This line of argument is ably rebutted in Peter C. Rollins, *Hollywood as Historian: American Film in a Cultural Context* (Lexington: University Press of Kentucky, 1983). Also see Robert A. Rosenstone, *Visions of the Past: The Challenge of Film to Our Idea of History* (Cambridge: Harvard University Press, 1995).

50. An interesting analysis is contained in Theodore S. Jojola, "Moo Mesa: Some Thoughts on Stereotypes and Image Appropriation," in Bird, *Dressing in Feathers*, 263–279.

51. See generally, Pauline Turner Strong, "Playing Indian in the 1990s: *Pocahontas* and *The Indian in the Cupboard*," in Rollins and O'Connor, *Hollywood's Indian*, 187–205.

52. Andrew L. Urban, "Black Robe," *Cinema Papers* (May 1991): 6–12. At p. 10, Beresford's production designer, Herb Pinter, is quoted as estimating that in material terms—costuming, props, and sets—about "99 percent of what you see [in the film] is accurate."

53. Kilpatrick, *Celluloid Indians*, 179–184; my *Fantasies of the Master Race*, 172–173.

54. Or, to borrow from Princeton professor-*cum*-U.S. President Woodrow Wilson upon viewing *Birth of a Nation*, D. W. Griffith's 1915 celluloid celebration of the Ku Klux Klan, "history written in lightening"; quoted in Wyn Craig Wade, *The Fiery Cross: The Ku Klux Klan in America*, 2d ed. (New York: Oxford University Press, 1998), 126.

55. We arrive thus at a fairly comprehensive validation of our earlier assertion that the Gramscian notion of hegemony is applicable to the context we are exploring (see note 15 and accompanying text). More precisely, we have staked out our terrain as the domain of hegemonic "colonial discourse" described by Edward Said in *Orientalism* (London: Routledge and Kegan Paul, 1978). Therein, "the arts"—especially literature (and presumably cinema)—are seen as inseparable and in many respects virtually indistinguishable from purportedly nonfictive or "scientific" modes of explanation. In Said's schema, all of them function in a contributory and mutually supporting and completing manner, forming the master narrative (see note 11) by which the dominant-subordinate relationship between Europe and its Others is rationalized.

56. Although it is never set forth in straightforward fashion, this idea appears to be a motive force underlying Ted Jojola's "Absurd Reality II: Hollywood Goes to the Indians," in Rollins and O'Connor, *Hollywood's Indian*, 12–26. It would also seem to inform much of what is written in Rollins's *Hollywood as Historian*.

57. Since Indians as well as settlers attend movies and watch TV these days, we are also systematically misrepresented to ourselves. Although the negative effects are somewhat wide of the scope of this chapter, they are substantial and are discussed in, among other sources, Strickland's "Tonto's Revenge."

58. This, as will be seen, applies primarily to certain strains of feminism, Marxism, "postmodernism," and, perhaps most explicitly, "postcolonialism"—each of which has "challenged" the prevailing order in ways that reinforce its cohesion. These will be addressed in due course.

59. For analysis of the myth, see Pearce, *Savagism and Civilization*; Berkhofer, *The White Man's Indian*. A classic if somewhat sentimental rendering of the mythic theme in a supposedly nonfictional format is found in Jay P. Kinney, *A Continent Lost—A Civilization Won: Indian Land Tenure in America* (Baltimore: John Hopkins University Press, 1937).

60. Brian W. Dippie, *The Vanishing American: White Attitudes and U.S. Indian Policy* (Middletown, CT: Wesleyan University Press, 1982); Christopher M. Lyman, *The Vanishing Race and Other Illusions* (New York: Pantheon, 1982).

61. Drinnon does a wonderful job of unraveling these codes of sign and signifier in the opening chapters of *Facing West*. One aspect he does not discuss, however, is the construction of savages as interlopers. The concept—or, more accurately, the "phobia"—appears to find its origins in the deepest recesses of the European mind, accruing from the trauma of such things as the sack of Rome and the Mongol invasion, each more than a thousand years hence; Roger Bartra, *Wild Men in the Looking Glass: The Mythic Origins of European Otherness* (Ann Arbor: University of Michigan Press, 1994).

62. The correspondence at issue was at times formalized as a matter of European/Euro-American law; see, e.g., Robert A. Williams Jr., *The American Indian in Western Legal Thought: The Discourses of Conquest* (New York: Oxford University Press, 1990).

63. Lest anyone deceive themselves into believing that such attitudes are consignable either to "the Past" or to only the more retrograde segments of contemporary settler society, see "progressive" commentator Christopher Hitchens's celebration of Columbus and the Columbian legacy in *The Nation* (19 October 1992).

64. In a truly bizarre twist, Griffith has his "Indians" cook and eat a puppy, the flesh of which he seems to have believed is imbued with psychedelic properties. In any event, those who ingest it shortly begin to exhibit clear signs of hallucinogenic intoxication.

65. For the moment, refer to the section "Ravages by Savages" in my *Fantasies of the Master Race*, 190–195. Alternately, see Tuska, *American West in Film*, 248–256.

66. Ralph K. Andrist, *The Long Death: The Last Days of the Plains Indian* (New York: Macmillan, 1964), 351–352; Dee Brown, *Bury My Heart at Wounded Knee: An Indian History of the American West* (New York: Holt, Rinehart, and Winston, 1970), 164–166, 401–402.

67. In fairness, the comparison should be reversed. There is no record of the Goebbels ministry having released a film claiming to "reenact" a similarly ferocious assault on SS personnel in an effort to transform the slaughter of Jewish infants into a heroic act of self-defense. Nor, for that matter, is there a record of the Nazi regime awarding decorations for gallantry to members of the SS for their service in the extermination squads. The U.S. Army, on the other hand, bestowed upwards of thirty Medals of Honor on troops participating at Wounded Knee. The massacre site was also formally designated a "battlefield"—the massacre itself a "battle"—until 1975. There is no record of the Germans making analogous references to, say, "the Battle of Babi Yar." See generally, Mario Gonzalez and Elizabeth Cook-Lynn, *The Politics of Hallowed Ground: Wounded Knee and the Struggle for Indian Sovereignty* (Urbana: University of Illinois Press, 1999).

68. Strickland, "Tonto's Revenge," 33.

69. Alternatively, extermination is sometimes employed as an object of humor. Witness Bob Hope's "comedy classic" *Son of Paleface* (1952), wherein the comic draws laughs by slaughtering a dozen Indians—two with a single bullet from his sixgun—all but one of whom fall in a neat pile. The wounded "recalcitrant," who staggers about for a few moments, is finally dispatched by Hope's hitting him in the head and adding his corpse to the stack. The sequence is included in *Images of Indians*. After viewing, it is good to ask what the likely response would be were the Germans to offer comparably "funny" movies depicting their elimination of Jews during the 1940s.

70. See Leah Renae Kelly, "The Auteurism of John Ford's 'Indian Films': A Brief Analysis," in her *Voice*, 98–107; Ken Nolley, "The Representation of Conquest: John Ford and the Hollywood Indian (1938–1964)," in Rollins and O'Connor, *Hollywood's Indian*, 73–88. For the phrase quoted, see Donald L. Davis, *John Ford: Hollywood's Old Master* (Norman: University of Oklahoma Press, 1995), 118.

71. Frederick F. Van de Water, *Glory Hunter: A Life of General Custer* (New York: Bobbs-Merrill, 1934).

72. Stan Hoig, *The Battle of the Washita* (Garden City, NY: Doubleday, 1976). As Hoig points out in his introduction, the word *battle* is used in his title only on "the basis of official convention" (i.e., to avoid confusing potential readers as to whether some different event is discussed therein). He is clear in the introduction, and more so in the body of his book, that what actually happened at the Washita was a massacre.

73. Brian Dippie, *Custer's Last Stand: The Anatomy of an American Myth* (Missoula: University of Montana Press, 1976); W. A. Graham, *The Custer Myth: A Sourcebook of Custerania* (Lincoln: University of Nebraska Press, 1986 reprint of 1953 original).

74. For a "scholarly" rendering of this ludicrous characterization, see Robert M. Utley, *Cavalier in Buckskin: George Armstrong Custer and the Western Military Frontier* (Norman: University of Oklahoma Press, 1988).

75. Van de Water, *Glory Hunter*, 168–177.

76. Donald Jackson, *Custer's Gold: The United States Cavalry Expedition of 1874* (Lincoln: University of Nebraska Press, 1966).

77. John E. Gray, *The Centennial Campaign: The Sioux War of 1876* (Norman: University of Oklahoma Press, 1988).

78. Far from being "the last man standing"—as not only Walsh's but every other Euro-American depiction has framed the scene—Custer was likely the first of his immediate command felled during his "Last Stand"; David Humphreys Miller, *Custer's Fall: The Native American Side of the Story* (New York: Penguin, 1992 reprint of 1953 original), 37, 129, 133.

79. It has been estimated that nearly 3,000 westerns were churned out between 1930 and 1960 (Nachbar, *Focus on the Western*, 9). Comparing this total to that offered in the text accompanying note 3 demonstrates the emphasis Hollywood has placed on depictions of "How the West Was Won."

80. The film—a TV miniseries, actually—was adapted from Evan S. Connell's best-selling biography, *Son of the Morning Star: Custer and the Little Big Horn* (San Francisco: North Point, 1984). The success of book and movie alike attests to the extent of the Custer myth's ongoing attraction.

81. See generally, Kasdan and Tavernetti, "Revisionist Western."

82. The comparison is in no sense intended rhetorically. The parallels are so close that U.S. Ambassador to Vietnam Maxwell Taylor referred to his country's military operations there as an "Indian War" (quoted in Drinnon, *Facing West*, 369), and American troops commonly referred to the combat zone as "Indian Country"; Noam Chomsky, *For Reasons of State* (New York: Pantheon, 1975), 120.

83. Actually, the "Colonel Iverson" character deployed in *Soldier Blue* more nearly resembles Colonel John Chivington, who perpetrated the 1864 Sand Creek Massacre in Colorado; Kilpatrick, *Celluloid Indians*, 77–79.

84. Such characters invite comparison to the "Good German" figure so prominent in that country's post-Nazi mythology. It was a similar wriggling in a different but distinctly

related context that led Sartre to remark that "there are neither good nor bad colonists: there are colonists"; Jean-Paul Sartre, "Introduction to Albert Memmi's *The Colonizer and the Colonized*," in his *Colonialism and Neocolonialism* (New York: Routledge, 2001), 51.

85. Stan Hoig, *The Sand Creek Massacre* (Norman: University of Oklahoma Press, 1961).

86. Friar and Friar, *"The Only Good Indian . . ."* 213.

87. As Sartre observed in a related connection, many "among them reject their objective reality: carried along by the colonial apparatus, they do each day, in deed, what they condemn in their dreams, and each of their acts contributes to the maintaining of oppression. They will change nothing, be of no use to anyone, and find their moral comfort in their malaise, that is all"; Sartre, "Introduction to Memmi" in his *Colonialism and Neocolonialism,* 51.

88. To be accurate, neither Penn nor Nelson created the model. They and certainly Costner patterned their rather clumsier efforts after those of English director David Lean, who developed and perfected the formula in his 1962 *Lawrence of Arabia*; see my "Lawrence of South Dakota," in *Fantasies*, 239–242. Also see Robert Baird, "Going Indian: *Dances With Wolves,*" and Jeffrey Walker, "Deconstructing an American Myth: *Last of the Mohicans,*" in Rollins and O'Connor, *Hollywood's Indian,* 153–169, 170–186.

89. See S. Elizabeth Bird, "Not My Fantasy: The Persistence of Indian Imagery in *Dr. Quinn, Medicine Woman*," in her *Dressing in Feathers*, 245–262.

90. Antonette Bosco, "Remembering Heaven-Bent Men Wearing Black Robes," *Litchfield County Times* (14 February 1992). On the actual roles played by missionaries during the invasion of North America, see George Tinker, *Missionary Conquest: The Gospel and Native American Cultural Genocide* (Minneapolis: Fortress, 1993).

91. Although it is never actually depicted, the horrors of "Iroquoian torture" comprises a sinister subtext throughout the first two-thirds of *Black Robe*, ultimately informing a dramatic sequence that is a crux point of the film. Tellingly, although it is set in the early seventeenth century, its hero a representative of Roman Catholicism, there is no whisper of the ubiquitous instrumentation of torture—the rack, body saws, and much worse—in the church's centuries-long and then-still-lingering Grand Inquisition; see Hoffman Nickerson, *The Inquisition: A Political and Military History of Its Establishment* (Port Washington, NY: Kennikat, 1968 reprint of 1932 original); Jean Guiraud, *The Medieval Inquisition* (New York: AMS, 1979).

92. Todorov explores this construction thoroughly in *Conquest of America*, as does Drinnon in the early to middle chapters of *Facing West*. Probably the best overview of the impacts attending the rationalization is found in David E. Stannard, *American Holocaust: Columbus and the Conquest of the New World* (New York: Oxford University Press, 1992). Also see "'Nits Make Lice': The Extermination of North American Indians, 1607–1996," in my *A Little Matter of Genocide: Holocaust and Denial in the Americas, 1492 to the Present* (San Francisco: City Lights, 1997), 129–288.

93. The indigenous population of North America has been credibly estimated to have numbered as many as 18.5 million in 1500. By 1890 it was less than a quarter million, a 99 percent reduction; see Russell Thornton, *American Indian Holocaust and Survival: A Population History Since 1492* (Norman: University of Oklahoma Press, 1987).

94. Quoted in Robert Jay Lifton, *The Nazi Doctors: Medical Killing and the Psychology of Genocide* (New York: Basic, 1986), 477. For context, see James M. Glass, *"Life Unworthy of Life": Racial Phobia and Mass Murder in Hitler's Germany* (New York: Basic, 1997).

95. See generally, Hoig, *Sand Creek Massacre*. It is noteworthy that Chivington was paraphrasing H. L. Hall, a noted Indian fighter in California who had several years earlier expressed the much-publicized view that native babies should be killed whenever possible because "a nit would make a louse." On Hall and for the quotation at issue, see Lynwood Carranco and Estle Beard, *Genocide and Vendetta: The Round Valley Wars of Northern California* (Norman: University of Oklahoma Press, 1981), chapter 4.

96. Witness the children's jingle, popular in the Massachusetts Colony that year, written in celebration of the colonists' recent "extirpation" of the Narragansetts: "A swarm of flies, they may arise / a Nation to annoy / Yea Rats and Mice or Swarms of Lice / a Nation may destroy"; reproduced in Drinnon, *Facing West*, 54.

97. These include everyone from Thomas Jefferson to Abraham Lincoln; see the quotations in Svaldi, *Rhetoric of Extermination*, throughout.

98. For a fairly comprehensive overview, see the section "The Most Savage of Practices" in my "'Nits Make Lice,'" 178–188.

99. Nolley, "Representation of Conquest," 83. Also see the relevant discussions in William Darby, *John Ford's Westerns: A Thematic Analysis With Filmography* (Jefferson, NC: McFarland, 1996).

100. See Carlos Clarens, *An Illustrated History of Horror and Science Fiction Films: The Classic Era, 1895–1967* (New York: Da Capo, 1997).

101. Friar and Friar, *"The Only Good Indian . . ."* 134.

102. Ibid., 215.

103. Stedman, *Shadows of the Indian*, 116.

104. Alan LeMay, *The Unforgiven* (New York: Harper and Bros., 1957).

105. In *Images of Indians* Will Sampson describes *The Unforgiven* as "the most racist movie about Indians ever made." For additional analysis, see Stedman, *Shadows of the Indian*, 124–125.

106. Capt. John Smith, *A Map of Virginia, With a Description of the Country, the Commodities, People, Government and Religion (1612)*. For an overview of this literary stream, see my "Literature and the Colonization of American Indians," in *Fantasies*, 1–18; Berkhofer, *White Man's Indian*; Stedman, *Shadows of the Indian*.

107. For framing, see, e.g., the essays collected in Gidley, *Representing Others*. Also see *Europe and Its Others: Proceedings of the Essex Conference on the Sociology of Literature, July 1984* (Essex: Essex University Press, 1985).

108. Published in *McClure's* magazine in 1910, London's short story is representative of its genre in every respect. See Richard Austin Thompson, *The Yellow Peril, 1890–1924* (New York: Arno, 1978); William F. Wu, *The Yellow Peril: Chinese Americans in American Fiction, 1850–1940* (Hamden, CT: Archon, 1982).

109. For analysis, see H. Bruce Franklin, *War Stars: The Superweapon and the American Imagination* (New York: Oxford University Press, 1988), 101–102.

110. Robert Jay Lifton and Eric Markusen, *The Genocidal Mentality: Nazi Holocaust and Nuclear Threat* (New York: Basic, 1988).

111. Griffith seems to have lifted the entire scene from David Belasco's 1893 Broadway play *The Girl I Left Behind Me*; Stedman, *Shadows of the Indian*, 109.

112. Tuska, *American West in Film*, 239.

113. For these and other relevant quotes, see Stedman, *Shadows of the Indian*, 105; ibid., 246, 250. Also see Jimmie Durham, "Savage Attacks on White Women, as Usual," in his *Lack of Coherence*, 120–125.

114. Jack Nachbar, "Ulzana's Raid," in *Western Movies*, ed. William T. Pilkington and Don Graham (Albuquerque: University of New Mexico Press, 1979), 139–147.

115. Probably the penultimate articulation of this theme comes in Burt Kennedy's *The Deserter* (1971), when the settler-hero's wife is captured, gang-raped, then skinned alive and left for him to kill; Tuska, *American West in Film*, 250.

116. The phrase is borrowed from Oneida comic Charley Hill.

117. This theme runs deep in the Euro-American psyche. The bloodthirsty "Ethan Edwards" portrayed by Wayne shares much in common with the revenge-crazed "Nathan Slaughter" constructed by Robert Montgomery Bird in his acclaimed 1837 novel *Nick of the Woods* (adapted by Louisa H. Medina for production as a stage play in 1838); Curtis Dahl, *Robert Montgomery Bird* (New York: Twayne, 1963), see esp. 97.

118. For a glimpse of the lengths to which mainstream critics have been willing to go in seeking to protect *The Searchers*—and Ford himself—from being categorized as racist, see Peter Lehman, "Looking at Look's Missing Reverse Shots: Psychoanalysis and Style in John Ford's *The Searchers*," in *The Western Reader*, ed. Jim Kitses and Gregg Rickman (New York: Limelight, 1998), 259–268.

119. This outcome should be usefully contrasted to that in *Unforgiven*, where Natalie Wood, portraying a young, fair-skinned native woman "taken in" as a child by "kindly" white raiders, is scripted to prove her "virtue"—and, more important, that she is "at heart really more white than not"—by killing her Kiowa brother when he comes to retrieve her.

120. Alan LeMay, *The Searchers* (New York: Harper and Row, 1954).

121. Zoe A. Tilghman, *Quannah: Eagle of the Comanches* (Oklahoma City: Harlow, 1958).

122. See generally, Cynthia Schmidt Hacker, *Cynthia Ann Parker: The Life and the Legend* (El Paso: Texas Western Press, 1990); quotation is from the dust cover. Also see Jimmie Durham, "Cowboy S-M," in his *Lack of Coherence*, 187–190.

123. Benjamin Franklin, letter to Peter Collinson, 9 May 1753, in *The Papers of Benjamin Franklin, Vol. 4*, ed. Leonard W. Larabee et al. (New Haven: Yale University Press, 1959), 481–482.

124. James Axtell, "The White Indians of Colonial America," in his *The European and the Indian: Essays on the Ethnohistory of North America* (New York: Oxford University Press, 1981), 177. He is quoting from William Smith, D.D., *Historical Account of Colonel Bouquet's Expedition Against the Ohio Indians, 1764* (Philadelphia: Remington's, 1765), 390–391; "Provincial Correspondence, 1750–1765," *Register of Pennsylvania* 4 (1839): 500; "Relation of Frederick Post of Conversation With Indians, 1760," *Pennsylvania Archive* 3 (1853). Hundreds—perhaps thousands—of similar observations might be quoted; see my "The Crucible of American Indian Identity: Native Tradition Versus Colonial Imposition in Postconquest North America," *American Indian Culture and Research Journal* 23, 1 (1999): 39–68.

125. Mary Rowlandson, *The Narrative of the Captivity and Restoration of Mrs. Mary Rowlandson* (Boston: Houghton-Mifflin, 1930 reprint of 1682 original).

126. "Isabella McCoy," in *Scalps and Tomahawks: Narratives of Indian Captivity*, ed. Frederick Drimmer (New York: Howard-McCann, 1961), 31–48.

127. Drinnon, *Facing West*, 61; Slotkin, *Regeneration*, 357. More broadly, see Jenny Sharpe, "The Unspeakable Limits of Rape: Colonial Violence and Counter-Insurgency," in *Colonial Discourse and Post-Colonial Theory: A Reader*, ed. Patrick Williams and Laura Chrisman (New York: Columbia University Press, 1995), 221–243.

128. To arrive at her desired conclusion—that men of all cultures are fairly consistently disposed to rape—Brownmiller often had to wildly distort the available evidence. With respect to the captivity narratives, for example, she is sweeping not only in her dismissal of native sources but also in discounting the accounts of the "victims" themselves. Meanwhile, the libidinal fantasies filling Mather's third-hand propaganda tracts are treated as credible sources. One can only wonder why she did follow through by citing the stories published during the 1930s in Julius Streicher's *Dur Stürmer* as "evidence" that Jews habitually ravaged fair Aryan maidens; Susan Brownmiller, *Against Our Will: Men, Women and Rape* (New York: Simon and Schuster, 1975), 140–145.

129. Drimmer, *Scalps and Tomahawks*, 13.

130. Morris Edward Opler, *An Apache Life-Way: The Economic, Social, and Religious Institutions of the Chiricahua Indians* (Chicago: University of Chicago Press, 1941), 228.

131. See "Sex, Race and Holy War" in Stannard, *American Holocaust*, 195–246. Also see Leslie Feidler, *Return of the Vanishing American* (New York: Stein and Day, 1968), 45–46.

132. The literature in this connection is burgeoning. See, as examples, Agnes Grant, *No End of Grief: Indian Residential Schools in Canada* (Winnipeg: Pemmican, 1996); Suzanne Fournier and Ernie Grey, *Stolen From Our Embrace: The Abduction of First Nations Children and the Restoration of Aboriginal Communities* (Vancouver: Douglas and McIntyre, 1997); Roland Chrisjohn and Sherri Young, with Michael Maraun, *The Circle Game: Shadows and Substance in the Indian Residential School Experience in Canada* (Penticton, BC: Theytus, 1997); John S. Milloy, *A National Crime: The Canadian Government and the Residential School System, 1879–1986* (Winnipeg: University of Manitoba Press, 1999).

133. The few films touching on the effects of Indian boarding schools in the United States—e.g., *Jim Thorpe, All American* (1951) and *Running Brave* (1981)—have been frankly celebratory. Even the somewhat more accurate depiction offered in *The Education of Little Tree* (1997) avoids any hint of sexual predation by the school's staff.

134. Cleaver's astute analysis of rapist psychology—offered through the lens of self-understanding attained by his own earlier affliction—is offered in his *Soul on Ice* (New York: Ramparts and McGraw-Hill, 1968); see esp. 16–17. For Brownmiller's incredibly distortive "interpretation"—it amounts to a complete inversion of Cleaver's argument—see *Against Our Will*, 248–252. The most recent regurgitation I am aware of is Judy Gumbo Albert's offhand comment during an interview on how "it's true that Eldridge Cleaver glorified rape as an insurrectionary act in his book, *Soul on Ice*"; "Thoughts on Subversion From Two Yippie Elders," *Green Anarchy* 6 (Summer 2001): 8. For a solid rejoinder, see Angela Y. Davis, "Rape, Racism, and the Myth of the Black Rapist," in her *Women, Race, and Class* (New York: Random House, 1981), 172–201.

135. There are, of course, exceptions, albeit of a rather peculiar sort. In her recent *Cartographies of Desire: Captivity of Race and Sex in the Shaping of the American Nation* (Norman: University of Oklahoma Press, 1999), Rebecca Blevins Faery, to offer a prime example, follows both Cleaver and the facts to conclude that red-on-white rape has been mostly nonexistent. To explain the virulent mythology that has nonetheless attended issues of red-white sexuality, she also "borrows"—intact and in its entirety—the quadrilateral typology of interracial sexual archetypes Cleaver set forth quite brilliantly in "The Allegory of the Black Eunuchs" (*Soul on Ice*, 155–175). Having thus dredged Cleaver for

his undeniable explanatory utility, Blevins Faery repays her debt by making absolutely no reference to him. *Cartographies,* which is in my opinion an otherwise admirable work, must therefore be seen as a classic illustration of intellectual imperialism.

136. I say "predictable" since such results have long been known to attend acute psychological trauma, especially that of a recurrent, protracted variety, inaugurated at an early age. For an excellent overview—which nonetheless neglects all mention of the residential–boarding school context in North America—see Judith Herman, *Trauma and Recovery,* 2d ed. (New York: Basic, 1997).

137. A stunning example is Mary Daley, *Gyn/Ecology: The Metaethic of Radical Feminism* (Boston: Beacon, 1978).

138. The Euro-feminist equation of nationalism to "masculinist dominance" commenced at least as early as Barbara Burris's "The Fourth World Manifesto" (in *Radical Feminism,* ed. Anne Koedt [New York: Quadrangle, 1973], 322–357) and has seen continued refinement in essays such as those collected by Miranda Davis in *Third World/ Second Sex: Women's Struggles and National Liberation* (London: Zed, 1983); those collected by Roberta Hamilton and Michèle Barrett, eds., *The Politics of Diversity: Feminism, Marxism and Nationalism* (London: Verso, 1987); and, most recently, attempts to discredit the work of Third World anticolonial theorists like Frantz Fanon spearheaded by mainstreamers such as Diana Fuss (see, e.g., her "Interior Colonies: Frantz Fanon and the Politics of Identification," in *Rethinking Fanon: The Continuing Dialogue,* ed. Nigel C. Gibson [Amherst, NY: Humanity, 1999], 294–328). A firm rejoinder is found in Gayatri Chakravorty Spivak, "Feminism in Decolonization," *Differences* 3, 3 (1991): 139–170.

139. For explication, see Gayatri Chakravorty Spivak, "French Feminism in an International Frame," in her *In Other Worlds: Essays on Cultural Politics* (New York: Methuen, 1987), 134–153; Linda Alcolff, "The Problem of Speaking for Others," *Cultural Critique* 20 (1991–1992); Chandra Talpade Mohanty, "Under Western Eyes: Feminist Scholarship and Colonial Discourses," in Williams and Chrisman, *Colonial Discourse and Post-Colonial Theory,* 196–220.

140. Gayatri Chakravorty Spivak, "Can the Subaltern Speak?" in *Marxism and the Interpretation of Culture,* ed. Carey Nelson and Lawrence Grossberg (Urbana: University of Illinois Press, 1988), 297.

141. The issue of white women's complicity in racism and colonialism is a matter of considerable inconvenience to Euro-feminist pretensions of victim status. This perhaps explains the recent spate of works seeking to separate women from the imperial project by setting forth the ways in which their "travel writing about the non-Western world," for example, "was markedly different from men's in form, thematic preoccupations and political positionality," thus allegedly posing "a subtle challenge to the dominant masculinist discourse of imperialism by 'helping to build a reservoir of mutual understanding' between the races, which was to smooth the way for decolonization"; Moore-Gilbert, *Postcolonial Theory,* 214, citing Helen Callaway, *Gender, Culture and Empire* (Urbana: University of Illinois Press, 1987); Mary Louise Pratt, *Imperial Eyes: Travel Writing and Transculturation* (London: Routledge, 1992); Sara Mills, *Discourses of Difference: An Analysis of Women's Travel Writing and Colonialism* (London: Routledge, 1993); Lisa Lowe, *French and British Orientalisms* (Ithaca: Cornell University Press, 1991). One need only undertake the most cursory comparison of men's writing during the classical colonial era—Kipling's to Melville's, for instance, or Sartre's to Graham Greene's—to

apprehend equal or greater "differences in form, thematic preoccupation and political positionality." For analysis of the transparency in Euro-feminism's "'common oppression' rhetoric and . . . attempts to deny white women's privilege in an antiblack culture," see T. Deneane Sharply-Whiting, "Fanon's Feminist Consciousness and Algerian Women's Liberation: Colonialism, Nationalism and Fundamentalism," in Gibson, *Rethinking Fanon*, esp. 350–351.

142. See Joel Kovel, *White Racism: A Psychohistory*, 2d ed. (New York: Columbia University Press, 1984).

143. George Lipsitz, *The Possessive Investment in Whiteness: How White People Profit From Identity Politics* (Philadelphia: Temple University Press, 1998). Relatedly, see David Roediger, *The Wages of Whiteness: Race and the Making of the American Working Class* (London: Verso, 1991).

144. For background, see, e.g., Eric Wolf, *Europe and the People Without History* (Berkeley: University of California Press, 1982); Vassilis Lambropoulis, *The Rise of Eurocentrism: Anatomy of Interpretation* (Princeton: Princeton University Press, 1993).

145. Norman Cohn, *Warrant for Genocide: The Myth of the Jewish World Conspiracy and the Protocols of the Elders of Zion*, 2d ed. (London: Serrit, 1996). Also see, e.g., the reproduction of the first page of the "Special Edition on Jewish Ritual Murder" put forth by *Dur Stürmer* in May 1934; Randall L. Bytwerk, *Julius Streicher: The Man Who Persuaded a Nation to Hate Jews* (New York: Dorset, 1983), fig. 16.

146. A dated but still useful examination of this script is found in "The Savage Art of Discovery: How to Blame the Victim," in William Ryan's *Blaming the Victim* (New York: Vintage, 1971), 3–29.

147. Probably the best-known example is that of "Little Horse," a lispingly stereotyped *heemaneh* portrayed by Lakota actor Robert Little Star in *Little Big Man*; Kasdan and Tavernetti, "Revisionist Western," 131. Unpacking this trope can be difficult, given the misperceptions of native homosexuality engendered by such pop treatments as Paula Gunn Allen, *The Sacred Hoop: Recovering the Feminine in American Indian Cultures* (Boston: Beacon, 1986), and Walter L. Williams, *The Spirit and the Flesh: Sexual Diversity Among Native Americans* (Boston: Beacon, 1986). The most straightforward indicator of the sorts of problems riddling both books is found in the juxtaposition of Gunn Allen's initial (and entirely accurate) representation of homosexuality as uncommon to the point of uniqueness—and therefore "special"—in most indigenous societies to her later insinuation that it was so common as to comprise a normative orientation. Obviously, the matter cannot be had both ways. Something is either common (banal) or special (unique). Thus, far from offering an accurate rendering of the facet of traditional native life she purports to depict, the author plays to the crowd, deliberately distorting her subject matter in a manner greatly appealing to a contemporary school of mostly non-Indian gay rights activists who demand that their constituencies be treated as if they were both special *and* "normal." Such posturing may make for good politics, but it is lousy scholarship.

148. Probably the first two movies to pursue this theme were *An Indian Maiden's Choice* and *The Indian Girl's Romance* (both 1910), and they have continued in a torrent ever since; see my *Fantasies of the Master Race*, 193–196. The matter is handled in more depth—and rather well—by Blevins Faery in *Cartographies of Desire*. Also see Robert S. Tilton, *Pocahontas: The Evolution of an American Narrative* (Cambridge: Cambridge University Press, 1994).

149. This is brought out in an endless stream of films about the "problems of mixed-bloodedness," e.g., *The Halfbreed* (1916; remade as *The Half Breed* in 1922 and as *The Half-Breed* in 1952), *The Dumb Half-Breed's Defense* (1910), *The Half-Breed's Way* and *The Half-Breed's Sacrifice* (both 1912), *The Barrier of Blood, The Half-Breed Parson,* and *The Half-Breed Sheriff* (all 1913), *Indian Blood* (1914), *The Ancient Blood* and *The Quarter Breed* (both 1916), *One-Eighth Apache* (1922), *Call Her Savage* (1932), and on and on. The Friars list 108 films devolving upon such themes by 1970; *"The Only Good Indian . . ."* 300–301.

150. Sheridan's actual statement was that "the only good Indians I ever saw were dead"; quoted in Paul Andrew Hutton, *Phil Sheridan and His Army* (Lincoln: University of Nebraska Press, 1985), 180.

151. An excellent montage sequence including dozens of such scenes is found in *Images of Indians*.

152. Arguably, Cooper found a model for his Good Indian character in that of "Friday," the faithful native constructed by Daniel Defoe in *Robinson Crusoe*; Stedman, *Shadows of the Indian,* 52–54, 179, 260. Also see William P. Kelly, *Plotting America's Past: James Fenimore Cooper and the Leatherstocking Tales* (Carbondale: Southern Illinois University Press, 1983).

153. Be it noted that the Mohicans still exist. Lumped together with several other small eastern peoples under the heading "Stockbridge-Munsee Indians," they reside on a small reservation near Green Bay, Wisconsin; Patrick Frazier, *The Mohicans of Stockbridge* (Lincoln: University of Nebraska Press, 1992).

154. Rayna Green, "The Only Good Indian: Images of Indians in American Vernacular Culture," Ph.D. dissertation, Indiana University, Bloomington, 382.

155. Daniel Francis, *The Imaginary Indian: The Image of the Indian in Canadian Culture* (Vancouver: Arsenal Pulp, 1992), 167.

156. Tilton, *Pocahontas,* 56.

157. Walker, "Deconstructing an American Myth."

158. On the concept of "the Man Who Knows Indians," see Slotkin, *Gunfighter Nation,* 47.

159. See generally, James Van Hise, *Who Was That Masked Man? The Story of the Lone Ranger* (Las Vegas: Pioneer, 1990).

160. Bird, "Not My Fantasy" in her *Dressing in Feathers.* Also see Richard Zoglin, "Frontier Feminist," *Time* (1 March 1993), and "The Other Side of Postfeminism: Maternal Feminism in *Dr. Quinn, Medicine Woman,*" in Bonnie J. Dow's *Prime Time Feminism: Television, Media Culture, and the Women's Movement Since 1970* (Philadelphia: University of Pennsylvania Press, 1996), 164–202.

161. Rudyard Kipling, *Gunga Din and Other Favorite Poems* (New York: Dover, 1991).

162. For exploration of levels of colonialist virulence in Kipling often ignored even by radical critics, see Patrick Williams, "Kim and Orientalism," in Williams and Chrisman, *Colonial Discourse and Post-Colonial Theory,* 480–489. Also see Zoreh T. Sullivan, *Narratives of Empire: The Fiction of Rudyard Kipling* (Cambridge: Cambridge University Press, 1993).

163. Bird, "Not My Fantasy" in her *Dressing in Feathers,* 249.

164. Ibid.

165. A hint of how the Vichy–Free French were juxtaposed in contemporaneous American cinema is found in Michael Curtiz's 1942 classic, *Casablanca.*

166. See generally, Geoffrey Warner, *Pierre Laval and the Eclipse of France* (London: Macmillan, 1968).

167. A good analysis is found in Frank Manchel, "Cultural Confusion: *Broken Arrow* (1950)," in Rollins and O'Connor, *Hollywood's Indian,* 91–106.

168. See Edwin R. Sweeny, *Cochise: Chiricahua Chief* (Norman: University of Oklahoma Press, 1991).

169. For relatively accurate views of "Geronimo" (Golthlay), see Britton Davis, *The Truth About Geronimo* (Chicago: Lakeside, 1951 reprint of 1929 original); Obie B. Falk, *The Geronimo Campaign* (New York: Oxford University Press, 1969).

170. See, e.g., Mari Sandoz, *Crazy Horse: Strange Man of the Oglalas* (New York: Alfred A. Knopf, 1942). It can be worthwhile to have students read this fine biography, then view what director George Sherman did with it in his 1955 *Chief Crazy Horse.*

171. With respect to such exposure "increasing," consider the program recently inaugurated by the Canadian government—which never seems to have funds to meet its actual treaty obligations in terms of providing adequate housing, medical services, and the like in exchange for its claimed land base—to install a satellite dish in every remote northern village so the kids there will share the "opportunity" to see reruns of John Ford movies; Jerry Mander, *In the Absence of the Sacred: The Failure of Technology and the Survival of Indian Nations* (San Francisco: Sierra Club, 1992), 97–119.

172. Strickland, "Tonto's Revenge" in his *Tonto's Revenge,* 18.

173. Strickland, "You Can't Rollerskate in a Buffalo Herd, Even if You Have All the Medicine: American Indian Law and Politics," in his *Tonto's Revenge,* 53. On Canada, see *Choosing Life: Special Report on Suicide Among Aboriginal People* (Ottawa: Canada Communication Group, 1994).

174. Geoffrey York, *The Dispossessed: Life and Death in Native Canada,* 2d ed. (Toronto: McArthur, 1999), 1–21; Gary Remington and Brian Hoffman, "Gas Sniffing as Substance Abuse," *Canadian Journal of Psychiatry* 29 (1984): 31–35; Fournier and Grey, *Stolen From Our Embrace,* 115–117.

175. See Leah Renae Kelly, "The Open Veins of Native North America," in her *Voice,* 112–115.

176. The issue is covered in "Let's Spread the 'Fun' Around: The Issue of Sports Team Names and Mascots" and "In the Matter of Julius Streicher: Applying Nuremberg Standards in the United States," in my *From a Native Son: Selected Essays in Indigenism, 1985–1995* (Boston: South End, 1996), 439–444, 445–454. Also see Carol Spindel, *Dancing at Halftime: Sports and the Controversy Over American Indian Mascots* (New York: New York University Press, 2000); C. Richard King and Charles Frueling Springwood, eds., *Team Spirits: The Native American Mascots Controversy* (Lincoln: University of Nebraska Press, 2001).

177. "Squaw" is a corruption of the Mohawk word for female genitalia, analogous when used as slang to the term *cunt*; Barbara Alice Mann, *Iroquoian Women: The Gantowisas* (New York: Peter Lang, 2000), 364. The pervasiveness of this descriptor in settler discourse is to some extent evident in the titles of scores of potboiler films like *The Squaw Man* (1913, 1918, 1938) and *The Fate of the Squaw* (1914). Even more striking is the fact that about a thousand officially designated place names in North America include the word—Squaw Valley, Squaw Peak, Squaw Creek, and so on. The effect on native women—not to mention six-year-old girls—of being referred to in this fashion is anything but "harmless";

see, e.g., Rayna Green, "The Pocahontas Perplex: The Image of Indian Women in American Culture," *Massachusetts Review* 16, 4 (1975): 698–714.

178. The relationship between denial of genocides past and the perpetration of genocides present and future is bought out well by Roger W. Smith, Eric Markusen, and Robert Jay Lifton in "Professional Ethics and the Denial of the Armenian Genocide," *Holocaust and Genocide Studies* 9 (1995): 1–22.

179. The implications are brought out well in Wolf, *Europe and the People Without History.*

180. Strickland, "Tonto's Revenge" in his *Tonto's Revenge,* 20.

181. The matter is discussed at several points in Allan L. Wald and Randall H. Miller, *Ethics and Racial Images in American Film and Television: Historical Essays and Bibliography* (New York: Garland, 1987). On Ford's fixation on Monument Valley in particular, see Maltby, "A Better Sense of History."

182. The largely Hollywood-induced deficit in geographical understanding suffered by American schoolchildren had become something of a scandal by the late 1960s. But then, what might one have expected of a culture that believes the European subcontinent is not only a continent in its own right but *"the* Continent"? See generally, Kenneth C. Davis, *Don't Know Much About Geography: Everything You Need to Know About the World But Never Learned,* 4th ed. (New York: Avon, 1999).

183. This sort of thing, which was and still is rampant, was addressed by Dan Georgakis in "They Have Not Spoken: American Indians in Film," *Film Quarterly* 25 (1972): 26–32. Also see Ralph E. Friar and Natasha A. Friar, "White Man Speak With Split Tongue, Forked Tongue, Tongue of Snake," in Bataille and Silet, *Pretend Indians,* 92–97.

184. Strickland, "Tonto's Revenge" in his *Tonto's Revenge,* 20.

185. Indigenous people are not alone in having protested this. As early as 1914, Alanson Skinner, curator of anthropology at the American Museum of Natural History, decried in a *New York Times* guest editorial the "ethnographically grotesque farces" embodied in such cinematic travesties as "Delawares dressed as Sioux" and "the Indians of Manhattan . . . dwelling in tipis"; quoted in ibid., 32. Given this and many subsequent criticisms of the same sort, it is untenable to argue—as have apologists like Lenihan and Nachbar—that Hollywood's systematic misrepresentation of native culture has been in any sense "unintentional" or "unwitting."

186. Maltby, "A Better Sense of History," 35.

187. Ralph and Natasha Friar provide a list of 350 noteworthy white actors, both male and female, who appeared in redface between 1910 and 1970; *"The Only Good Indian . . ."* 281–283. Suffice to say that the list of Indians cast as whites is a bit shorter.

188. The effect, as Charley Hill has put it, was "like casting Wilt Chamberlain as J. Edgar Hoover." Connor discusses his role without discernible embarrassment in *Images of Indians.*

189. Aside from the Mohawk Jay Silverheels, who found steady work playing Tonto in the *Lone Ranger* epics, the last overtly native actor before the 1990s to win name recognition in movie theaters was the Cherokee Will Rogers during the 1930s; see my and Leah Renae Kelly's *"Smoke Signals* in Context: An Historical Overview," in her *Voice,* esp. 123–125.

190. In this there is a striking parallel to the arrogant assertion made by many "American Indianist" anthropologists—and undoubtedly harbored as an unstated belief by most

others—that they "know more about Indians than the Indians themselves"; see Wendy Rose, "The Great Pretenders: Further Reflections on White Shamanism," in *The State of Native America: Genocide, Colonization and Resistance,* ed. M. Annette Jaimes (Boston: South End, 1992), 403–422.

191. Bird, "Not My Fantasy" in her *Dressing in Feathers,* 251.

192. The 1955 movie was a sequel to *Davy Crockett, Indian Scout* (1950) and was fashioned from segments run on Disney's popular Sunday night TV series. A third film, *Davy Crockett and the River Pirates,* was released in 1956. The package was such a hit that for a while it seemed every grade-school boy in the United States was running around in a coonskin cap resembling that Fess Parker wore in the title role; Slotkin, *Gunfighter Nation,* 516. More fully, see Margaret J. King, "The Recycled Hero: Walt Disney's Davy Crockett," in *Davy Crockett: The Man, the Legend, the Legacy, 1786–1986,* ed. Michael J. Lofaro (Nashville: University of Tennessee Press, 1986), 137–158.

193. An unnamed critic observed in *Film Quarterly* at the time of its release that "stripped of its pretensions, *Horse* parades the standard myth that a white man can do everything better than an Indian. Give him a little time and he will marry the best-looking girl (a princess, of course) and will end up chief"; quoted in Kilpatrick, *Celluloid Indians,* 82.

194. On *Cheyenne Autumn*—another devastating corruption of a fine book by Mari Sandoz—see ibid., 67–70; Noley, "Representations of Conquest," esp. 79–82; V. F. Perkins, "Cheyenne Autumn," in Bataille and Silet, *Pretend Indians,* esp. 153.

195. Loosely based on the book cited in note 169, the movie should really have been titled "The Britton Davis Story." In any event, see Kilpatrick, *Celluloid Indians,* 143–148.

196. Ibid., 154–156.

197. Durham, "Cowboys" in *Lack of Coherence,* 176. His entirely appropriate inclusion of Queequag and Kesey's "Bromden" ("Chief Broom") character along with Tonto is instructive insofar as most analysts have considered both Melville's and Kesey's works counterhegemonic; see, e.g., H. Bruce Franklin, "From Empire to Empire: Billy Budd, Sailor," in *Herman Melville: Reassessments,* ed. A. Robert Lee (London and Totowa, NJ: Vision and Barnes and Noble, 1984), 199–216.

198. Durham, "Cowboys" in *Lack of Coherence,* 176.

199. Ibid. A deliberate irony is imbedded in Durham's metaphor devolving upon a curious insistence among anthropologists—despite a total lack of evidence—that American Indians were in preinvasion times anthropophagi. This "scientific" assertion serves much the same "blood libel" purpose discussed earlier with respect to rape; see my "Science as Psychosis: An Analysis of *Man Corn* by Christy and Jacqueline Turner," *North American Archaeologist* 21, 3 (2000): 268–283.

200. Europe even developed a legal principle—*territorium res nullius*—as a subset of its Doctrine of Discovery to accommodate the notion of "vacant land"; see "The Tragedy and the Travesty: The Subversion of Indigenous Sovereignty in North America," in my *Struggle for the Land,* esp. 43–50. For a good survey of the sorts of effects that attend application of this construction in the "real world," see Boyce Richardson, *The People of Terra Nullius: Betrayal and Rebirth in Aboriginal Canada* (Seattle and Vancouver: University of Washington Press and Douglas McIntire, 1993).

201. Once again a clear interface exists between myth and "science" in the public consciousness. The standard estimate put forth by the Smithsonian Institution for most of the twentieth century was that only about a million indigenous people were residing in

North America when the European invasion commenced. Over the past thirty years it has been conclusively established that, beginning in the early nineteenth century, generations of settler academics deliberately falsified their data to make the preinvasion native population appear far smaller than it actually was (thereby making the continent appear to have been relatively uninhabited); for analysis, see "Widowed Land" in Francis Jennings, *The Invasion of America: Indians, Colonialism and the Cant of Conquest* (Chapel Hill: University of North Carolina Press, 1975). For honest estimates, see Thornton, *American Indian Holocaust,* note 93.

202. See "Deconstructing the Columbus Myth: Was the 'Great Discoverer' Italian or Spanish, Nazi or Jew?" in my *A Little Matter of Genocide,* 81–96.

203. As Deloria has aptly observed, "The white man is haunted by the knowledge that he can never be alone" on the land of North America; "American Fantasy" in *The Pretend Indians,* xvi.

204. Such information—including the fact that self-anointed federal "trustees" have "misplaced" as much as $40 *billion* in funds belonging to destitute Indians over the years, plowing the money into programs benefiting the settler populace—is readily available in the mass media; see, e.g., Peter Maas, "Broken Promise," *Parade Magazine* (9 September 2001). Overall, see Kelly, "Open Veins," and my "The Indigenous Peoples of North America: A Struggle Against Internal Colonialism," in *Struggle for the Land,* 15–36.

205. Sartre, "Colonialism Is a System" in his *Colonialism and Neocolonialism,* 39.

206. The standard rejoinder to this is that we did not/do not "really" constitute nations and thus cannot comprise colonies in the sense contended. In response it can be pointed out that under both customary law and Article 1, Section 10 of its own constitution, the U.S. government has never been empowered to enter into treaty relationships with any entity but another nation. On record, the federal government has entered into and duly ratified around 400 treaties with Native American peoples, each of which conveys formal legal recognition that the other parties were or are separate nations; Vine Deloria Jr. and Raymond J. DeMallie, *Documents of American Indian Diplomacy: Treaties, Agreements and Conventions, 1775–1979,* 2 vols. (Norman: University of Oklahoma Press, 1999). The same principle applies to Canada; see *Canada: Indian Treaties and Surrenders From 1680 to 1890,* 3 vols. (Ottawa: Queen's Printer, 1891; reprinted by Fifth House [Saskatoon], 1992). Overall, see Sir Ian Sinclair, *The Vienna Convention on the Law of Treaties* (Manchester: Manchester University Press, 1984).

207. For the relevant texts, see Burns H. Weston, Richard A. Falk, and Anthony D'Amato, *Basic Documents in International Law and World Order,* 2d ed. (St. Paul: West, 1990). For elaboration of principles, see John Howard Clinebell and Jim Thompson, "Sovereignty and Self-Determination: The Rights of Native Americans Under International Law," *Buffalo Law Review* 27 (Fall 1978): 669–714; Lee C. Buchheit, *Secession: The Legitimacy of Self-Determination* (New Haven: Yale University Press, 1978); Ved Nanda, "Self-Determination Under International Law: Validity of Claims to Secede," *Case Western Journal of International Law* 13 (1981): 257–280; Michla Pomerance, *Self-Determination in Law and Practice* (The Hague: Marinus Nijhoff, 1982).

208. The famous phrase was first uttered by Chief Justice of the Supreme Court John Marshall in his 1803 *Marbury* opinion (1 Cranch [5 U.S.] 137). For analysis, see "It's the Law," in Rodolfo Acuña, *Sometimes There Is No Other Side: Chicanos and the Myth of Equality* (Notre Dame: Notre Dame University Press, 1998), 33–56.

209. This seems to pertain not just in North America but to all comparable contexts. See Ronald Weitzer, *Transforming Settler States: Communal Conflict and Internal Security in Northern Ireland and Zimbabwe* (Berkeley: University of California Press, 1992).

210. Durham, "Cowboys" in *Lack of Coherence,* 174–175. The final query plainly ties back to the suicide and gasoline sniffing epidemics afflicting native youth, mentioned in conjunction with notes 173 and 174.

211. "Conquest was achieved by violence; exploitation and oppression demand the maintenance of violence. . . . Colonialism [thus necessarily] denies human rights to people it subjugates by violence, and whom it keeps in poverty and ignorance by force"; Sartre, "Introduction to Memmi" in his *Colonialism and Neocolonialism,* 50.

212. Neither the idea of internal colonialism nor its applicability to North America is unique to Durham. Probably the best-known study is Michael Hector, *Internal Colonialism: The Celtic Fringe in British National Development, 1536–1966* (Berkeley: University of California Press, 1975). Actually, the concept seems to have originated with Antonio Gramsci in his 1920 essay, "The Southern Question" (in his *The Modern Prince and Other Writings* [New York: International, 1957], 28–51). It was adapted by Cherokee anthropologist Robert K. Thomas to describe the situation of American Indians in his "Colonialism: Classic and Internal" (*New University Thought* 4, 4 (Winter 1966–1967). Since then, it has been employed by numerous scholars, including myself, working on indigenous issues (both in North America and globally). Rodolfo Acuña, among others, has also used it to good effect in analyzing the circumstances of Mexican Americans in the southwestern United States; see esp. Acuña, *Occupied America: The Chicano's Struggle Toward Liberation* (San Francisco: Canfield, 1972).

213. Durham, "Cowboys" in *Lack of Coherence,* 175.

214. Ibid.

215. Ibid., 174.

216. On the concept of White Skin Privilege, see Allan G. Johnson, *Power, Privilege, and Difference* (Mountain View, CA: Mayfield, 2000).

217. See, e.g., Allan Bloom, *The Closing of the American Mind* (New York: Touchstone, 1988); Arthur M. Schlesinger Jr., *The Disuniting of America: Reflections on a Multicultural Society,* rev. ed. (New York: W. W. Norton, 1998).

218. For especially telling comments in this connection, see Tuhiwai Smith, *Decolonizing Theory,* 98; Aijaz Ahmad, *In Theory: Classes, Nations, Literatures* (London: Verso, 1992), 7.

219. Although the term *ludic* is typically employed as signifying "playfulness," I use it in the sense of "ludicrous." For further explication, see Teresa Ebert, *Ludic Feminism and After: Postmodernism, Desire, and Labor in Late Capitalism* (Ann Arbor: University of Michigan Press, 1996).

220. A devastating critique of this tendency is found in J. Sakai, *Settlers: The Myth of the White Proletariat* (Chicago: Morningstar, 1983). Also see Roediger, *Wages of Whiteness;* Lipsitz, *Investment in Whiteness.*

221. For abundant quotations to this effect, see the opening chapter of Walker Connor, *The National Question in Marxist-Leninist Theory and Strategy* (Princeton: Princeton University Press, 1984). For the best overall critiques of Marxian ethnocentrism at the level of high theory, see Jean Baudrillard, *The Mirror of Production* (St. Louis: Telos, 1975), and Said, *Orientalism.* Still, one finds echoes of Marx's outlook on "the benefits of colonialism" in the unlikeliest of places; see, e.g., Gayatri Chakravorty Spivak, "Bonding in Difference:

Interview With Alfred Arteaga," in *The Spivak Reader,* ed. Donna Landry and Gerald MacLean (New York: Routledge, 1996), esp. 19.

222. Robert J.C. Young, "Preface: Sartre: The African Philosopher," in Sartre, *Colonialism and Neocolonialism,* xix. For greater detail, see Young, *White Mythologies,* 28–47.

223. See Vijay Mishra and Bob Hodge, "What Is Post (-) colonialism?" in Williams and Chrisman, *Colonial Discourse and Post-Colonial Theory,* 276–290; Stephen Slemon, "The Scramble for Theory," in *The Post-Colonial Studies Reader,* ed. Bill Ashcroft, Gareth Griffiths, and Helen Tiffin (New York: Routledge, 1995), 45–52.

224. Anne McClintock, "The Angel of Progress: Pitfalls of the Term 'Post-colonialism,'" in Williams and Chrisman, *Colonial Discourse and Post-Colonial Theory,* 294. Stuart Hall also does an excellent job of debunking "postcolonialist" temporality in "When Was 'the Post-colonial'? Thinking at the Limits," in *The Post-Colonial Question: Common Skies/ Divided Horizons,* ed. Iain Chambers and Lidia Curti (London: Routledge, 1996), 242–260.

225. McClintock, "Angel of Progress," 294.

226. Diana Brydon, "New Approaches to the New Literatures in English," in *A Shaping of Connections: Commonwealth Studies, Then and Now,* ed. Hena Maes-Jelinek, Kristen Holst Peterson, and Anna Rutherford (Mundelstrup: Dangaroo, 1989), 95.

227. See R. S. Mathews, "The Canadian Problem," in *Commonwealth Literature: Unity and Diversity in a Common Culture,* ed. John Press (London: Heineman, 1965), 157–167. Also see Deepika Bahri, "Once More With Feeling: What Is Postcolonialism?" *Ariel* 26, 1 (1995): 51–82.

228. Arif Dirlik explores these issues rather thoroughly in *The Postcolonial Aura: Third World Criticism in the Era of Global Capitalism* (Boulder: Westview, 1997). For what is probably the strongest debunking to date of the whole notion of "postcoloniality," see Gayatri Chakravorty Spivak, *A Critique of Postcolonial Reason: Toward a History of the Vanishing Present* (Cambridge: Harvard University Press, 1999).

229. In addition to the various "posts" discussed here, we find an intellectual terrain littered with outgrowths of "post-Marxism" and "postfeminism," even "posthistory," a landscape of overall "postality" inhabited in part by—you guessed it—"post-Indians." See, as examples, Stuart Sim, *Post-Marxism: An Intellectual History* (New York: Routledge, 2001); Imelda Wheleman, *Modern Feminist Thought: From the Second Wave to "Post-Feminism"* (New York: New York University Press, 1995); Ken Harper, *The Third Millennium: Living in the Posthistoric World* (San Francisco: Harper, 1996); Masid Zavarzadeh, *Post-Ality: Marxism and Postmodernism* (Washington, DC: Maisonneuve, 1995); Gerald Vizenor, *Manifest Manners: Postindian Warriors of Survivance* (Middletown, CT: Wesleyan University Press, 1994).

230. Teresa Ebert, "Political Semiosis in/of American Cultural Studies," *American Journal of Semiotics* 8, 1–2 (1991): 117.

231. For what may be the key exposition on narrative totalization, see Jean-François Lyotard, *The Postmodern Condition: A Report on Knowledge* (Minneapolis: University of Minnesota Press, 1985). Also see Manfred Frank, *What Is Neostructuralism?* (Minneapolis: University of Minnesota Press, 1989); Derek Attridge and Robert Young, eds., *Post-Structuralism and the Question of History* (Cambridge: Cambridge University Press, 1989).

232. "It is a mistake to confuse hierarchy with elitism. . . . 'Hierarchy,' a term which originally denoted the three categories of angels, has come to mean any kind of graduated

structure. In its broadest sense, it refers to something like an order of priorities. In this broad sense of the word, everyone is a hierarchist, whereas not everyone is an elitist. Indeed you may object to elites because they offend your order of priorities"; Terry Eagleton, *The Illusions of Postmodernism* (Oxford: Blackwell, 1996), 93–94.

233. Essentialism reduces, *essentially*, to the proposition that "things are made up of certain properties, and that some of these properties are actually constitutive of them, such that if they were removed or radically transformed the thing in question would become some other thing, or nothing at all"; ibid., 97. This is rather different from the doctrine holding that there are "core properties, or clusters of properties, present, necessarily, in all and only those things which bear the common name" assailed by Wittgenstein; Garth L. Hallet, *Essentialism: The Wittgensteinian Critique* (New York: State University of New York Press, 1991), 2.

234. In simplest terms, "teleology" means only "the assumption that there is some potential in the present which could result in a particular sort of future." This is very different from the typical postmodernist contention that it implies "the belief that the world is moving purposefully toward some predetermined goal which is immanent within it even now, and which provides the dynamic of this inexorable unfurling"; Eagleton, *Illusions of Postmodernism*, 108. 45.

235. The antirationalist impulse is discussed at length in Horace L. Fairlamb, *Critical Conditions: Postmodernity and the Question of Foundations* (Cambridge: Cambridge University Press, 1994).

236. See, as examples, Barbara Hernstein Smith, *Contingencies of Value* (Cambridge: Harvard University Press. 1988); Richard Rorty, *Contingency, Irony, Solidarity* (Cambridge: Cambridge University Press, 1989); Zygmunt Bauman, *Postmodern Ethics* (Oxford: Blackwell, 1993).

237. Christopher Lasch, "Learning From Leipzig . . . or Politics in the Semiotic Society," *Theory, Culture and Society* 7, 4 (1990): 145–158.

238. Eagleton, *Illusions of Postmodernism*, 64. For a dose of the real thing, see Jean Baudrillard, *Simulacra and Simulation* (Ann Arbor: University of Michigan Press, 1995).

239. Gerald Vizenor, *The Trickster of Liberty: Tribal Heirs to a Wild Baronage* (Minneapolis: University of Minnesota Press, 1988), 3. Also see Homi K. Bhabha, "Of Mimicry and Man: The Ambivalence of Colonial Discourse," in his *Location of Culture*, 85–92.

240. See, e.g., Gayatri Chakravorty Spivak, "The Post-modern Condition: The End of Politics?" in her *The Post-Colonial Critic: Interviews, Strategies, Dialogues* (New York: Routledge, 1990), 17–34. Also see the essays collected in Andrew Ross, ed., *Universal Abandon? The Politics of Postmodernism* (Minneapolis: University of Minnesota Press, 1988). The implications are brought out rather sharply in Terry Eagleton's observation that the "belief that values are constructed, inherently variable and inherently revisable has much to recommend it, though it fares rather better with Gorky than it does with genocide"; *Illusions of Postmodernism*, 97.

241. Homi K. Bhabha, "DissimiNation: Time, Narrative and the Margins of the Modern Nation," in his *Location of Culture*, 145.

242. See, e.g., Homi K. Bhabha, "The Postcolonial and the Postmodern: The Question of Agency," in *Location of Culture*, 171–197.

243. Ahmad, *In Theory*, 68–69. Benita Parry makes much the same point in "Signs of Our Times: A Discussion of Homi Bhabha's *The Location of Culture*," *Third Text* 28–29 (1994).

244. Moore-Gilbert, *Postcolonial Theory,* 138. The assessment pertains directly to Bhabha's (mis)reading of Frantz Fanon, most notably in his "Interrogating Identity: Frantz Fanon and the Postcolonial Prerogative" (*Location of Culture,* 40–65) and "Remembering Fanon: Self, Psyche, and the Colonial Condition" (in Gibson, *Rethinking Fanon,* 179–198). For further critique, see Neil Lazarus, "Disavowing Decolonization: Fanon, Nationalism, and the Problematic of Representation in Current Theories of Colonial Discourse," *Research in African Literatures* 24, 2 (1993): 69–98; Quadric Robinson, "The Appropriation of Frantz Fanon," *Race and Class* 35, 1 (1993): 79–91.

245. Eagleton, *Illusions of Postmodernism,* 105, 120, 132. Very similar characterizations are advanced with respect to postcolonialism in Amada, *In Theory*; Dirk, *Postcolonial Aura*; Spivak, *Critique of Postcolonial Reason*; Abdul R. JanMohamed, "Worldliness-Without-World, Homelessness-as-Home: Toward a Definition of the Specular Border Intellectual," in *Edward Said: A Critical Reader,* ed. Michael Sprinker (London: Blackwell, 1992), 96–120.

246. Eagleton, *Illusions of Postmodernism,* 122. Much the same criticism is advanced by Vicki Coppock, Deena Hayon, and Ingrid Richter in *The Illusions of Post-Feminism: New Women/Old Myths* (London: Taylor and Francis, 1995).

247. The phrase is taken from Zavarzadeh, *Post-Ality.*

248. The confluence is exemplified in Slavoj Zizek, "Class Struggle or Postmodernism? Yes, Please!" in *Contingency, Hegemony, Universality: Contemporary Dialogues on the Left,* ed. Judith Butler, Ernesto Laclau, and Slavoj Zizek (London: Verso, 2000), 90–135.

249. This is said despite the best efforts of Stanley Aronowitz, Henry Giroux, Peter McLaren, and others to achieve an "organic" or "grassroots" version of postmodernism that might lend itself to genuinely liberatory pursuits. See, as examples, Stanley Aronowitz and Henry Giroux, *Postmodern Education* (Minneapolis: University of Minnesota Press, 1991); Peter McLaren, *Critical Pedagogy and Predatory Culture: Oppositional Politics in a Postmodern Era* (New York: Routledge, 1995); Gustavo Esteva and Madhu Suri Prakash, *Grassroots Postmodernism: Remaking the Soil of Cultures* (London: Zed, 1998).

250. This is not to argue that neocolonialism does not exist or that it is unworthy of study and address but simply that conflating it with the ongoing internal colonization of indigenous peoples—as postcolonialists habitually do—is deforming of both concepts; see, e.g., Moore-Gilbert, *Postcolonial Theory,* 30–31. On the distinction that should be drawn between internal and "neo" colonial modes, see Hector, *Internal Colonialism*; Kwame Nkrumah, *Neo-Colonialism: The Highest Stage of Imperialism* (New York: Monthly Review, 1967).

251. Jean-Paul Sartre, "On Genocide," *Ramparts* (February 1968) (reprinted in Jean-Paul Sartre and Arlette El Kaim-Sartre, *On Genocide and a Summary of the Evidence and Judgements of the International War Crimes Tribunal* [Boston: Beacon, 1968]).

252. See Sartre, "Introduction to Memmi" in his *Colonialism and Neocolonialism,* 51.

253. Ngugi Wa Thiongo, *Decolonizing the Mind: The Politics of Language in African Literature* (Oxford: James Curry, 1986).

254. See, e.g., Julian Henriques, Wendy Holloway, Cathy Urwin, Couze Venn, and Valerie Walkerdine, *Changing the Subject: Psychology, Social Regulation and Subjectivity,* 2d ed. (London: Routledge, 1998).

255. "It is interesting to note that at the very moment when celebrated Euro-American cultural theorists have pronounced the collapse of 'grand narratives' the expressive culture

of [the] black poor is dominated by the need to construct them as narratives of redemption and emancipation"; Paul Gilroy, "One Nation Under the Groove: The Cultural Politics of 'Race' and Representation in Britain," in *Anatomy of Racism,* ed. David Theo Goldberg (Minneapolis: University of Minnesota Press, 1990), 278. On the idea that Grand Narratives can serve liberatory as well as hegemonic purposes, see Patrick Taylor, *The Narrative of Liberation: Perspectives on Afro-Caribbean Literature, Popular Culture, and Politics* (Ithaca: Cornell University Press, 1989). Also see Mario Sáenz, "Memory, Enchantment and Salvation: Latin American Philosophies of Liberation and Salvation," *Philosophy and Social Criticism* 17, 2 (1991): 149–173.

256. To appreciate the depth of the relationship between the two, it is useful to juxtapose major contemporaneous texts describing each: e.g., say, Albert Szymanski, *The Logic of Imperialism* (New York: Praeger, 1981) to Richard Falk, *Predatory Globalization: A Critique* (Cambridge: Polity, 1999).

257. Kwame Nkrumah, *Consciencism: Philosophy and Ideology for Decolonization* (New York: Monthly Review, 1970); Amilcar Cabral, *Revolution in Guinea* (New York: Monthly Review, 1969). Also see Jomo Kenyatta, *Facing Mount Kenya* (New York: Vintage, 1962); Julius K. Nyerere, *Freedom and Unity: Uhuru Na Umoja* (Washington, DC: Africa House, 1973).

258. Frantz Fanon, *The Wretched of the Earth* (New York: Grove, 1963); *A Dying Colonialism* (New York: Grove, 1965); *Black Skin, White Masks* (New York: Grove, 1965); *Toward the African Revolution* (New York: Grove, 1967). Also Albert Memmi, *The Colonizer and the Colonized* (New York: Orion, 1965); *Dominated Man* (New York: Orion, 1968).

259. Peter Worsely, *The Third World,* 2d ed. (London: Weidenfeld and Nicholson, 1967); Heydar Reghaby, ed., *Philosophy of the Third World* (Davis, CA: D-Q University Press, 1974).

260. George Manuel and Michael Posluns, *The Fourth World: An Indian Reality* (New York: Free Press, 1974). On the fundamental nature of these conflicts, see my and Glenn T. Morris's essay, "Between a Rock and a Hard Place: Left-Wing Revolution, Right-Wing Reaction, and the Destruction of Indigenous Peoples," in my *Since Predator Came: Notes on the Struggle for American Indian Liberation* (Littleton, CO: Aigis, 1995), 329–348; Bernard Neitschmann, "The Fourth World: Nations Versus States," in *Reordering the World: Geopolitical Perspectives on the Twenty-First Century,* ed. George J. Demko and William B. Wood (Boulder: Westview, 1994), 225–242.

261. See "I Am Indigenist: Notes on the Ideology of the Fourth World," in my *Struggle for the Land,* 367–402. Also see Guillermo Bonfil Batalla, *Utopia y Revolutión: El Pensamiento Politico Contemporáno de los Indios en América Latina* (Mexico City: Editorial Nueva Imagen, 1981).

262. The Gramscian concept of internal colonialism was adapted by the Communist Party USA during the 1930s to describe the situation of rural blacks in the Deep South; see generally, Harry Haywood, *Black Bolshevik: The Autobiography of an Afro-American Communist* (Chicago: Liberator, 1978). Black Panther Party founder Huey P. Newton in particular later reworked the idea for application to inner-city blacks as well; see, e.g., "Speech Delivered at Boston College, November 18, 1970," in *To Die for the People: The Writings of Huey P. Newton* (New York: Random House, 1972), 20–38. James Boggs, however, should probably be credited with the clearest and most comprehensive articulation

of the idea in relation to peoples of color in the United States; see his *Racism and Class Struggle: Further Pages From a Black Worker's Notebook* (New York: Monthly Review, 1971).

263. See, e.g., Mario Barrera, Carlos Muñoz, and Charles Ornelas, "The Barrio as an Internal Colony," *Urban Affairs Annual Review* 6 (1972): 465–498. Also see the latest iteration of Rodolfo Acuña's *Occupied America* (New York: Addison-Wesley, 1999).

264. Recall that degraded socioeconomic status was once assigned to certain groups within the settler populace itself, largely on the basis of the Anglo-American racial elite perceiving them as "colored"; Matthew Frye Jacobson, *Whiteness of a Different Color: European Immigrants and the Alchemy of Race* (Cambridge: Harvard University Press, 1998). The result, especially for those such as the Irish and Scots-Irish colonized at home, has been outright colonization in the New World as well; see Helen M. Lewis, Linda Johnson, and Donald Askins, eds., *Colonialism in Modern America: The Appalachian Case* (Boone, NC: Appalachian Consortium Press, 1978); Ada F. Haynes, *Poverty in Appalachia: Underdevelopment and Exploitation* (New York: Garland, 1996).

265. "The idea of a master narrative's 'phallic trajectory' into the telos of historical destiny needs to be discredited, yet the idea of totality as a heterogeneous and not homogeneous temporality must be recuperated"; Peter McLaren, "Multiculturalism and the Postmodern Critique: Towards a Pedagogy of Resistance and Transformation," in Giroux and McLaren, *Between Borders,* 210.

266. See, e.g., David Horowitz, *Hating Whitey and Other Progressive Causes* (Los Angeles: Spense, 2000).

267. "The flip side of the tyranny of the whole is the tyranny of the fragment. . . . Without some positive and normative concept of totality to counter-balance the poststructuralist/postmodern emphasis on difference and discontinuity, we are abandoned to the seriality of pluralist individualism and the supremacy of [those capitalist] competitive values" that have begotten the world we now inhabit; Steven Best, "Jameson, Totality and Post-structuralist Critique," in *Postmodernism/Jameson/Critique,* ed. Doug Kellner (Washington, DC: Maisonneuve, 1989), 361.

268. There has been a veritable torrent of drivel over the past twenty years—that is, since the success of Third Worldism in vanquishing the classic form of European imperialism—about how "inappropriate" the ideology was and how its supposed defects have led to "a historic defeat of socialism." Such criticisms have ranged from contentions that the "sexism" inherent to the Third Worldist perspective paved the way for the rise of Islamic fundamentalism in the newly decolonized states to claims that decolonization leads inevitably to outbreaks of industrial capitalism and similar maladies. The questions always evaded in these critiques are, to quote Terry Eagleton, "what if this 'defeat' never happened in the first place? What if [the appearance to the contrary results mainly from] a gradual failure of nerve, a creeping paralysis" preventing those who now condemn Third Worldism—especially self-interested First World critics—from following through its liberatory potentials; Eagleton, *Illusions of Postmodernism,* 19. For representative critiques, see Robert Malley, *The Call From Algeria: Third Worldism, Revolution, and the Return to Islam* (Berkeley: University of California Press, 1996); Nigel Harris, *The End of the Third World: Newly Industrializing Countries and the Decline of an Ideology* (New York: New Amsterdam, 1990).

269. On the conception of a "Fanonist pedagogy"—an idea entirely consistent with those referenced in notes 23, 29, and 32—see Kenneth Mostern, "Decolonization as

Learning: Practice and Pedagogy in Frantz Fanon's Revolutionary Narrative," in Giroux and McLaren, *Between Borders,* 251–271. Also see Peter McLaren, ed., *Revolutionary Multiculturalism: Pedagogies of Dissent for a New Millennium* (Boulder: Westview, 1997).

270. McLaren, "Multiculturalism and Postmodern Critique," 218. This would seem commensurate with Catherine Clément's staid but much better-known axiom that one must first "change the imaginary in order to act on the real"; quoted in Spivak, "French Feminism" in her *In Other Worlds,* 145.

271. Karl Marx, *The German Ideology* (New York: New World, 1963), 197.

272. "But what if the [colonized] asserts himself as a [human being], as the colonist's equal? Well, then, the colonist is wounded in his very being; he feels diminished, devalued: he not only sees the economic consequences of the accession of 'wogs' to the world of human beings, he also loathes it because of his personal decline. In his rage, he sometimes dreams of genocide"; Jean-Paul Sartre, "A Victory," in his *Colonialism and Neocolonialism,* 75–76.

5
EL ESPEJO/THE MIRROR
Reflections of Cultural Memory

CARMEN HUACO-NUZUM

It is because this "New World" is constituted for us as a place, narrative of displacement, that it gives rise so profoundly to a certain imaginary plenitude, recreating the endless desire to return to "lost origins" . . . to go back to the beginning.

—Stuart Hall[1]

The diaspora of cultural dislocation, myth, memory, and discovery described by Stuart Hall in the new Caribbean and Third World cinema is also present in *El Espejo/The Mirror* (Frances Salomé España 1991). The video pays homage to ancestors, family, culture, and nation—pivoting between spatial realities that serve as ground and foreground to an examination of cultural trauma, social displacement, and the (re)positioning of the Chicana subject.

This chapter addresses several aspects of *El Espejo*: the reproduction of memory, nation, the body as site of inscription and memory, the mirror as metaphor of social gender inscription, *testimonio* discourse, and pedagogy.

España does not adhere to the traditional linear narrative found in many Hollywood films and videos with predictable plots and dialogue, fancy camera work, fast-paced editing, popular music, and happy endings. It is difficult to sconce *El Espejo* into any particular category that closely resembles a documentary or an experimental video. Rather, *El Espejo* is an art form—a visual poetic, sociopolitical tone poem that functions as a didactic visual text challenging the spectator to examine social, cultural, gender, and political issues that impact the Chicana/o community and the politically responsible society at large. España

113

focuses on the primacy and aesthetic composition of each shot. The narrative is disjunctive, held together by numerous unorthodox cinematic techniques reminiscent of Goddard's early work. The repetitive use of jump cuts forces the viewer to gain necessary distance from the image, thus transforming the work into a self-reflexive experience of listening to the filmmaker recount a storylike dream of deterritorialization and reterritorialization.

El Espejo briefly looks back to the historical space of trauma to show how the Chicana/o has been impacted by the social conditions of the past. This is best exemplified in España's use of *testimonio* discourse that situates the spectator as bearing witness to contestations of race, remembrance, and the ever-looming threat of cultural erasure found throughout the video.

El Espejo does not express a desire to return to the beginning, which Hall has described as the "Archeological past, that like the imaginary in Lacan can never be fulfilled."[2] Rather, España is more concerned with addressing the present while never losing sight of the legacies of colonialism that have helped to forge the present social conditions. She examines the tension in the positioning of the Chicana who must learn to oscillate between past and present spaces of historical memory. This shift between temporal spaces brings to mind Homi Bhabha's claim that, within the separation of national identities articulated in overlapping temporalities that exist between the present and an unknowable future, we—"as social minorities"—must attempt to comprehend our present reality, which is remembered through the resonance of the past. Even though Bhabha refers to England, his cultural assessment is applicable to the United States as well. We are continually looking back, he notes, to cope with the urban, social, and racial problems of postmodernity.[3]

For Bhabha, the fear of diversity remains attached to the specter of the past in a frenetic attempt to revive genres of music, fashion, film, and diverse art forms of past decades. The need to recapture the past signals an anxiety that uncovers the unstable indeterminate future of postmodernity, encouraging aspects of society to romanticize the nostalgia of the past.[4] Although España draws on the past to contextualize a sentient portrayal of experience, she does not romanticize this temporal space but rather uses the recollection of memory as a means through which Chicana identity is negotiated.

Bhabha draws on a nationalist discourse to show how the metaphor of the gendered patriarchal family functions as a means through which moral ethics are measured and mirrored back to citizens in the form of "self-identity." It is a reflection of a romanticized nostalgia, he notes, to recapture a space in time that represents familiarity and sameness.[5] He further reminds us that the component of nation as a familial metaphor that privileges the father's presence or absence is responsible for instilling respect, morality, ethics, and civic duty. Although this emanates from the peripheral space of the father's relation to the family, the father's presence serves as a mirror from which the child (subject) derives its self-worth. Thus the subject is constituted in the space of the "splitting gaze . . . between presence/absence reflected in the national mirror whose temporality is consequently . . . in a disjunctive present-past."[6]

One could argue that the national mirror of the United States continues to function as metaphor for the gendered white patriarchal family. Therefore the self-worth that is mirrored back is solely in terms of the dominant culture. This omits from the social contract the Chicana/o and other people of color who must find their own cultural mirror through which they can negotiate terms of self-worth and subject identity.

España contests the nation's mirror by forcing the spectator to bear witness to a discourse that uncovers the nation's inability to accurately reflect and implement constitutional ideals for all its citizens. España suggests that the desire to return to the past is a last-ditch attempt to retain cultural hegemony.

THE REPRODUCTION OF MEMORY

The opening shots of *El Espejo* depict a slow-moving train, apple trees, the front yard of a farm, and chickens, followed by a shot of España's feet in an intimate setting that invites the spectator to participate in a dialogue with the filmmaker, who is the main narrator of the story. España at times looks directly at the camera while engaged in a conversation that is almost inaudible to the audience. Long shots of a freight train—followed by successive medium shots of the filmmaker's grandparents' farm, stacked wooden chairs, a beat-up blue pickup truck—all serve as visual markers that contextualize the cultural space of memory. España's narration begins to capture the unsettling position of being a divided subject: "I knew it wasn't so bad; things were never quite clear then, you know. Heaven was the sky and hell was somewhere under the dirt. It was pretty clear where I was."[7]

Repetitive shots of España's bare feet conjure up the ancient practice of binding female feet while also serving as a Brechtian self-reflective device to prevent identification with España's image. The sounds and shots of a freight train function as a recurring cultural motif and historical social marker that links the space between the United States and Mexico. The train triggers a historical collective memory of disruption, separation, and loss experienced in the 1930s by hundreds of Mexicans and Mexican Americans. It is well documented that during this period of "ethnic cleansing," Mexicans and Mexican Americans were indiscriminately rounded up like cattle, packed into freight trains, and sent across the Mexican border without due process of law.

Moreover, the train, as a commercial carrier, is used to transport farm goods across the nation for general consumption by the public. The farmworker, as part of the labor force, does not own or have access to the means of production. Rather, the labor of the Mexican American farmworker has been and continues to be used as surplus value to increase the nation's wealth.

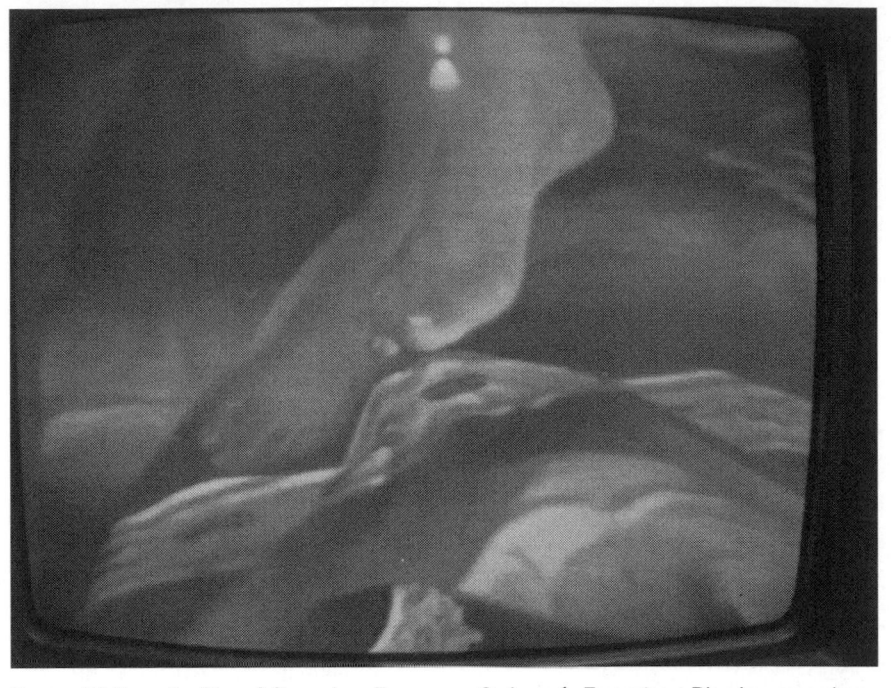

From *El Espejo/The Mirror* by Frances Salomé España. Photo courtesy Frances Salomé España

THE BODY: SITE OF REMEMBRANCE

España's dreamlike narrative of social transculturation opens up a discourse of deterritorialization experienced in her homeland. España addresses the relationship of the Chicana/o body to the city of Los Angeles (City of Angels)—a city known as wonderland, a place where dreams are forged and celluloid fantasies are re-created. Los Angeles is a geographic location of ancestral remembrance and loss of historical placement, a city that beckons marked Chicana/o bodies not to forget their ancestral roots while dispossessing them from participation in the polity of dominant culture.

In "Bodies and Cities" Elizabeth Grosz looks at the relationship between corporeality and the city in regard to the way the subject is constructed by different variables of social production—environmental, socioeconomic, gender, race, and class variables, in addition to architecture, geographic location, and all forms of media.[8] The body, Grosz notes, is produced by the city, and the city is produced by the body in the context of environmental elements continually changing in time and space relationships. In defining the connection between corporeality and the city, Grosz examines two models of corporeal production she finds problematic because they prove to be megalithic and, to some degree, fixed in a causal time relation between body and city.[9]

The first model contends that the city is "a reflection, projection, or product of bodies."[10] Since bodies exist before cities, they construct cities that become reflections, projections, and experiences of the human undertaking. The problem with this model, Grosz notes, is that it "subordinates the body to the mind while retaining their structure as binary opposites." Moreover, "it posits, at best, a one-way relation between the body . . . and the city, linking them through a causal relation in which body or subjectivity is conceived as the cause, and the city the effect."[11]

The second model proposes that city and body function in a parallel context "between the body and the city, or the body and the state."[12] The difficulty with this model, as Grosz claims, is that it is hierarchical, racial, and gender coded. From this perspective the body functions not only independently but also from a collective space that claims a right to impose its politics for the good of the whole: "The human body is a natural form of organization that functions not only for the good of each organ but primarily for the good of the whole."[13] It is a hierarchical, hegemonic model that dictates and subordinates bodies to the body politic or state.

Grosz provides a third model that incorporates some aspects of the first two models but serves as an alternative to the relationship between body and city: "What I am suggesting is a model of the relations between bodies and cities that sees them, not as megalithic total entities, but as assemblages or collections of parts, capable of crossing the thresholds between substances to form linkages, machines, provisional and often temporary sub- or micro-groupings."[14] In this model the connection between body and city is one of fluid exchange that allows interconnected linkages between subjects to come together temporarily to meet the independent or larger needs of the community. Grosz elaborates further, noting that "this model is practical, based on the productivity of bodies and cities in defining and establishing each other."[15] Her model seems more inclusive and socially based, inviting marginalized bodies to engage in the production of the body's relationship to the city. The model is not fixed in a causality, in a time and space relationship, but rather provides possibilities for temporary coalitions and linkages between groups that are focused on a specific purpose for the good of the group or the greater community.

The relationship of the Chicana/o body to the city of Los Angeles is one of displaced historical fragmentation because that body did not participate in the construction of corporeal production vis-à-vis city to body, body to city. The relationship is one of produced marginalization, away from the center; it is geographically contained and socially and economically ghettoized—one that reflects more accurately the first two models described by Grosz. The experience of deterritorialization and cultural displacement is so intense that the marked body seeks resolution and wish fulfillment, escaping through the fantasy of the dream. The narrative in *El Espejo* is the outcome of conscious and unconscious material. The wish fulfillment emerges from a distressing need to belong, to be part of the city and the nation's community in which one ceases to be a marginalized "other"—a city wherein one can retain the cultural aspects of identity and pride in one's ancestral home without feeling devalued and subordinate; a city that provides opportunities to participate in its production without engaging in the production of the stereotyped body; a space where social and interpersonal hypervigilence ceases to be a recurrent experience that later becomes a reproduction of distressful memories and coerced cultural dislocation.

España's narration conveys emotional, painful events that appear to emerge from a disjointed manifest dream. Eventually, however, by recounting the dream, the narrator is able to recognize the realization of cultural displacement projected onto the spectator/witness. For the act of testimony and bearing witness has the potential, like that of psychoanalysis, to bring forth material that was once repressed, as I will show later.

The dream narrative becomes the sanctuary as well as the repository experience of psychic pain. Unable to maintain the safety childhood once offered, the narrator finds herself caught between two cultures. On the one hand she is told she does not belong, and on the other she is reminded that she lives in *maravilla,* in wonderland.

> I was being beckoned the hell out of here, so I jumped on a cloud that carried me across the burning sun. The air was full of giant bees. These *moscos* were telling me to get out of East L.A. *Volaban por todos lados esos* bees. One of them spoke to me and said: *Hay Rosario, por donde andas?* Why do you want to get out of this place, girl, don't you know you are already in wonderland? (see note 7)

España, perceiving that some forms of knowledge are social constructs established and mediated by institutions of power from which she cannot escape, gestures in reconciliation: "I tried to wave goodbye but by then it was too late, and with a long last look back I saw them sealing everything up with this invisible stuff like glue . . . the people, the *gente,* could not see beyond it" (see note 7). The *gente* could not see how the nation moved systematically and swiftly, taking on political momentum in the effort to force the assimilation of Mexican Americans and other Latinas/os to comply to a political agenda of sameness. By peeling away at affirmative action and the right to bilingual education, the road was left open to Anglosize the population and, in time, eradicate all vestiges of Latina/o culture. If the city is, as Grosz contends, "a site for the body's cultural saturation, its takeover and transformation by images, representational systems, the mass media, and the arts [makes it] the place where the body is representationally reexplored, transformed, contested, reinscribed."[16]

The Chicana/o body is definitely a site of cultural hegemonic reading and social inscription—produced, marked, and reinscribed by representational media systems of dominant culture. A troubling example is found in a television commercial that portrays a hyper, emotionally labile Chihuahua whose vulnerability and lack of power are inscribed in his body. The dog is always pursuing attractive young Latinas, connoting sexual bestiality and promoting further semiotic implications of male Mexican/Chicano sexual prowess. Moreover, such images—a puny-looking dog devoid of power—function as double messages, reinforcing racial difference while attempting to diffuse fear of the "other."

THE MIRROR SYMBOLISM IN *EL ESPEJO*

One function of the mirror dates back to the fifteenth century when the mirror as object of frivolity came to be associated with female representation, symbolizing what John Berger has described as "the vanity of woman." Underlying this male inscription of woman and her relationship to the mirror was the true function of the mirror, which as Berger has pointed out was "to make woman connive in treating herself as, first and foremost, a sight."[17] España shatters the patriarchal inscription of mirror through the use of *testimonio* narrative that works as metaphor for a site of resistance and contestation. España looks at herself looking at the spectator looking at her. She becomes the object but not the objectification of the look. Her contested gaze destabilizes established positions of filmic objectification. At times España's gaze is confrontational but always changeable, containing a shifting spiral of emotional affect that ranges from seriousness to sadness to laughter. In the self-disclosure *testimonio* España makes an effort to find herself reflected in the nation's mirror. She is told she lives in *maravilla*, so why does the nation's mirror betray her? For Bhabha, the perception of difference circulates in the periphery and cannot be seen, or rather it is visually denied to reduce the nation's anxiety.[18]

España often reels in the spectator/witness through a direct gaze sustained only momentarily, whereas on other occasions her gaze is directed toward one side of the frame or the other, as though she were conversing with an imaginary witness. Feminist film theory has addressed the way relations of power function in relation to the female gaze. bell hooks takes the notion of the gaze one step further in her discussion of "the Oppositional Gaze." She claims the gaze was used as a means of control and power over slaves.[19] They were punished for looking, and out of that attempt to repress the slave came a "longing to look, a rebellious desire, an oppositional gaze." The declaration was, "Not only will I stare, I want my look to change reality."[20] So for hooks, returning the look opens up space for oppositional resistance. It is a look that learns to resist hegemony, one that constitutes "awareness and politicizes looking relationships."[21] Even though hooks's oppositional gaze makes reference to the spectator, I find the experience can also function for the narrator as well, and *El Espejo* is one example.

From El Espejo/The Mirror by Frances Salomé España. Photo courtesy Frances Salomé España

One finds a contested gaze throughout España's work, and it is readily defined in this video. As I previously noted, even though España sustains the gaze only momentarily, it is sufficient to partake in the reciprocity of exchange and power relations between narrator and spectator. The power of the contested gaze is found in the incongruity of emotional affect expressed by España and in the process of what is transcribed between what is said (the content) and what is perceived and felt (affect) by the narrator. España smiles and says "I was an illegal, right? And it's like I could not wake up until I showed them my papers. Isn't that a trip [continues smiling]. . . . You've got to show them this, you've got to show them that, you have to show them something all the fucking time" (see note 7).

What is perceived as España's incongruous affect as she recounts painful events is precisely what helps to destabilize established power relations of looking. España's contested gaze is one of resistance. It is as though she were declaring "I want my look to change reality."[22] The power of resistance is in the knowing that even though power relations and social conditions may not readily change in the present, an indeterminate temporal space in the unknowable future holds the potential for transformation. The Chicana cannot permit the emotional content of the experience to detract from her ability to resist tyrannical conditions that threaten to destabilize the subject. Furthermore, the discourse of resistance in *El Espejo* is conveyed through linguistic forms of bilingual code switching that reinforce cultural validation and destabilize dominant narratives of postcolonial hegemonic practice.

TESTIMONY AND BEARING WITNESS

The spectator as witness to *testimonio* is engaged in a relationship with the visual text and with the experience conveyed by the narrator. Shoshana Felman has extended this view in "Education and Crisis, or the Vicissitudes of Teaching" when she writes: "In the age of testimony . . . testimonial teaching fosters the capacity to witness something that may be surprising, cognitively dissonant. The surprise implies a crisis. Testimony cannot be authentic without that crisis, which has to break and to transvaluate previous categories and previous frames of reference."[23]

So the importance of testimony is that the information transmitted to the witness not be restricted to a congruent message. Rather, the dissonance of the experience and of the message received helps to facilitate a "crisis" for the spectator. Testimonial narratives of racial and social dislocation inevitably function as dissonant messages because of historical implications that inevitably (re)stimulate for narrator and spectator (sender and receiver) the Hegelian dialectic of historical remembrance between self and other, past and present, and the precarious unknowable future that awaits both. Such is the case in *El Espejo* when España looks at the spectator and says: "That I was always on the trees so I was safe. That this place had a *corazon* unto itself something very special, something that we had to learn to embrace. It was a beautiful thing you trying to figure that one out—that we cleared our breath from an urban area, something far removed and yet so close to the homeland" (see note 7).

As Felman further reminds us, the listener/spectator must be deeply impacted by what he or she hears and sees, and the level of dissonance has to be strong enough to cause discomfort so a "crisis" can take place for the one bearing witness.[24] One can speculate that España's *testimonio* received by the spectator of dominant culture is perceived to be dissonant not only because of the discourse of race and cultural dislocation but also because the linguistic code switching augments the dissonance of the message being conveyed.[25]

In "Bearing Witness or the Vicissitudes of Listening," Dori Laub's analysis of trauma is focused on Holocaust narratives of a survivor's testimony and the relationship of the narrator to the listener who bears witness.[26] In drawing from the discourse of testimony and bearing witness, I do not intend to diminish the important significance of Holocaust narratives. But her analysis is also useful to examine the process and close association between the narrator of the *testimonio* (España) and the spectator who bears witness to her story. Individuals experience various degrees of trauma, and the traumas of social displacement and racial difference are two of those variants.

Laub contends that cognition between sender and receiver occurs at the moment of enunciation when the narrator utters the testimony and it is received by the listener/spectator. It is at this place of exchange, she writes, that "cognizance of the 'knowing' of the event is given birth to."[27] When España testifies "I was being beckoned the hell out of here. . . . These *moscos* were telling me to get out of East L.A. . . . I tried to ignore all of that, but I was getting stung real bad," the spectator/listener, as Laub suggests, becomes a partial "co-owner" of the traumatic events being heard and seen.[28] Thus the act of listening and being present is one of dissonant discomfort experienced by the spectator who bears witness to España's *testimonio* of being asked to leave the country and of the pain attached to the consequences of that action.

España's subsequent narration discloses the trauma contained in her experience of events that occurred in the past but that are also part of a present reality: "They would not let me cross over until I showed them something. I needed some kind of documentation. I was an illegal, right? . . . Even awake I can see them flying around" (see note 7). According to Laub, it is through the process of cognitive awareness by the witness/spectator and the internal and external feelings stimulated by the exchange that a "crisis" is ignited between testimony and bearing witness that is then transcribed into knowledge.[29] The listener/spectator is placed in a unique position of bearing witness to traumatic events the narrator may not have yet cognitively processed, even though they are historically known.[30] So the moment of enunciation of the events that produced the pain and the witnessing by the listener/spectator ultimately initiates the creation of a new form of knowledge they now mutually share.

To begin the process of healing and reconciliation, the narrator of the testimony must reconstruct a narrative of the experience that, as Laub informs us, "has to be set into motion. This re-externalization of the event can occur and take effect only when one can articulate and transmit the story, literally transfer it to another outside oneself and then take it back again inside."[31] España's testimony is effective in re-externalizing traumatic memory events of the past, and even though the painful events may continue to impact the narrator in the present, the *testimonio* has nevertheless expelled some of the internalized pain. What has been achieved is a momentary re-externalization of a hurtful traumatic experience that finds resolution in the process of testimony and bearing witness. The impetus of the *testimonio* is also representative of a much larger collective consciousness of Chicana/o experience that needs to be played out many times over and in different arenas of political discourse. Clearly, the *testimonio* needs to be conveyed not from a position of victimization but rather from a place of empowered resolution.

Through *testimonio* and bearing witness, *El Espejo* facilitates for the Chicana spectator an opportunity to uncover the untapped potential for political social action. For the white spectator, bearing witness opens a better understanding of race and power relations between the two groups. The dissonance conveyed in *El Espejo* provides the degree of "crisis" and distanciation needed to produce a shift of consciousness, it is hoped, among both white and Chicana spectators.

The healing process begins with the externalization of the pain through which *testimonio* is the conduit of that expression. *Con el corazón en la mano,* España ventures into the private, intimate space where dreams are forged. She invites the spectator to witness her pain, her alienation, her anger, and her accommodation. Through this process of self-disclosure España offers the spectator an opportunity to gain a new form of knowledge. In the end, the process of *testimonio* and bearing witness serves as a bridge toward a better understanding of and reconciliation among self, other, community, and nation.

El Espejo reflects multiple facets of Chicana/os' attempt to participate in the social and corporeal construction of the subject's relationship to the city and the nation. This failed attempt often leads to overwhelming feelings of loss, depersonalization, social exploitation, disenfranchisement, and deterritorialization. Ultimately, a form of resolution is achieved through testimony and bearing witness, opening a space where reconciliation and self-healing can at last be achieved through mutual social reciprocity.

PEDAGOGY AND PRAXIS IN *EL ESPEJO*

In the 1920s the Russian formalist Viktor Shklovsky wrote that the action of unconscious habits is so pervasive that "life fades into nothingness. Automatization eats away at things, at clothes, at furniture, at our wives, and at our fear of war."[32] Art has the ability to make us see beyond what is commonplace, and *El Espejo* has the capability to help us see things as different and innovative. As previously noted, España does not adhere to the traditional linear narrative often found in many Hollywood films and videos, which makes this work more challenging for students.

How, then, does one approach avant-garde Chicana/o cinema and video pedagogically? How does one teach students to see beyond what is commonplace? This is the problematic for educators who must compete with students' historical and experiential place of reference, level of sophistication, cultural conditioning, and visual memory that seem greatly influenced by MTV, video games, and other forms of media. This referential memory is often revealed through students' short attention spans and difficulty seeing or accepting difference, which can be traced to years of conditioning by television and Hollywood films. Unfortunately, this experience has resulted in many young students becoming passive spectators who can only relate to the mediocre action and coming-of-age films Hollywood pumps out in an assembly-like fashion.

Given this resistance, prior to showing *El Espejo* I prepare the class by exposing them to relevant readings by Bertold Brecht, Ernesto Canclini, Tomas Ibarra Faustro, Gomez-Peña, and others. Brecht's concern with the notion of distanciation and self-reflexivity as well as readings by Chicano/a cultural theorists reflect the contemporary concerns and disjunction of deterritorialization and reterritorialization visually expressed and contextualized in *El Espejo.*

Students are encouraged to stretch their imaginations and to temporarily put aside their visual experiential prejudices in the hope that they will become active and responsible spectators. Furthermore, while viewing the video, I ask students to place themselves in oppositional frames of reference, a point raised in the Chicano film *Mi Otro Yo/My Other Self* (directed by Amy Brookman and Peter Brookman, 1988). Here, performance artist Gomez-Peña asks the audience, "What if you were me and I were you, mister?" Having contextualized some relevant frames of reference, students are asked to dig deeper into these questions: How do cultural identity, social dislocation, and border politics impact the lives of Chicanas/os, Latinas/os, and the rest of society? How is the use of cultural memory reproduced in the video? Does sound help to reinforce the image? How does España utilize the metaphor of the mirror to contextualize the concept of nation? Does the use of distanciation help the spectator engage in self-reflexivity; if so, how is this accomplished? Finally, how does España negotiate terms of cultural identity?

I have found that students often feel motivated to explore beyond that which is visually presented to them once the material is properly introduced prior to showing any nontraditional video. Consistently, students are able to find linkages among the written and the visual text, their own history, and their own notions of cultural remembrance. These connections establish a foundation that often gives students a sense of accomplishment at having understood a different form of visual coding than the one they are used to seeing on television and in Hollywood cinema. Film and video that functions as an art form and a political social statement does have, as Shklovsky informed us, the ability to help us see beyond what is commonplace, and *El Espejo* can be used effectively to such end.

NOTES

1. Stuart Hall, "Cultural Identity and Cinematic Representation," *Framework* 36 (1989): 80–81.

2. Ibid., 80.

3. Homi Bhabha, "Anxious Nation, Nervous States," in *Supposing the Subject,* Joan Copjec (New York: Verso, 1994), 202.

4. Ibid., 203–206.

5. Ibid., 205–206.

6. Ibid., 206.

7. This and subsequent quotes are from *El Espejo* (Frances Salomé España, 1991).

8. Elizabeth Grosz, "Bodies and Cities," in her *Space, Time, and Perversion* (New York: Routledge, 1995), 108.

9. Ibid., 108–109.

10. Ibid., 105.

11. Ibid.

12. Ibid.

13. Ibid., 106.

14. Ibid., 108.

15. Ibid.

16. Ibid.

17. John Berger, *Ways of Seeing* (London: British Broadcast Corporation, 1972), 51.

18. Bhabha, "Anxious Nation," 202–205.

19. bell hooks, "The Oppositional Gaze," in her *Black Looks: Race and Representation* (Boston: South End, 1992), 115.

20. Ibid., 116.

21. Ibid.

22. Ibid.

23. Shoshana Felman, "Education and Crisis, or the Vicissitudes of Teaching," in Shoshana Felman and Dori Laub, *Testimony Crises of Witnessing in Literature, Psychoanalysis and History* (New York: Routledge, 1992), 53–54.

24. Ibid.

25. This, of course, is contingent upon whether the spectator is white or Chicana of color.

26. Dori Laub, M.D., "Bearing Witness or the Vicissitudes of Listening," in Felman and Laub, *Testimony Crises of Witnessing in Literature, Psychoanalysis and History,* 58–59.

27. Ibid., 57.

28. Ibid., 59.

29. Ibid., 58.

30. Ibid., 58–60.

31. Ibid., 59.

32. Viktor Shklovsky, *Theory of Prose,* trans. Benjamin Sher (Elmwood Park, IL: Dalkey Archives, 1990), 5–6.

6
MISSISSIPPI MASALA
Crossing Desire and Interest

ADELEKE ADEEKO

To be human is to be called by the other.

—Gayatri Spivak[1]

Toward the end of *Mississippi Masala,* two members of an immigrant family—both motel owners in Greenwood, Mississippi—confront each other about the contradictory exactions of cultural continuity and disruption on transnational migrants. In their heated conversation Jammubhai (Anjan Srivastava), angry that his son is severing ties with an older male member of a closely related family in a culturally inappropriate way, closes his admonition with the statement "you behave like Americans!" He intends the words to be a grave moral indictment of his son's alienation from Hindu ways of dealing with relatives. To the father's surprise, the son, Anil (Ranajit Chowdhry), blasts back, "So what! I live here in America. If you don't like it, go back to India." Jammubhai, discounting the implications of his family's permanent residency in the United States, believes immigrants should traverse cultures like excursionists whose true culture is that into which their ancestors are born. Anil's response implies a contrary view: the predominant culture within which one earns a living is one's true culture.

Several other episodes in the film reflect—with a depth unusual for a Hollywood production—the practical difficulties of cultural mingling, and they invite a reassessment of the goals of producing ethical citizenry implied in multiculturalist pedagogic and political activism. In the controversy summarized in the previous paragraph, for example, Jammubhai wants to insulate culture from the vagaries of physical movements across geopolitical boundaries and the economic intercourse that attends to those movements. If he is right, efforts at creating multiculturalist curricula are clearly wrongheaded. But multiculturalist teaching has little else to go on if it lacks the tendency for vigilant differentiation Jammubhai advocates, albeit in the extreme. At the same time, the family's migration and profitable participation in the economic life of its new location illustrate the basis of another axiom of multicultural pedagogy, which is also reflected in Anil's response to his father: culture abhors absolute difference. But one cannot unequivocally say Anil is right without rendering multiculturalist pedagogy redundant.

I suggest that the dilemma that haunts Anil and his father—the temptation either to separate culture from other things or to make everything cultural—dogs multiculturalist scholarship and activism ceaselessly. Multiculturalist pedagogy cannot escape the question of how to balance, on the one hand, the demands of ancestral forms of expressing desires and, on the other hand, full participation in the necessarily changing environment in which one's material interests are at stake. This chapter stresses that multicultural teaching stands a chance of being effective if the tension is not resolved in favor of either position. As Mira Nair's *Mississippi Masala* (1991) shows, debilitating anxieties about productive cultural crossing diminish when the tension is perpetuated and individuals are free to work out the most comfortable place that accommodates their cultural dilemmas. Even so, choosing a comfort level in multicultural transnational existence will not eradicate the tension, since its cause is social.

CROSSING CULTURES

The film begins on 7 November 1972, two days before the expiration of the three-month deadline set by the dictatorship of General Idi Amin for all noncitizen Asians to leave Uganda. (Amin initially said the expulsion decree was divinely revealed to him in a dream. Later he accused the Asians of being economic saboteurs, arrogant haters of black people, and disloyal citizens who love India [their ancestral home] and England [the country of the colonizers that underwrote their immigration] more than Uganda.[2]) Caught in this order is Jay Loha (Roshan Seth), a lawyer of Indian descent, who because he is a citizen is not immediately affected by the quit order. As an outspoken opponent of Amin's racist nativism, however, Jay is arrested for calling Amin a madman during a critical interview on the world service of the British Broadcasting Corporation. Jay's black childhood friend, Okello (Konga Mbandu), bribes the police to secure Jay's release. During an argument over the appropriateness of Jay's interview, the two friends offend each other deeply. Jay believes that what he calls

From *Mississippi Masala,* Columbia/Tristar Studios, 1991

Amin's madness must be resisted with every measure possible, whereas Okello—for no reason explained in the film—parrots Amin's slogan "Africa for Africans, black Africans."[3] Okello, one is left to speculate, probably thinks—as do many of his countrymen and women—that Amin is right. Whatever the case, Okello's words, coming from someone Jay has always regarded as a brother, devastate Jay. If Okello can barefacedly call him an illegitimate African, then Jay thinks his claim to legal citizenship carries little significance. Therefore he decides to take his wife, Kinnu (Sharmila Tagore), and only daughter, Mina (Sahira Nair), out of the country. The reason for Jay's precipitous decision to leave Uganda is depicted in a flashback much later in the movie. Initially, he is only shown among a dejected multitude of Asians being forced out of their homeland.

The family lives in England for ten years before moving to the United States in 1982, where they settle in Greenwood, Mississippi. There Kinnu operates a liquor store she buys with a loan from a relative, and twenty-one-year-old Mina (Sarita Choudhury) works as a maid in a hotel owned by another relative. Jay, who was a successful lawyer in Uganda, is still unable to find permanent employment. He files endless court petitions against subsequent Ugandan governments, demanding the restoration of his property and citizenship, which were "forcibly and illegally" taken from him.[4]

Jay's family's experiences in Uganda last a very short while—only about 10 of the film's 113 minutes. The decade-long sojourn in England is left out, except in the camera's brief pause over the British Isles on the world map used to trace the journey from Kampala to Greenwood. The central narrative concern is with the family's U.S. immigration experience, although the Ugandan background shapes its unfolding.

The U.S. segment of the narrative—which clearly foregrounds Mina's experience—opens with a "literal" collision of Indo-African and Afro-American peoples when Mina, driving her boss's huge American car, rear-ends a carpet cleaning truck owned by two African American men, Demetrius (Denzel Washington) and Tyrone (Charles S. Dutton). Later, at the car owner's wedding, Mina is asked out by Harry Patel (Ashok Lath), an obviously well-to-do bachelor who many Indian mothers want as a son-in-law. Mina and Harry go to a black working-class nightclub, forebodingly named the Leopard, where she runs into Demetrius again. Demetrius does a very slow dance with her to make his former girlfriend jealous. Harry, who from the start is uncomfortable with Mina's warm rapport with the black women she knows from work, asks that they leave at once. The black women persuade Mina to stay, promising to drive her home, and Harry stomps out of the club. That night begins what later develops into a very intense but forbidden love affair between Demetrius and Mina.

The auto accident spawns the two principal subplots that sustain the narrative. The first subplot deals with Anil's anxiety about repairing his car, his escalating worries about Mina's carefree attitude, and his desire to prevent

Demetrius from filing a lawsuit against him. All the worries are manifested in his inability to consummate his marriage. Parallel to this subplot is the apparently fulfilling love that keeps growing between Demetrius and Mina—an affair the Indian family is unaware of but that gains the acceptance of most of the blacks. The main conflict that develops out of the second story line comes to a head when Anil—a blood relative of Mina's mother—and two of his friends discover that Mina has sneaked away to Biloxi with Demetrius. They force their way into the couple's hotel room, screaming sacrilege. In the encounter, the physically stronger and sexually virile Demetrius roughs up the thin and sexually dysfunctional Anil. The police, called in by Anil's bewildered friends, who are possibly venting their own sexual animosities, arrest the lovers and let off the aggressors.

From this point on, the profitable economic alliance of the local motel owners,[5] "immigrant and native," and the black American–owned carpet cleaning outfit unravels in direct proportion to the expanding trouble experienced in Mina and Demetrius's Indo-African and Afro-American libidinal relationship. In place before the conflict is a complex cultural and economic community: Demetrius and his partner, two self-employed African American males, obtain cleaning contracts from white American female and Asian male motel owners; African American Demetrius and Afro-Asian Mina engage in a love affair that is satisfying to both. The emerging libidinal, cultural, and economic harmony is shattered when some Asian male immigrants violently rebuff Demetrius's move into their culture. After the fracas, cranky old white male motel operators call their Asian colleagues about their "nigger" trouble. In response, the Asian motel owners ally with the whites to mount a devastating economic ambush by terminating their cleaning contracts with Demetrius and his partner, which causes the black partners to default on their credit obligations. The local bank forecloses on the cleaning truck, in part because of what one of its officials refers to as "character issues" that have impeded the business projections underlying the loan.

On the Indian immigrant community's home front, Anil threatens to evict Mina and her family—at once kinsfolk, employee, and tenants—from his property. A frustrated Jay initially decides to return to Uganda with his family, believing his petitions that are finally set for a hearing will succeed and that he will be able to begin anew in familiar terrain. Anil's father, Jammubhai, however, prevails upon his son not to act "American," and he allows the Loha family to stay. Meanwhile, Mina finds Demetrius and convinces him that they can escape from Greenwood together and establish a life free of family, culture, and traditions. Jay returns to Uganda alone to a distressing homecoming. He learns that shortly after he left in 1972, his childhood friend, Okello, whom he believed supported Amin's policies, had been murdered by Amin's death squad. His cherished lakefront property was taken over by goats. Jay writes to his wife that he is coming back to where his heart lies—in Mississippi, his future permanent home. Although the film starts and closes in Uganda, the difficulties of minority cultures cohabiting peacefully in the United States take up the greatest share of narrative time.

BEYOND THE IMAGE: THE DILEMMAS OF TEACHING

The positive resonance of the film's closure makes it a virtuous text—the love between Mina and Demetrius fortifies them enough that they defy their cultural backgrounds and march eyes wide open into a union whose interracial character will likely cause them endless headaches; Jay's love for his wife convinces him that he might secure a peaceful permanent future in a foreign country; individuals who attempt to stall the realization of the will to create relationships that can successfully overcome cultural restrictions seem to fail in the end. As the story closes, cultural mixing is endorsed, and the fleeting value of origins is rejected. Because of these obvious virtues, praising or criticizing the film's triumphant multiculturalism comes easily. According to Mark Reid, for instance, "Mina and Demetrius fight the prejudice that censures people of brown, black, yellow, and red complexions from loving outside their racial and ethnic communities."[6] The major characters reconcile themselves to the multicultural fate that awaits their transnational migration in a manner that indicates the kind of cultural differences that will have to be negotiated and embraced in the future. For bell hooks and Anuradha Dingwaney, who mounted an internationalist critique against the film, its too apparent multicultural virtue is troubling not just because it simplistically turns a specifically American yearning for honest interracial relationships into a global concern but primarily for concealing the devious role of the centers of (post)colonial and imperial domination—the very profiteers from the agonies of displacement—that force the two lovers into the cultural conflicts they are left alone to resolve: "The American dream of a love that triumphs over politics is a negation of our need to seriously examine the West's relationship to India, Africa, and global liberation movements for national freedom and self-determination."[7]

Beneath arguments about whether the film is adequately multicultural—as reflected in the different positions taken by Reid on one hand and hooks and Dingwaney on the other—sit two divergent views on the nature of intercultural dynamics. Reid's praise endorses the tendency to see intercultural relationships strictly within nationalist confines. In the words of Gayatri Spivak, multiculturalism here stands as "a nice name for the exoticism of the outsider" who finds a place within our nation, a self-congratulatory exhibition of sorts. hooks and Dingwaney's critique views the film's endorsement of U.S. exceptionalism as an attempt to make one nation's problem into "reason as such."[8] In this discursive orbit, Mina and Demetrius signify either the positive integration of two minority groups and the path to accepting the hybridity of culture or the imaginative projection of an American dilemma into a universal theoretical status.

Multiculturalist curricular reforms reflect these two tendencies as well, often with little attempt to bring them together. In my English Department at the University of Colorado, students can fulfill the multicultural component of their degrees with one course in either the cultures and literatures of demographically framed minority groups in the United States or of the former colonies of England. We hope students who take the American option will learn to appreciate the multiplicity of histories and traditions that constitute the national U.S. literary heritage. Those who take the "postcolonial" option, we expect, will also learn the operation of other "English" traditions. Within the postcolonial rubric under which I usually teach *Mississippi Masala,* I focus on "native" self-conscious reflections on historical experiences, believing I am diversifying my students' bases for knowing and organizing the world. I also tell myself that I am teaching them, as Homi Bhabha advises in his writing, to recognize the "performative" relationship of cultures to their geopolitical environments. I teach students that the nationalist constructions that favor continuist and "accumulative" narratives, which work to establish a unifying nationalist ideology, usually repress the performative—the repetitive, recursive, and contingent character of living cultures.[9]

But this egalitarian view of culture, which experience reveals is easily teachable, risks becoming the model it is intended to supplant if diversity (performativity) is presented in a way that conceals its inventedness (or historicity) as a category. In other words, correcting the errors of nationalist unitarian discourses whose coherence depends on the exclusion of formations that "do not add up" should not focus solely on identifying a "nation split within itself, articulating the heterogeneity of its population"[10] to the extent that the forces of unity that operate within the component culture or that make a specific constellation possible are repressed. Such a grotesque "exhibition" may easily deny the existence of "reason" or, to borrow terms from structuralist linguistics, may claim that some "syntactic" order is totally absent. Nationalist or postmodernist cultures are coded, contentless means of grounding difference.[11] Their constituent parts therefore do not "add up" to a fully representative whole. As long as cultural codes condense and extract from other material practices, the "adding to" sought in multicultural pedagogy may still not result in full representation. Resolving the dilemmas by favoring either "reason" or "exhibition" can only be counterproductive, and that is why the component parts of one do not "add up" and the radical "adding to" sought by the other may still fall short.[12]

But the "reason-exhibition" pulls are not the only forces tugging at the heart of multiculturalist humanities. Because texts taught under the multicultural heading are often viewed as allegorizing the political predicaments of the social group to which the major characters in the texts belong, regardless of whether these are explicit concerns in the narratives, the relationship of the internal texture of a narrative to the political imperatives of the milieu of its production and teaching can also be a source of pedagogic tension when characters pursue "exogamous" libidinal interests.

It is perhaps worth restating here, in spite of the observations made later, that political reading predominates in multiculturalist studies because the practical consequences of racist exclusion in the consciousness of the politically disadvantaged was not a serious concern of humanities education until the intervention of minority studies. Reckoning the seminal character of slave narratives in American letters, determining the multiplicity of ethnic and national literary languages within English, fathoming how the representation of non-white peoples furthers white American self-definition, to give a few examples, became paradigmatic issues in English studies only as a result of the trenchantly political scholarship on the cultural impact of minority confrontation with exclusion in the metropolitan United States, Great Britain, and their former colonies. These initial ethnocentric studies, not infrequently viewed as mere provincial inquiries, are now means of understanding the nature of crossing cultures—a crossing that is inherently conflicting because it traditionally involves resisting hegemonic orders.

Nonetheless, the insights gained from the predominance of political considerations in ethnic, cultural, and literary studies have led to the repression of deep studies of individual libidinal interests to the extent that they are only read as expressions of collective impulses. The main questions then become, Do characters in minority texts have libidinal drives at all, and if they do, are they culturally specific? Are libidinal drives always subordinated to material interests? Thinking about the relationship of group material interests to individual libidinal desires without privileging one over the other may redirect our theoretical and pedagogic interests to formulate fresh means of thinking about nations and cultures.

Mississippi Masala allows considerable latitude for analyzing the intertwined texture of both the material and the libidinal preoccupations of multicultural literatures. Beyond its conventional forbidden romance narrative, which is intensified by interracial sex and the exoticism of non-Caucasian peoples, the film elaborates the cultural factors that underlie characterization and action in such texts by connecting Mina and Demetrius's different ancestral histories to their behaviors in the present time. The forbidden romance, especially important because it occurs between minorities,[13] becomes a vehicle for staging the complex calculations that circumscribe action and thought when individuals balance material interests and libidinal desires. For one, the "interracial" sex, given Mina's (and her father's) Ugandan childhood and her calling herself an African on more than one occasion, is really not interracial. The black and Asian families' disapproval of the lovers' choice of partners—repressed until the trouble with the police—is also riddled with irresolvable contradictions: Jay is an Indo-Ugandan who fought virulent monoculturalism in his country of birth, but he now condones same; the not-quite-not-American Asian motel owners separate the personal from the economic, but they conflate the personal and the cultural, entering freely into multicultural economic intercourse but disapproving a genuine love affair between their trusted business acquaintance and a female member of their extended family. As many actions in the film show, the terms of living with cultural difference shift constantly according to whether political, economic, or libidinal interests are at stake.

Although the affirmative choice the two lovers make at the end of the film suggests that the freedom to live as one desires necessarily involves admitting that a living culture is an interaction of differences,[14] many preceding episodes support the notion that culture—"a regulator of how one knows"[15] and acts— also abets the concealment of interest-driven manipulations. Kanti's behaviors— he is the most loquacious of the Asian motel owners—illustrate these truisms well. His character carries the villain's burden visibly: he looks unkempt in his dull-colored Nehru jacket, his shifty eyes suggest something untoward, his central role in the ambush of Demetrius and Tyrone's cleaning company betrays his faked conviviality. More than these generic markers of a villain, however, his exploitation of the conditions of racial tension in the United States speaks to the fact that an enthusiastically expressed desire for multicultural alliances may be a ruse for consolidating exploitative economic interests.[16] Early in the movie, Kanti exploits multicultural solidarity to persuade Demetrius, who cleans the carpet in his motel, not to sue Anil.

> Kanti: Your people are very good at sports. No? Kareem Abdul Jabbar, Freddy Brown from downtown, Hector Macho Man, Camacho.
>
> Demetrius: No, Macho ain't black, though.
>
> Tyrone: No, Macho's Puerto Rican.
>
> Kanti: Black, brown, yellow, Mexican, Puerto Rican, all the same. As long as you're not white means you're colored. Isn't that so?
>
> Demetrius: [Puzzled] Yeah. Yeah, I guess.
>
> Kanti: Hey Demetrius, a girl had an accident with your van yesterday.
>
> Demetrius: Uh uh.
>
> Kanti: But no damage was done to your person or to your van.
>
> Demetrius: That's right.
>
> Kanti: Thank God. You know the person whose car she was driving is my very good friend. Also Indian. You get me?
>
> Demetrius: No.
>
> Kanti: He's worried because in this country people are suing all the time.

Demetrius: Oh! [Knowing laughter] I got you now. This is good tea. [Kanti looks as if he is waiting for bad news.] I didn't mean to laugh. You tell your friend he ain't got nothing to worry about.

Kanti: [Looking relieved] I told him. I told him not to worry. You're a good man. *All of us people of color must stick together.*

Tyrone: That's right. 'Cause you and your brothers, you all done right by us. And me and my brother we gonna do sure nuff by you all.

Kanti: [Standing and sitting to dramatize his words] United we stand, divided we fall.

Tyrone: That's right. Right on, brother. Power to the people.

We know immediately that Kanti is not trying to build a political coalition with the black contractors when he mocks Tyrone's "power to the people" in the call he makes to Anil about the "deal" he had just struck. Kanti's manipulation succeeds in spite of his obvious cynicism because the sentiment that minority peoples should form large social blocks makes sound political sense. When Kanti tells Demetrius that the car that rear-ended his truck belongs to a fellow victim of the racially unjust country they all inhabit, he waves the solidarity proverb "united we fall, divided we stand." In other words, members of racially oppressed groups, regardless of their privilege and rank, must not employ the often abused civil litigation processes—actually meant to protect the property rights of all—to distress each other because that will make them less capable of forming the unified front necessary to face the larger social injustice. "As long as you are not white," Kanti says, "we are one."

The narrative later exposes Kanti's interest-driven sham solidarity when "black" Demetrius's libidinal desires cross "brown" Mina's desires and shatter the transnational "colored" family rhetoric. At the bail hearing for the lovers, Kanti very reluctantly accepts the handshake of Tyrone—Demetrius's partner—and when Tyrone tries to engage him further in a friendly conversation, Kanti rebuffs him sharply. Kanti also joins white motel owners to boycott and destroy Demetrius's business. Likewise Anil, the proud new American whose disagreement with his father was discussed earlier, assaults Demetrius in defense of Hindu cultural integrity. As soon as Demetrius files a lawsuit against Anil over the "forgotten" auto accident, Anil decides to do away with the Loha family to cut his economic losses. His callous individualism—ostensibly American—does not prevent him, however, from willingly participating in a Hindu marriage celebrated publicly.

Although the film discourages the easy conclusion that Anil's and Kanti's acts indicate the priority of material interests over libidinal desires in the choice of cultural affiliations, it nonetheless stresses their interconnectedness in the details of Mina and Demetrius's elopement. After her release on bail to her father, Mina's parents try to convince her that the violent confrontation between

From *Mississippi Masala,* Columbia/Tristar Studios, 1991

Demetrius and the Indian men who barged into their room portends the trouble that will follow if she continues a relationship with someone of a different culture. Here is an excerpt of the conversation:

Mina: I love him. That is not a crime, is it?

Kinnu: You call this love? When all you've done is bring this shame on our heads?

Mina: I didn't do anything. They barged in. . . .

Jay: Don't answer back. Have the decency at least to be sorry.

Mina: I am sorry about this mess. But I am not sorry I'm in love with him.

Here Mina's argument rests upon her right to choose membership in a cultural group that is not that of her parents. When she later goes to elope with her lover, she convinces him not only with additional evidence of her genuine affection but also with her ability as a worker.

Demetrius: I'm thinking about going somewhere. . . .

Mina: Demetrius, can I come with you?

Demetrius: What!

Mina: Can I come with you?

Demetrius: Come with me where?

Mina: I don't know. Where are you going?

Demetrius: Well, I didn't say I was going anywhere. I said I was thinking about it.

Mina: Think about it. You said we're gonna travel. And see the world.

Demetrius: Well, what we gonna live on? Fresh air?

Mina: No. You've got the van. I could be your partner. I know how to clean rooms.

Mina seems to realize that to give her chosen immigrant, working-class relationship with Demetrius any chance of success, she will have to abandon both her father's unstated anxieties about her uncertain future outside the professional or mercantile middle class and the Indian community's ethnocentrism.[17] Although her father justifies his decision to live permanently in the United States and abandon his yearning for a homeland by citing his affection for his wife, he reaches that resolution narratively only after ascertaining that the level of material comfort he used to enjoy in Uganda can no longer be attained. He justifies his decision with his desire for his wife, writing "home is where the heart is" in a letter to her. For father and daughter, it seems, crossing cultures involves balancing libidinal desires with material interests.

The film further dramatizes the inherently conflictual nature of cultural crossing with the difficulties the Loha family experiences as it confronts Mina's choice of a lover. Here we have a family of postcolonial expatriates with roots on two continents (Asia and Africa), who lived for a decade on a third (Europe) and is grappling with life on a fourth (North America). Ordinarily, cultural mixing should come easily to them. Mina describes herself as a Masala—a potpourri of hot experiential spices—to Demetrius's African American family to reflect her family's diverse cultural identities—which have included Indian, Ugandan, British, and American at different times. Her reference, initially taken to mean exotic sexuality by Demetrius's African American acquaintances, encodes and represses—like all cultural metaphors—the long history of conflicts and involuntary migration that has kept her family on the move.

Jay's grandfather went to Uganda as one of the Asian laborers the British took to East Africa during the 1890s to build the railway project that connected the landlocked Uganda to the Indian Ocean coast in Kenya. After the railroad was completed, the grandfather, like many others, settled in East Africa.[18] The finished railroad opened the East African hinterland to Asians who had formerly settled on the coast and served in the civil and commercial services of the Mediterranean conquerors of the coastline. European takeover and partition allowed the established group of Asians to expand inland, supplying goods, services, and transport first to the railroad builders and later to Africans living in the hinterland.[19] At independence in 1962, Uganda's Asian population constituted the country's largest immigrant group. To avert a crisis of citizenship after their departure, the British, on the eve of independence, worked out an arrangement that gave Asians the chance to take either British citizenship or that of their country of residence. According to Thomas and Margaret Melady,

> The bulk of the Asians eventually applied for British passports, and thus
> became foreigners. They feared the changes that might take place under the
> African leadership and somehow believed that being under British protection
> was better than being a mistrusted minority in a nation struggling for unity.
> Many believed that even though they may have a piece of paper to indicate
> citizenship, in the long run they would always be considered foreigners in the
> eyes of the African, and thus they never even attempted to legalize a national-
> ity which they feared they might not be able to keep.[20]

In a pedagogic context, this synoptic historical background to Mina's "I am African" or "I'm a Masala" enlarges the seemingly uncomplicated, anxiety-free, joyous immigrant story and shows—in the extreme, of course—that migration or nontourist cultural crossing is usually involuntary and always takes place in conflictual psychic and political circumstances.

The film thus presents an opportunity to teach students two facts about cultural crossing: one, that permanent immigration to the United States as a place of refuge for those seeking to improve their lives is not historically unique; and two, that crossing cultures does not always result in improved opportunities for the emigrant. The Loha family's emigration practically renders them destitute.

Ten years into immigration Jay—the successful lawyer who lived in a large lakefront house attended by a retinue of servants—is jobless in Mississippi, living in a motel on the limited income his wife gathers from her liquor store and the wages his daughter earns cleaning motels. The reality that the family is not doing well, despite the fact that Kinnu is always counting money with a contented smile whenever she is in her store, is obvious as Jay laments their inability to send their only daughter to college. Immigration has definitely impoverished the younger Loha. When Mina runs away with her lover, she not only establishes her independence, but she also places an otherwise well-to-do migrant from a postcolonial state on a very low rung on the socioeconomic ladder of a metropolitan neocolonial country. True, emigration has liberated Mina from her parents' desires, but it has not improved her material well-being. Pointing out this aspect of Mina's life is meant not to denigrate working-class realities but to highlight the material hardship that may follow immigration or other cultural crossing. To argue that her rebuffing her father's plea that they return to Uganda with "I'm not coming back. . . . What will I do there?" means she has absorbed the irreversibility of migrancy tells only part of the story.

I will close with another aspect of Mina's heated argument with her parents over Demetrius. When Kinnu asks her daughter "Who is he? What do you know about him? What about his family?" Mina replies, "This is America, Ma! No one cares." The scandalous response leads Kinnu to say, "We care. Your father and I. You're our only child. If we don't care, who will?" In this exchange—the only episode in which all members of the Loha family scream at each other—an immigrant child is attempting to set out the parameters of Americanness for a parent. To Mina, and Anil in the episode discussed earlier, being American involves abandoning the traditional reverence for the unquestioned right of elders to have the final say on the actions most appropriate for an offspring's future. Emigrants embrace the aspects of their new cultures that they are convinced represent a superior means of negotiating their libidinal desires and material interests. Mina elopes with an African American man, a person of a different "kind" to her father, because she believes—contrary to her parents' view of Indian tradition, which they have only lived outside India—that she has a right to determine what constitutes happiness individualistically.[21]

If this discussion suggests skepticism about the ability of multiculturalist humanities to catalyze the cultivation of ethical citizenship, it is because I believe curricular content diversity—optimistic "exhibition"—alone cannot achieve that goal. It is not enough to assemble texts that celebrate the immitigable contingency of cultures, as the ending of *Mississippi Masala* seems to do. Equally inadequate is the false confidence in "reason" promoted by theoretical explanations that depict radical difference as the irremediable fate of nationalist cultures. Complicating the issues with knowledge of the material and libidinal purposes without privileging one over the other may only enhance the discovery of a fuller explanation of cultural crossing.

NOTES

1. Gayatri Spivak, *A Critique of Postcolonial Reason: Toward a History of the Vanishing Present* (Cambridge: Harvard University Press, 1999), 397.

2. Thomas P. Melady and Margaret B. Melady, *Uganda: The Asian Exiles* (New York: Orbis, 1976), 3–4. Thomas Melady was the U.S. ambassador to Uganda at the time of the crisis.

3. The motto was first formulated for the nationalist independence struggle and not for the racist use to which Amin put it.

4. Chapter 1 of H. S. Morris, *The Indians in Uganda* (Chicago: University of Chicago Press, 1968) provides a background summary of Indian immigration to East Africa. See also Daniel D.C. Don Nanjira, *The Status of Aliens in East Africa: Asians and Europeans in Tanzania, Uganda, and Kenya* (New York: Praeger, 1976). For discussions of the Asian expulsion, see Melady and Melady, *Uganda*; Bert N. Adams and Mike Bristow, "Ugandan Asian Expulsion," *Journal of Asian and African Studies* 14, 3–4 (1979): 191–203. For information on the pattern of resettlement in Europe, see United Nations High Commission on Refugees (UNHCR), *How They Did It: Resettlement of Asians From Uganda in Europe and North America* (Geneva: UNHCR, 1973).

5. For a good introduction to the dynamics of Indian presence in the U.S. motel industry and the employment of family members, see Suvarna Thaker, "The Quality of Life of Asian Indian Women in the Motel Industry," *South Asia Bulletin* 2, 1 (Spring 1982): 68–73.

6. Mark A. Reid, "Rebirth of a Nation," *Southern Exposure* (Winter 1992): 26–28; quotation on p. 28. See also Andrea Stuart, "Mira Nair: A New Hybrid Cinema," in *Women and Film: A Sight and Sound Reader,* ed. Pam Cook and Phillip Dodd (Philadelphia: Temple University Press, 1993), 210–216.

7. bell hooks and Anuradha Dingwaney, "Mississippi Masala," *Z Magazine* (July-August 1992): 41–43; quotation on p. 42.

8. The quotes are from the "Culture" chapter in Spivak, *Critique of Postcolonial Reason,* 354–355.

9. Homi Bhabha, *The Location of Culture* (London: Routledge, 1994), 139–170.

10. Ibid., 148.

11. Gayatri Chakravorty Spivak, "Acting Bits/Identity Talk," *Critical Inquiry* 18 (Summer 1992): 775.

12. The terms are from Homi Bhabha.

13. Binita Mehta, "Emigrants Twice Displaced: Race, Color, and Identity in Mira Nair's *Mississippi Masala,*" in *Between the Lines: South Asians and Postcoloniality,* ed. Deepika Bahri and Mary Vasudeva (Philadelphia: Temple University Press, 1996), 185–203.

14. Spivak's phrase is "culture at work is a play of differences" in *Critique of Postcolonial Reason,* 356.

15. Ibid.

16. See Arif Dirlik, "The Postmodernization of Production and Its Organization," in *The Postcolonial Aura: Third World Criticism in the Age of Global Capitalism* (Boulder: Westview, 1997), 186–219.

17. The agonizing exchange between the lovers makes it hard to understand why hooks and Dingwaney believe the film depicts romantic love as "that interaction which most powerfully enables individuals to move beyond systems of domination . . . to bond despite differences" (41).

18. According to H. S. Morris, "Relatively few coolies from the railway did in fact settle" in Uganda. From *The Indians in Uganda*, which contradicts the most popular view (8–9).

19. Ibid., 9.

20. Melady and Melady, *Uganda*, 45.

21. We should not construe Mina's words to mean that cultural origin is a "pathology." See Spivak, "Acting Bits," 781.

7
SKIN DEEP
Using Video to Teach Race and Critical Thinking

BRENDA J. ALLEN

As a result of societal pressures, many U.S. institutions of higher education now require students to take at least one course that addresses diversity. They also encourage faculty to weave multicultural issues into the curriculum.

At the same time, universities strive to ensure that students acquire and develop critical thinking skills. The critical thinking movement began in the 1980s as educators sought to counter traditional educational strategies that promoted rote learning.[1] These initiatives seek to move students from passivity to engagement and to empower them to be responsible for their learning and thinking.

In addition, some educators advocate teaching reform through methods that focus on experiential (affective) as well as the more traditional cognitive (rational) aspects of learning.[2] Proponents of this approach often tout the effectiveness of popular media in eliciting affective learning.[3]

In this chapter I discuss a teaching-learning situation that encompasses all of these contemporary topics in higher education by exploring the utility of documentary videos as tools for teaching students to think critically about diversity. Specifically, I discuss how I use a video entitled *Skin Deep* in a course on critical thinking and race at a predominantly white university. My goals are

143

to provide a specific example other instructors might employ and to offer general insight and information that might assist faculty members as they use video and film to teach about race and related topics.

I begin by providing an overview of the course, including its genesis and my teaching objectives. Then I describe pedagogical issues related to teaching critical thinking and multiculturalism. I also discuss challenges I face as a black female professor addressing the topic of race in a predominantly white university. Next I offer a synopsis and overview of the video, and I explain how and why this documentary provides a powerful and compelling means by which to help students "experience" the complexities of racial identity. Following that, I describe how I employ the video. I conclude with implications for using video to teach about race and critical thinking.

ABOUT THE COURSE

The mid-level undergraduate course entitled Current Issues in Communication (taught through the Department of Communication at the University of Colorado) qualifies as a core course in critical thinking. Communication majors are required to take the course; in addition, majors from other programs (e.g., education, fine arts, philosophy) often enroll to fulfill their critical thinking requirement. The department offers at least seven sections (twenty-five students each) per semester. Responsibility for teaching the course rotates among faculty members, who have free rein over content and focus.

When I teach the course, my primary objective is to help students increase their critical thinking skills. Thus I design course activities that will help students become independent thinkers, develop skills of inquiry, discern their reasoning processes, draw reasonable conclusions, recognize that multiple viewpoints can exist, and respect and value alternative perspectives. I also help them connect their emotions with their rationality—to understand relationships between feelings and thoughts. I also address egocentrism and ethnocentrism.

The first few times I taught the course I covered basic concepts of critical thinking. I relied on current events for discussion topics and assignments, often inviting students to identify and recommend them.

The last two times I taught the course I decided to focus on race. I had long avoided the topic for several reasons—mainly because, as the only faculty member of color in the department, I did not want to be stereotyped as the resident expert on race, particularly since race was not my area of study at that time. As a result of numerous developments in my life, however,[4] I decided to change my scholarly emphasis from computers and communication to identity and diversity issues. Consequently, I made a conscious decision to actively engage those topics in my teaching as well as my research.

Because of my personal experiences with race and my scholarly background, I believe I am well positioned to be an agent of social change in my role as a

From *Skin Deep*, Iris Films. Photograph by Kirsten Neff-Jones.

university teacher. If I can make a course interesting and challenging without alienating students, I can help them to realize their agency as it relates to social issues. I can empower them to transform society with their behaviors and perceptions. Although teaching race is a risky venture because it is difficult to predict how students will respond, I believe it is necessary if we wish to effect change.

To this end, I redesigned the course to explore how our social understanding of race is linked to our institutions and cultural norms and to examine the roles of communication and critical thinking. As course content I present factual information related to historical perspectives on race in addition to basic concepts of critical thinking. I also explain how identity is constructed through interaction with others and through messages we send and receive about ourselves and others. I stress the role of significant socializing sources such as the media, educational institutions, peers, and family members. Most important, I strive to help students understand that "races" are far from fixed, transparent, biological categories.

One salient challenge in teaching this course is my identity as a black female professor in a predominantly white university.[5] To a certain extent I am always aware of my identity as a black woman teaching white students, but I feel especially aware of my identity when I teach race and gender.

Another challenge in teaching the course stems from working with students who often have a limited awareness of their own racial identities and who tend

145

to view racism as rare on the one hand and limited to extreme acts on the other. At the beginning of the course, most white students seem apathetic—they do not view race as a significant topic; race does not concern them. Once exposed to the harsh realities of race in the United States, however, many begin to deal with complex emotions such as shame and guilt.

In contrast, the few students of color in my classes tend to be wary and weary. Their experiences in a predominantly white university have led them to expect to be either invisible (most of the time) or hypervisible (when race-ethnicity is the topic) in most of their classes. Therefore I face the challenge of creating a course and classroom environment in which everyone can delve openly and deeply into critical thinking about race.

PEDAGOGICAL ISSUES

Numerous pedagogical issues undergird the example I offer here, but I will not attempt to exhaust the huge body of relevant literature. Instead, to contextualize my experiences I provide a brief overview of select writings about critical thinking and multiculturalism.

Critical Thinking

Scholars hold varying views about how to teach critical thinking. Salient for the current discussion is the idea that effective teaching incorporates both cognition (rationality) and affect (emotions).[6] For instance, Mark Weinstein asserts that educators need to orchestrate information and experience, "informed throughout by an awareness of actual and preferred cognitive strategies and the criteria that warrant them."[7] Cognitive approaches should focus on key critical thinking dispositions including curiosity, objectivity, open-mindedness, flexibility, self-awareness, persistence, and respect for other viewpoints.[8] Proponents of this approach believe students' personal experiences are essential for critical thinking instruction.[9] They also advocate methods that allow students to explore relationships between thoughts and feelings. Other recommended methods to promote critical thinking dispositions include encouraging success and self-esteem, establishing a climate of trust and respect, developing a community of inquiry, striking a balance between teacher talk and student talk, and emphasizing thinking about thinking.[10]

Multiculturalism

Education literature is rife with research, guidelines, and discussions about challenges and effective approaches to teaching multiculturalism and diversity.[11] Increasingly, scholars advocate incorporating experiential (affective) methods in contrast with the propensity to focus mainly on knowledge (cognition).[12] Teachers, however, should include both the affective and cognitive domains to maximize the learning experience: they should employ the experiential system

From *Skin Deep*, Iris Films. Photograph by Kirsten Neff-Jones.

in an effort to shape attitudes and behaviors and implement the rational system to develop students' knowledge base.[13] Furthermore, "Teaching that simultaneously engages both systems may be the most effective."[14] Thus teachers should seek to balance learning objectives in rational and experiential domains.[15]

Rather than merely *tell* students about the experiences of others or merely *describe* cultural biases, teachers should incorporate methods that allow students to experience (even vicariously) "others" and then reflect on their own biases. Consequently, learning may occur at an unconscious level, and "students may not need to consider rational arguments, but may respond from their own experiential base in a manner that may be less ethnocentric."[16]

Multicultural scholars endorse strategies that help students experience the views of members of various racial, ethnic, and cultural backgrounds. One way to enrich students' experience is to present "the experience of others, whether in the form of first hand reports in the classroom or in the form of narratives in contemporary media, literature, history or sociology."[17] To provide such experiences, scholars frequently recommend using media based on narrative because of its potential for a strong, enduring impact on students.[18]

USING VIDEO TO TEACH ABOUT RACE AND CRITICAL THINKING

My course design strikes a balance between experiential and rational learning processes. I use the textbook *Thinking for Yourself*,[19] which nicely blends coverage of key critical thinking concepts (e.g., assumptions, inferences, facts, perspectives, viewpoints, opinions, evaluations) with experiential exercises. During the first few weeks of the course, I concentrate more on knowledge sharing than on affect. It is important to establish a safe climate for students before inviting them to share their feelings and experience subject materials.

I also develop a variety of assignments that touch upon one or both domains. For instance, students are required to keep a journal. Some record content-based information, and others express feelings, but most move between the two. I sometimes place students in groups corresponding to U.S. racial groups and direct them to "identify" with their group for the duration of the semester. The students and I employ a variety of media including print (magazines and newspapers), television shows, educational videos, and commercial films.

The video documentary *Skin Deep* (1995) provides an excellent means for striking a balance between cognition and affect. The video's synopsis reads: "A diverse group of college students come together to confront their country's racial legacy. Risking openness and candor, the young people share their anger, pain, confusion and hope in the effort to go beneath the surface of America's racial divide." Produced by Francis Reid and Iris Films, the video is fifty-three minutes, nineteen seconds long.

The video displays interactions among racially diverse college students who participated in a weekend retreat. Students in the video are self-identified as African American, Asian American, Mexican American, Native American, Jewish, and Caucasian. Through personal narratives and interactions with one another, the students bring up a variety of issues that are addressed in the course. Their stories and conversations reveal some of the complexities and nuances of racial identity according to young people in contemporary U.S. society. Some of the topics they raise include in-group challenges (e.g., skin color), affirmative action, white male privilege, white privilege, guilt (white students and family), diversity within racial groups, internalized racism, and institutionalized racism.

The video evokes many emotional responses in the classroom, and during the postviewing discussion we process our feelings. I also help students locate and label specific concepts we have covered in class. Examples include the assumptions the Jewish woman in the video faces when other people make comments around her about Jews because they do not know she is Jewish or the internalized racism evident in a Mexican American woman's uncle's comments about her dark skin.

Seeing other college students articulate fear and anger in response to their experiences empowers students in the class to also express themselves, both in their journals and during class discussions. Students also develop deeper and more enduring empathy than they seem to do after reading print versions of autobiographical narratives.

When I use this video, the class always views it in its entirety (the class meets for an hour and fifteen minutes). I ask them to take brief notes during the viewing. After the viewing I facilitate the discussion with broad-based, open-ended questions such as, What stood out for you? What upset you? With whom did you identify? What course concepts did this video exemplify? What did you learn that you never knew before? I also invite students to reflect on the video in their journals, and they often do so. The experience of viewing the video encourages students to engage in honest dialogue about racial issues.

IMPLICATIONS

My experience using a documentary video yields numerous implications for teaching critical thinking and race. It reinforces a need to address both affective and cognitive domains of learning. In addition, it demonstrates the potential power of film to evoke emotions as it develops intellect. Several factors contribute to creating a successful teaching-learning experience. These factors hold implications for anyone who may wish to incorporate videos into classes on race.

First, choosing an appropriate video is important. Because *Skin Deep* corresponds with my learning objectives, it is a good selection. It helps students experience firsthand some specific concepts from the course—for instance, to become aware of the worldviews and experiences of people from various racial-ethnic groups. In addition, the documentary format appeals to students because the people in the video are "real." Similarly, the fact that the people in the video are college students seems to enable closer identification. Moreover, the video is well produced, with smooth transitions. Experience has taught me to select contemporary media—unless, of course, the film has historical significance—because students will question the credibility of outdated films based on cues such as hairstyles and clothing. In addition, the video is neither too short nor too long.

Timing is another consideration. I do not show this video until well into the semester, after students have a sense of comfort within the classroom, with me, with their peers, and with the subject matter. By the time I show the video I have helped students master concepts such as assumptions, inferences, and stereotypes by using relatively "safe" examples, such as newspaper cartoons on relatively neutral topics and magazine ads. In other words, I ease them into more controversial and challenging topics rather than forcing them to confront them early on. As time passes I share some of my own narratives regarding race and critical thinking—including instances when I was guilty of stereotyping others, as well as when I felt as though I was the object of racism. This helps to set the tone for students to feel free to express their experiences and to be open to the experiences of the students in the video.

Thorough preparation is important as well. I watched the video a few times prior to airing it so I could develop discussion questions, assess my own responses, and try to anticipate students' reactions. In addition, I prepare students for viewing by announcing beforehand that we will watch the video and by giving them questions to consider as they view the film. I also actively view the film with them so I can monitor their responses.

In conclusion, video can be an effective means for faculty members to respond to educational initiatives related to diversity as well as critical thinking. Incorporating video can also help students use both affective and cognitive learning processes. Finally, using video to teach race may help students develop "attitudes and behaviors consistent with the acceptance and celebration of human diversity."[20]

NOTES

1. Valerie R. Swarts, "Critical Thinking: Friend or Foe of Higher Education," paper presented at the Annual Meeting of the Speech Communication Association, Chicago, IL, 29 October–1 November 1992.

2. Seymour Epstein, "Integration of the Cognitive and the Psychodynamic Unconscious," *American Psychologist* 49, 49 (1994): 709–724.

3. J. Michael Tyler and Lorraine J. Guth, "Using Media to Create Experiential Learning in Multicultural and Diversity Issues," *Journal of Multicultural Counseling and Development* 27, 3 (1999): 153–169.

4. See Brenda J. Allen, "Feminism and Organizational Communication: A Black Woman's (Re)view of Organizational Socialization," *Communication Studies* 47 (1996): 257–271.

5. For an analysis of black women's socialization experiences in academe, see Brenda J. Allen, "'Learning the Ropes': A Black Feminist Critique," in *Rethinking Organizational and Managerial Communication From Feminist Perspectives*, ed. P. Buzzanell (Thousand Oaks, CA: Sage, 2000), 177–208.

6. Mark Weinstein, *Critical Thinking and the Psycho-logic of Race Prejudice*, Resource Publication Series 3, 1, Montclair State College (Upper Montclair: New Jersey Institute for Critical Thinking, 1990).

7. Ibid., 17.

8. Debbie Walsh, "Critical Thinking to Reduce Prejudice," *Social Education* 52, 4 (1988): 280–282.

9. Weinstein, *Critical Thinking.*

10. Ibid.

11. Tyler and Guth, "Using Media."

12. Cynthia Breaux, William M. Liu, and Donald B. Pope-Davis, "A Multicultural Immersion Experience: Filling a Void in Multicultural Training," in *Multicultural Counseling Competencies: Assessment, Education, Training, and Supervision*, ed. Donald B. Pope-Davis and Hardin L.K. Coleman (Thousand Oaks, CA: Sage, 1997), 227–241.

13. Tyler and Guth, "Using Media."

14. Ibid., 156.

15. Epstein, "Integration of the Cognitive."

16. Tyler and Guth, "Using Media," 159.

17. Weinstein, *Critical Thinking,* 16.

18. Tyler and Guth, "Using Media."

19. Marlys Mayfield, *Thinking for Yourself: Developing Critical Thinking Skills Through Reading and Writing* (New York: Harcourt College Publishers, 1996).

20. Tyler and Guth, "Using Media," 162.

PART III
ETHNICITY, RACE, GENDER, SEXUALITY, AND THE POLITICS OF REPRESENTATION

Anna May Wong from *Slaying the Dragon,* produced by Asian Women United of California

8

CONFRONTING GENDER STEREOTYPES OF ASIAN AMERICAN WOMEN

Slaying the Dragon

MARILYN C. ALQUIZOLA AND LANE RYO HIRABAYASHI

In this chapter we delineate how we approach a number of key issues revolving around gender stereotypes of Asian and Asian American women using the documentary film *Slaying the Dragon* (1988), directed by Deborah Gee. Although it is only sixty minutes long and thus could be shown in one sitting, we will outline an alternative way to introduce, show, and analyze the film to make it an even more effective tool for examining gender stereotypes of women of Asian descent.

The description on the box states that *Slaying the Dragon* "traces sixty years of Hollywood's inaccurate stereotyping of Asian women. . . . Through film clips and interviews with critics and actresses we are shown how little these images have changed from bygone days. Asian American women [also] reflect on the ways these stereotypes have affected their lives."

Basically, we break *Slaying the Dragon* into three episodes. We reinforce each episode by posing study questions and then set up small discussion groups to promote a reflexive and critical reading of the documentary. Although *Slaying the Dragon* does have limitations, they can be raised openly, and in fact they serve as additional themes to be explored through discussion. *Slaying the Dragon* was widely circulated, so it is available in many university media libraries, as well as in public collections across the country.

THESIS

Media representations have markedly and indelibly shaped the way members of society at large and, by extension, Asian American women perceive images of Asian women. We believe it is necessary to expose these representations explicitly and critically in terms of both their content and their dynamics. Moreover, we do not fear that by presenting such images we will reinscribe them in viewers' minds, either subconsciously or consciously, because although doing so may pose a certain risk, we believe the risk entailed in avoiding the topic of gendered stereotypes of women of color altogether seems much greater. After all, if one does not know what these images are and how they "work," one can neither defend against them nor generate alternative representations.

We do not assume, however, that the reinscription of racist and stereotypical images cannot or does not happen. Rather, in this chapter we delineate a number of techniques we have used in the past to actively counter the reinscription of racist stereotypes even as we bring them forward and present them to audiences for critical deconstruction.

We also suggest ways *Slaying the Dragon* can be used to introduce audiences to feminist perspectives on the Asian American experience. Given that patriarchy remains a powerful force in many new Asian immigrant families, it seems imperative that *Slaying the Dragon* be used to encourage men and women to reflect upon how we may be reinforcing gendered stereotypes of Asian American women in our communities and lives.

SETTING UP THE FIRST EPISODE

We often set up *Slaying the Dragon* by reviewing key concepts that are an integral part of an introductory Asian American or ethnic studies course. First, we review lecture and reading material on racial prejudice,[1] racial stereotypes,[2] and the elements of "racial formation theory."[3] Although racial formation theory is complex, undergraduates should be exposed to its basic elements. "Race" is not a scientific or a biological fact; rather, it is a construction, and as such, "racial" categories and classifications are continually subject to politicization. Thus the manifestations of "race" are constantly a site of negotiation and struggle. This is why, when examined over time and through space, "race" is unstable and inherently subject to shifts and flux. What we look at in ethnic studies has more to do with *processes of racialization* than anything else. We also introduce the concept of gender, emphasizing its socially constructed nature.[4] This is also the time to expose students to the concept of patriarchy, which can be done through a combination of readings, lecture materials, and discussion, depending on the level of the students.[5]

Next we assign a short paper students are expected to finish before viewing the first episode. For the paper we ask students to consider these questions: (1) In your opinion, what common images of Asian women are held by members of the larger public? (2) Where do these images come from? (3) Do these same images have any impact on Asian American women (that is, women of Asian or part-Asian descent in the United States)? (4) If so, how and why?

In the session after the papers have been submitted, the responses can be processed in different ways. One is to ask for responses in a collective, open-ended fashion by reiterating the questions and writing students' responses on the blackboard. It is worth noting that students may have reservations about identifying various stereotypes "out loud" (especially if they are Euro-Americans). This can be mitigated by reassuring students that they are being asked to report on images held by members of the dominant society; the images they voice are not necessarily ones they endorse. Alternatively, students can be divided into small discussion groups randomly, by gender, or by ethnicity and race. "Group reports" can be called for after a ten-to-fifteen-minute discussion period, then the responses can be listed on the blackboard. Reserve a block of time so items can be discussed as they are put on the board.

It is useful as well to ask students why they think given images can be classified as stereotypical and why they might be applied to Asian and Asian American women. We have been surprised by the fact that so many basic images are still widely known, suggesting they are still in circulation. Here are some stereotypical images of Asian women: they are exotic, sexual, beautiful, mysterious, possibly dangerous or even overtly evil, dutiful, polite, quiet, conservative (in terms of language, custom, and a tendency to be virgins), obedient, subservient, and so on. Occasionally, we get other interesting responses; a person may note that because of Asian patriarchal orientation, Asian and Asian American women find Asian men too oppressive; concomitantly, they may prefer Euro-Americans.

After these images have been shared and discussed, it is useful to discuss where and how the images have been generated and circulated and whether they impact Asian and Asian American women. This provides an excellent introduction for the first episode of *Slaying the Dragon*.

THE FIRST EPISODE

Before showing the first episode of *Slaying the Dragon* (approximately the first twenty minutes), we usually write a set of questions on the board. We do not assume students will get the key points on their own, although they may. Visual media are complex because they involve our senses of sight and sound while also stimulating our thoughts and emotions.[6] For this reason we give students questions to consider before films or videos are screened to help them key into certain information or points they might otherwise miss, especially if they will

From *Sayonara*, MGM/UA Studios, 1957

only view the film once.[7] Our initial questions for the first episode include: (1) What stereotypes of Asian women are presented? (2) Where do they seem to come from, and as of what dates? (3) Are the stereotypes fairly structured and consistent over time, or do they shift? (4) If they shift, how and why do they change over time?

Slaying the Dragon presents the three "classic" representations of Asian women: (1) the Dragon Lady, an image of an evil, amoral vamp; (2) the geisha/

Anna Mae Wong

bar girl/prostitute, an image of Asian women as sexual playthings for Caucasians; and (3) the "good, conservative" Asian woman, typically a virgin or a wife and mother. Deborah Gee argues that Hollywood feature films bear much

From *A Study in Scarlet,* World Wide Pictures, 1933

responsibility for presenting and inscribing these images in U.S. society's popular consciousness (and, we would add, unconscious). *Slaying the Dragon* highlights clips from a wide range of "old" movies—including series such as *Flash
Gordon* (1936) and the *Fu Manchu* (1956) films, footage featuring actresses
such as the famed Anna Mae Wong, and classics such as *The Good Earth* (1937)
and *Sayonara* (1957)—to illustrate these three key portrayals of Asian women.

After screening the first episode, the instructor can return to the list of
images on the blackboard—most of which can be directly linked to the three
basic gendered and racialized representations of Asian women featured in *Slaying the Dragon.* Students should also critically assess Gee's argument. Although
Hollywood bears a great deal of responsibility for circulating and reinforcing
these images, it is crucial to remember that the images are actually very old—
dating back to the West's initial contact and interaction with China, Japan, and
the rest of Asia.[8] The images were reinscribed in the late nineteenth and early
twentieth centuries, when Euro-American exclusionists trumpeted the dangers
of "the Yellow Peril" and pushed for an end to open immigration from Asia to
the United States—which they accomplished for the Chinese in 1882 and for
the Japanese and Koreans in 1908.[9] Gee does an excellent job of showing that
these images respond to and thus reflect the state of international relations

From *The Tea House of the August Moon,* Warner Studios, 1956

between the United States and various Asian nations. Although she does not use that framework, her thesis illustrates compellingly the elements of a "racial formation" perspective on gender stereotypes of Asian women.

Initially, Chinese and Japanese were portrayed as mysterious, exotic, sexual, sinister, and dangerous; but when Japan became a threat to Western imperialism and colonization in Asia during the 1940s, Japanese men were depicted as brutal warmongers. This transpired as images of the Chinese (as allies of the

161

From *The Tea House of the August Moon,* Warner Studios, 1956

United States) received a more sympathetic treatment in feature films such as *The Good Earth.* After the creation of the People's Republic of China (PRC) in 1949, however, sympathetic portrayals of Chinese began to shift. On the one hand, the PRC and communist Chinese (and shortly afterward communist Koreans) were vilified as a ruthless, faceless horde (in essence, a new "Yellow Peril") capable of sweeping over democratic, capitalist countries. As a number of authors have pointed out, these shifting images subtly yet powerfully determined the way Euro-Americans perceived Americans of Asian descent.

On the other hand, the image of the geisha/prostitute came to the fore during the 1950s and 1960s vis-à-vis occupied Japan and the Western presence in such colonial holdings as Okinawa, Hong Kong, Singapore, Hawaii, and the Philippines. Gee clips scenes from *Tea House of the August Moon* (1956), *Sayonara*

(1957), *The World of Suzy Wong* (1960) to illustrate this image. Concomitantly, Japanese (and Japanese American) men were suddenly desexualized—witness, for example, the portrayal of these men as servants, houseboys, and sidekicks during the 1950s. Thus although clear continuities exist regarding racialized gender stereotypes, it is fascinating to note how these representations have shifted between images of "good Asians" versus "bad Asians," echoing the shifting patterns of international relations and the resulting alliances and disjunctures between the United States and various Asian countries.

THE SECOND EPISODE

During the following class session, we show the second episode of *Slaying the Dragon* (approximately another twenty minutes). This episode revisits an old debate: namely, do Hollywood movies perpetuate racial stereotypes by reinscribing them in the popular imagination, or are such movies merely "harmless entertainment" that has no lasting impact or effect?

The centerpiece of this episode is the infamous movie *The World of Suzy Wong*. The narration in *Slaying the Dragon* revolves around the "present-day" commentary of the lead actress, Nancy Kwan, on the one hand, who argues that the film is basically entertainment and that the images it presents are harmless and could not be applied to Asian women as a whole. On the other hand, a number of Asian American women, who appear to be of college age, share personal anecdotes that indicate that the Euro-American men whom they have met have stereotypical assumptions about women of Asian descent that were influenced by *The World of Suzy Wong* and similar films. Gee intersperses clips from more recent films such as Michael Cimino's *Year of the Dragon* (1985) to show that the trope of an Asian woman as the sexual plaything of a domineering white man is alive and well.

Gee also explores other productions and actresses. Clips from the feature-length movie *The Flower Drum Song* (1961) suggest a step forward because the film was based on a novel by Asian American writer C. Y. Lee and featured actors of Asian descent. Similarly, Gee presents interview footage with the Asian American actress Nobu McCarthy. From a young age, McCarthy played a range of roles in Hollywood feature films but, by her own account, was sensitive to representations that stereotyped Asian and Asian American women and refused to play such roles.

Following the second episode a reflection paper can be assigned along the line of questioning in the next paragraph. Or sometimes when we show the video in a humanities-oriented course, we have asked students to do short research papers if time permits. One line of research asks students to address the life, work, and images of specific actresses such as Anna Mae Wong, Nancy Kwan, Nobu McCarthy, or news personalities such as Connie Chung, who is also featured in *Slaying the Dragon*.

Depending on the class and the students' maturity, discussion groups might pursue another dimension of this episode of *Slaying the Dragon*. Gee has included interviews with several Asian American women—including biracial and multiracial women of part Asian descent—in which the women speak about a range of interpersonal relationships that have been impacted by racial stereotypes, from the benign to the offensive. In addition, students should be invited to grapple with questions about whether the visual media have affected both the attitudes and behaviors of Asian and Asian American women. Students often have strong views on this subject, so it may be helpful to remind them that much debate surrounds this complex question that has not been resolved even by media experts.[10] Students may wish to research these contradictory findings by studying the large bodies of empirical data that have been gathered in the communications field, among others.

Another point to consider is the fact that *Slaying the Dragon* is approximately fifteen years old. To be open to changing realities, in terms of either stereotypic images or the reception of such images, discussions of the second episode should be fairly open-ended. In this sense *Slaying the Dragon* can serve as a kind of "ink blot" in which students can explore their own and their peers' experiences to see whether Gee's messages are useful. Regardless of whether students find *Slaying the Dragon* relevant to their own lives, their reactions to Gee's arguments and presentation of visual evidence can help expose what they may be experiencing and thinking. In sum, it will be important to be open to the unexpected, with the understanding that as the times change, so do students' interpretations of what representations are at play and what they entail.

THE LAST EPISODE

The final segment of *Slaying the Dragon* (the last twenty minutes) addresses alternative representations of Asian American women. Gee features outtakes from filmmaker Wayne Wang's early prototype of the movie that eventually became *The Joy Luck Club* (1993). As Wang explains, his original idea was to feature a group of young Asian American women who were friends—depicting them individually to illustrate their diversity but also depicting the ways their lives intersect. Although this approach was abandoned because the plot became too complex, the outtakes illustrate Wang's vision of a new genre: films that are by, about, and for Asian Americans; films that provide alternative images of women based on the lived experience of Asian Americans; and films that are also suitable for non-Asian audiences. This is a very important point that deserves further emphasis in lectures and small discussion groups.

It might be valuable to contrast Wang's "emic" approach with clips of Caucasian actors such as Marlon Brando and Katharine Hepburn, who are shown early in *Slaying the Dragon* in yellow face. Parallels can be made to black face and what it means when people of color are played by Euro-Americans in makeup. Or—and this becomes more subtle—what does it mean when non-Korean Asian American actors play Korean Americans, say, in a program such as *M*A*S*H* or in Margaret Cho's TV family sitcom *All American Girl* (1994–1995). One could argue that such practices might amount to pretty much the same thing as the use of yellow face—that is, they are premised on the assumption that "most Americans cannot tell the difference anyhow."[11]

Other questions worth exploring are whether it is realistic to expect that audiences who are not of Asian descent will go to see—let alone understand and value—films that revolve around insiders' views of the Asian American experience. Reference might be made to film studies that delineate the complexities of political economy in the production and reception of films about people of color. Studies along these lines indicate that independent films are expensive to produce, and even when they are of excellent quality, they may lack the financial backing and thus the eventual circulation to have any sustained impact on the popular imagination.[12]

TOWARD ASIAN AMERICAN FEMINIST PERSPECTIVES

At the same time that we praise Deborah Gee and highlight the many useful dimensions of her film *Slaying the Dragon* as a tool for learning about racialized gender stereotypes, we can also supplement Gee's analysis by inviting critical examination of several related points. To what extent, for example, can Gee's analysis be extended from her Chinese and Japanese examples to other Asian American and Pacific American women? To be fair to Gee, it could be argued that since the former were the first two large populations of Asians in the United States, the stereotypical images that plagued the early Chinese and Japanese—both men and women—were then successively applied to the other Asian immigrant groups that followed. Thus in terms of women, the early stereotypes were reinscribed—in many cases with few variations other than those inflicted by "racist hate," which reflected historical situations such as competition or war, or "racist love," which reflected the sympathy or alliances prompted by other historical events.[13] Moreover, Gee does try to incorporate other populations, referencing the Korean War in the 1950s, as well as the war in Southeast Asia—particularly Vietnam—and cinematic representations of women in the latter in such feature films as *Rambo* (1985) and *The Deer Hunter* (1978), which repeat the same old clichés.

We think it is worthwhile to ask whether the stereotypical images of Asian and Asian American women Gee presents are valid for other populations, such as Koreans and Korean Americans, South Asians and South Asian Americans, or Filipinos and Filipino Americans. Do real differences exist—concerning generation, history, and culture—that we need to highlight that may be erased if we simply project what has happened to Chinese and Chinese Americans and

Japanese and Japanese Americans onto all subsequent populations of Asian descent? It may, in fact, not be possible to resolve this issue without focusing on a specific population and doing empirical research on the matter. Nevertheless, we should raise the question and invite our audience to carry out the necessary work to try to clarify, if not resolve, the matter.

Other questions worthy of exploration are, As the global positioning of Asian women laborers has shifted, how have stereotypical images been reinscribed, and how have new ones been reinvented?[14] *Blood, Sweat, and Lace* (1994)—a film made by supporters of the grassroots organization Asian Immigrant Women's Advocates (AIWA)—could be used to spark such a discussion. *Blood, Sweat, and Lace* is also notable because it is overtly politicized: it presents a critical analysis of the way sweatshops exploit Asian immigrant women's labor but also highlights how these women have organized to resist and oppose those responsible for their working conditions.[15]

Finally, *Slaying the Dragon* invites us to go beyond Gee's analysis, since we cannot and should not blame non-Asians and non–Asian Americans alone for sexist images and attitudes. We need to confront the fact that sexist and patriarchal images of Asian and Asian American women can come from, or be supported by, the inside as well. In this sense, people of Asian descent in the United States have to be willing to examine the ways their family and community institutions may knowingly or unknowingly stereotype and thus limit women.

Moreover, these negative images may be reproduced at the interpersonal level in school, the workplace, the neighborhood, or between lovers, husbands and wives, parents and children, brothers and sisters, and so on. Asian American men should also grapple with the role they have played in the past in this regard so they can help to reconstruct the future by developing and disseminating alternative images.[16]

In the end, Deborah Gee's *Slaying the Dragon* is a very useful tool for exploring a range of gender issues in contemporary Asian American communities. It does not provide all the answers—nor does it claim to—yet the documentary presents a solid analysis of stereotypical images of the past. With the right presentation, *Slaying the Dragon* also offers a vehicle to move discussion beyond the film itself. Thus we can ask our students collectively, even as we ask ourselves, Do we need Asian American feminisms and feminist perspectives? If so, what forms should they take?[17]

NOTES

1. Racial prejudice has to do with a negative prejudgment against a given group of color or against people of color in general. See Richard T. Schaefer, "Prejudice," in his *Racial and Ethnic Groups* (New York: HarperCollins, 1990), 53–86.

2. Racial stereotypes are prejudicial but are often differentiated in terms of presenting specific racialized images: e.g., Japanese and Japanese Americans specifically are deemed to

be inherently sneaky and treacherous. See Philip Q. Yang, *Ethnic Studies: Issues and Approaches* (Albany: State University of New York Press, 2000).

3. See Howard Winant, *Racial Conditions: Politics, Theory, Comparisons* (Minneapolis: University of Minnesota Press, 1994), for a succinct overview of racial formation theory.

4. The concept of gender is effectively glossed in Maggie Humm, ed., *The Dictionary of Feminist Theory* (Columbus: Ohio State University Press, 1995). We sometimes use this short entry and others from this volume as a convenient reference of key terms for students.

5. Patriarchy is given a sophisticated treatment in Sylvia Walby, *Theorizing Patriarchy* (Oxford: Basil Blackwell, 1990). Walby's treatment appeals to us because she addresses the complexities of patriarchy, arguing that its manifestations and its impact in different cultures and different historical contexts must be looked at empirically because they vary.

6. This point is borrowed from Jun Xing, Chapters 2 and 13 in this volume.

7. As presenters, we have often seen a given program many times. (Lane Hirabayashi, for example, has probably shown *Slaying the Dragon* every semester over the past twelve years.) We should thus realize that our students might not "get" everything in a video or film after only the first viewing. Some semesters, when featuring documentaries that we discuss extensively, we have put them on reserve in the library so students can study them in more depth.

8. A recent book by Robert Lee is a useful source for tracing early stereotypical images of Chinese, as well as the ways these images have impacted popular perceptions of Asians in the United States. In particular, Lee traces "Orientalism" through a variety of domains of popular culture. See Robert G. Lee, *Orientals: Asian Americans in Popular Culture* (Philadelphia: Temple University Press, 1999). For a treatment of similar images in Hollywood feature films, see Eugene Wong, *On Visual Media Racism: Asians in American Motion Pictures* (New York: Arno, 1978) and the award-winning book by Gina Marchetti, *Romance and the Yellow Peril: Race, Sex and Discursive Strategies in Hollywood Fiction* (Berkeley: University of California Press, 1991). Marchette does a thorough job of identifying a wide range of gender stereotypes of Asian women, although again these are primarily permutations of the three key images Gee treats in *Slaying the Dragon*.

9. For a history of Asian immigration to the United States and the related legislation, see Bill Ong Hing, *Making and Remaking Asian America Through Immigration Policy, 1850–1990* (Palo Alto: Stanford University Press, 1993).

10. The Columbine shootings in Littleton, Colorado, in 1999 brought many pundits to the air waves, debating whether the tragic incident had been primed in any way by violent feature films portraying teen-on-teen shootings or by the violent video game the killers, Eric Harris and Dylan Kliebold, were reputed to have played for hours on end. Somewhat related incidents seem to be fairly commonplace in the United States; for example, see *Newsweek*, 4 December 2000, 46, in which John Horn discusses yet another case in which a heavy-metal band—in this case Slayer—has been named in a wrongful-death suit. Supposedly influenced by Slayer's image and lyrics, the alleged perpetrators are reputed to have killed a fifteen-year-old acquaintance to "make a sacrifice to the Devil" and to make a name for themselves and their garage band, Hatred. Horn notes that in addition to "unspecified monetary damages," the parents of the victim are seeking "restrictions on the marketing of violent music to minors." As of mid-December, the case was still pending. Also see "Hollywood Won't Lobby its Way out of This One" in *Business Week*, 25

September 2000, 43, in which Ronald Grover writes as a father who does not like the fact that his daughter listens to Eminem. He objects to Eminem's messages and says that parents ought to make media accountable for the production and distribution of these pieces.

11. A useful discussion of racial stereotypes and images in prime-time television is presented in Darrell Y. Hamamoto, *Monitored Peril: Asian Americans and the Politics of TV Representation* (Minneapolis: University of Minnesota Press, 1994).

12. See, for example, Jesse A. Rhines, *Black Film, White Money* (New Brunswick: Rutgers University Press, 1996), which discusses the political economy of black film.

13. See Frank Chin and Jeffery Paul Chan, "Racist Love," in *Seeing Through Shuck,* ed. Richard Kostelanetz (New York: Ballantine, 1972), 65–79.

14. Two good resources for instructors, which could be used with seniors or graduate students, are Laura Hyun Yi Kang, "Si(gh)ting Asian/American Women as Transnational Labor," *Positions* 5, 2 (Fall 1997): 403–437, and Evelyn Hu-DeHart, "Women, Work, and Globalization in Late 20th Century Capitalism: Asian Women Immigrants in the United States," Working Paper 24, American Ethnic Studies Program (Pullman: Washington State University, 1999).

15. AIWA is treated in an excellent article by Miriam Ching Louie, "Immigrant Asian Women in Bay Area Garment Sweatshops: After Sewing, Laundry, Cleaning, and Cooking, I Have No Breath Left to Sing," *Amerasia Journal* 18, 1 (1992): 1–26.

16. For an exposition of how Jachinson Chan raises feminist issues in his Asian American men's courses at University of California–Santa Barbara, see Jachinson W. Chan, "Contemporary Asian American Men's Issues," in *Teaching Asian America: Diversity and the Problem of Community,* ed. Lane Ryo Hirabayashi (Lanham, MD: Rowman and Littlefield, 1998), 93–102.

17. For an intriguing essay that raises many relevant questions on feminism and Asian Americans, see Sonia Shah, "Presenting the Blue Goddess: Toward a National Pan-Asian Feminist Agenda," in *The State of Asian America: Activism and Resistance in the 1980s,* ed. Karin Aguilar San Juan (Boston: South End, 1994), 147–158.

9

SCREENS AND BARS

Confronting Cinema Representations of Race and Crime

Lee Bernstein

In 1953 Daniel Bell wrote, "Crime is an American way of life."[1] We can take this observation in at least two ways. First, crime occupies a central place in U.S. art, history, and literature, not to mention news, film, and television. But crime is also an "American way of life" in a second way. Crime and punishment are much more than stories about which we read or watch: people are robbed and violated; others spend large portions of their lives behind bars or are executed by the U.S. government. The number of people behind bars eclipsed 2 million on 15 February 2000. Thousands of people are on our nation's death rows—with an even higher proportion of people of color than that among the general prison population. At the same time, the mass media is saturated with misleading images of crime and punishment that are either unduly menacing or follow the models established by video-store employee turned director Quentin Tarantino's fantasies of vicarious transgression.

This saturation of crime images creates unique challenges for teaching courses on crime in U.S. history and culture. Crime stories are among the most popular Hollywood fare while also serving as the basis of independent cinema. Whether we like it or not, these crime stories shape the way we and our students understand actual criminal and policing practices; they also shape how many people think about racial, ethnic, and class differences. Uncovering—and, it is hoped, transforming—some of these links and distortions is a necessary part of my pedagogy. According to Bureau of Justice statistics, "Black offenders are 50 to 60 percent more likely to be sentenced for larceny than white offenders, and twice as likely as whites to be sentenced for weapons offenses."[2] The disparities for drug offenses are even greater: whereas 65 percent of crack users are white, 92.6 percent of those convicted for the crime are African American. Clearly, it is irresponsible to talk about the representation of crime without talking about the representation of race. Our understandings of the causes of crime and punishment often grow from our understandings of racial and class stereotypes in U.S. popular culture.

This chapter will explore the textual, social, and pedagogical possibilities of comparing mainstream and incarcerated people's perspectives on the racial context for crime and punishment. The comments of those behind bars about their crimes and experiences with the justice system are useful counterhegemonic perspectives. Teachers should use them whenever screening Hollywood films, regardless of the race of the writer, producer, or director. Although these comments may reinforce some assumptions about race, class, and criminality, their connection to a long tradition of creative expression behind bars helps us to see incarceration within the context of oppression—that is, voices and visions coming from our prisons often force audiences to make links among histories of class, gender, and racial inequality.

PART I: SCREENS

Hollywood has long boasted about the realism of its crime stories. *Scarface* (1932) opened by telling viewers that the film's intention was to outrage them into doing something about the violence and corruption in urban America, staging well-known gangland killings such as Al Capone's St. Valentine's Day massacre. The 1980s remake featured actual news footage of the Mariel boat lift. Both films featured highly sensationalized images of immigrant gangsters. Despite classic ethnic stereotypes of violent ethnic men who covet Waspy women, the films were heralded as examples of "realism." Think of all the films that package criminal fantasies within the guise of realism: from *Blackboard Jungle* (1955) to *In Cold Blood* (1967) and the televised crime-of-the-moment docudramas. The films seem to grant access to both policing and the criminal underworld that would otherwise be unavailable. They serve as a kind of curriculum about crime that our students and colleagues accept.

A white male student from southern California, for example, told a story in class about getting lost while driving through Los Angeles and ending up in Latino East Los Angeles. Although he lived only a short drive from that neighborhood, his only contact had been from films such as *Colors* (1988) and evening

He was a nobody; a black man in a white man's prison.
She was a somebody; a notorious, beautiful, radical black professor.
Their love story shocked the nation.

This film is that story.

EDWARD LEWIS PRODUCTION OF 'BROTHERS'
STARRING BERNIE CASEY · VONETTA McGEE · RON O'NEAL
WRITTEN AND PRODUCED BY EDWARD AND MILDRED LEWIS
DIRECTED BY ARTHUR BARRON · EXECUTIVE PRODUCER LEE SAVIN
IN ASSOCIATION WITH ROBERT H. GREENBERG
MUSIC COMPOSED AND PERFORMED BY TAJ MAHAL
FROM WARNER BROS Ⓦ A WARNER COMMUNICATIONS COMPANY

From *Brothers,* Warner Bros., 1977

news crime updates. His perception of what he saw had been almost entirely shaped by the camera lens. Perhaps even more disturbing, his assumptions about what to do if he encountered criminal behavior were shaped by representations of paramilitary police occupying alien territory. A simple explanation of the difference between reality and representation could not solve this problem; in this case the representation stood in for the reality. Correcting the misperception of students from privileged backgrounds acquires added urgency if one is sensitive to the reality that others in the room have had firsthand experience with the criminal justice system—as victims of criminals, perpetrators of crime, or targets of police harassment. The most common crimes on college campuses are theft, liquor and drug law violations, sexual assault, and rape. Because of these experiences, many students are prepared to explore the differences between glitzy images of outlaws and the relationship of criminality to social injustice.

To some, the remedy to negative stereotypes lies in changing the images. If people create a broader range of images and image makers, then the gangster stereotype would be less dangerous. Those who critiqued racism in the mass media used to hope that greater diversity would ultimately bring about a broader range of vision and less reliance on these negative stereotypes. Hollywood has not given directors of color enough chances to prove this thinking wrong, and it would be premature to critique that vision. The few examples we do have, however, indicate that inclusion will never be a cure-all when it comes to the links between crime and mass-media representation. Jacquie Jones, editor of *Black Film Review,* has shown that inclusion does not always result in more desirable images and stories. In her critique of the spate of early 1990s films that she dubbed "the new ghetto aesthetic"—*New Jack City* (1991), *Boyz N the Hood* (1991), and the gangster films of the Hughes brothers—Jones showed that "the [movie] industry's wholesale investment in films that explore only ghettoes and male youth ignores the existence of a Black community beyond these narrow confines—inclusive of women as valuable participants—as well as films that refuse to cater to these prescriptions." Not only do these films amplify and distort a small minority of African Americans, they often reaffirm the more transparently racist images of black criminality so prevalent in films made by white directors. Although Jones concedes that films by African American directors tend to "be executed with a greater degree of truth and sensibility," they ultimately take a small range of unrepresentative characters and make them stand in for an entire range of African American lives.[3]

Mario Van Peebles's *New Jack City*, which grossed over $40 million in less than four months, was among the first of the genre to break through to a wide audience. Van Peebles's Harlem is peopled with African Americans unwilling to make changes in their lives. Most problematic in this film is the standard it set for future films in the genre. As Jones put it, "That one 'bitch' is elevated to the

From *New Jack City*, Warner Studios, 1991

status of psychopathic murderer hardly seems an achievement." The next such film to reach a wide audience was twenty-three-year-old John Singleton's *Boyz N the Hood*. The film, based in part on Singleton's upbringing, details the difficult personal and communal decisions necessary to avoid the violence of south-central Los Angeles. The biographical connections and interpersonal dynamics—including a sensitive depiction of the conflicting factors that lead one character to commit crimes—made this film stand out from other early 1990s films. Despite the strides Singleton made in lending depth to the evening news broadcasts, the politics of the film, according to some critics, continued the pattern of Van Peebles when it came "dangerously close to blaming Black women for the tragedies currently ransacking Black communities."[4]

Few women of color have directed Hollywood crime films. Several notable crime films feature women as central characters, including *Set It Off* (1996) and *Mi Vida Loca* (1994). Both present relatively complicated images of women who make difficult decisions to commit crimes. In *Set it Off*, one character's decision to go from bank teller to bank robber comes after she has already faced false accusations of criminality. The film gives us a typical "crime does not pay" ending, but along the way we are reminded that deindustrialization, racism, and sexism influenced the crime spree, so inclusion is far from unimportant. Still, showing *Set it Off* instead of *New Jack City* seems a paltry response to the saturation of the violent, sexist images of black men driven to a life of crime by overbearing or absent black women. Rather, we need to explicitly pose questions that begin with the assumption that all these images are—at best—misleading by demonstrating that our expectations have consequences.

The excitement of bank robbery and the depression of death depicted in *Set it Off* appear quite different when placed next to the words of those who create from behind bars. The women Assata Shakur met during her time behind bars "who weren't doing time for the numbers were in for some form of petty theft, like shoplifting or passing bad checks. Most of those sisters were on welfare and all of them had been barely able to make ends meet."[5] These women will not appear in a Hollywood film, but their voices are available to us. Their voices do more than correct the misperceptions doled out with licorice twists. They immediately raise crucial questions about what we know and the sources of that knowledge. If false or misleading, why are the sensational images most attractive to studios and audiences? Most important, what effects do they have on those who actually spend portions of their lives behind bars?

PART II: BARS

Hollywood images are misleading, but they also provide direction. That is, they lead us toward conclusions and serve as evidence to support responses to criminality. We need to do more than just add to these images or tell our students that they are wrong. That is, telling them that crime stories are hegemonic constructions that encourage consent to a racist, classist, and sexist hierarchy might work for some students, but teachers need to be cultural workers who expose students to counterhegemonic visions to improve critical thinking skills and promote social justice. Perhaps the most successful strategy is to ask students to explain their attraction to crime stories. What do they like about them? What assumptions do they carry about the causes of crime or about possible solutions? Once they articulate their unstated assumptions, questioning them becomes much easier. Marshall McLuhan's famous line is apropos here: "I don't know who discovered water, but I'm pretty sure it wasn't a fish." Identifying unstated assumptions helps locate the cultural and political contexts for our beliefs and reactions.

Identifying unstated assumptions, however, is not the ultimate goal. A useful next step toward elucidating the connection between images of criminality and the walls they create is to provide our students with the criticism that comes from behind bars.

Incarcerated people are avid consumers of mass-media texts. Songs, magazines, and television programs provide crucial links to life outside prison. Music reviews, such as Mumia Abu-Jamal's cogent remarks about R. Kelley's "You Remind Me of Something" and Tupac Shakur's "Dear Mama," provide insightful connections between rap and soul, but they also elucidate for a younger generation the cultural politics of popular music. In addition to critiquing music, incarcerated people are particularly well suited to debunking menacing evening news broadcasts. Abu-Jamal's discussion of an inmate sentenced at age fifteen to fifteen to thirty years for armed robbery reminds students that there are boys behind the "get tough" rhetoric. Abu-Jamal wrote:

> He has been "corrected" in precisely the same way that hundreds of thousands of others have been, that is to say, warehoused in a vat that sears the very soul. He has never held a woman as a mate or lover; he has never held a newborn baby in his palm, its heart athump with new life; he hasn't seen the sun rise, nor the moon glow, in almost fifteen years. For a robbery, 'armed' with a pellet gun, at fifteen years of age.[6]

Others make similar connections between Hollywood realism and the practice of incarceration. Wilbert Rideau and Ron Wikberg, former editors of the Louisiana State Penitentiary's *Angolite,* have written about the filming of a movie on prison grounds. CBS filmed scenes of *The Outside Woman* (1989)—a made-for-television film about a dramatic real-life helicopter escape from a Tennessee prison—at Angola in the late 1980s. Rideau and Wikberg interviewed actors, the producer, and prison employees, emphasizing the contrasts and similarities between prison and the media. Max Gail, an actor known for his role in the police comedy *Barney Miller* (1975), told the incarcerated reporters that "working on a movie is much like a prison. . . . On *Barney Miller,* we used to work around the clock all the time. You just stay at it until you get it done. We've got an [assistant director] who is the equivalent of your warden, who makes arbitrary decisions—Do this, Do that, Don't ask why, Just do it 'cause I say do it."[7] The writers ask their readers to see past the glitz of Hollywood, emphasizing the connections between life behind bars and the mythmaking machine. In this way the *Angolite* demystifies popular culture in its strained link between acting and life as a convict.

These essays provide an incarcerated review of Hollywood cinema, which seeks to close the gap between representation and reality. Closing the gap between screens and bars is a crucial step in a larger process that can include fictional and autobiographical stories and films by incarcerated people. When we look at media criticism by the *Angolite* or listen to a Mumia Abu-Jamal radio broadcast, we implicitly accept that Hollywood establishes the terms of the debate. Under these terms we can do little more than critique and unmask its images. Ultimately, however, we should do more. In particular, classroom strategies that expose and explore the unique tradition, culture, and politics of life behind bars provide students with more than a response to mainstream cinema. Literature and films by or featuring inmates follow generic conventions that point to an alternative way of understanding the problem of crime and its relationship to assumptions about racial difference within the criminal justice system and U.S. society.

Criminality and U.S. culture have almost always been intertwined. In colonial America many colonies, particularly those in the Chesapeake Bay region, received mass shipments of convicts. This continued until the revolution, when the flow shifted to Australia. For this population, stories and literature that featured criminals were among the most popular early texts. The first of these were confessionals. A poem by Philip Kennison, a man executed in Cambridge, Massachusetts, for burglary in 1738, was widely distributed:

> Good People all both great and small,
> to whom these Lines shall come,
> A warning take by my sad Fall,
> and unto God return.
> You see me here in Iron Chains,
> in Prison now confin'd,
> Within twelve Days my Life must end,
> My Breath I must resign.[8]

Many others were conversion tracts written by prisoners and distributed by tract publishers to other prisoners as part of their missionary work. In 1807 Henry Tufts published *A Narrative of the Life, Adventures, Travels and Sufferings of Henry Tufts*. In it Tufts wrote: "Should any of the rising generation, by a perusal of my story, learn to avoid the quicksands of vice, on which I have been so often wrecked, I shall feel myself amply compensated for the trouble I have taken in its compilation." But this was entertainment as much as moralizing. If the moral "crime doesn't pay" comes at the end, it does so only after he keeps several wives, commits adultery, and passes counterfeit money, among other things. The condemned did not always cooperate. Another way convicts' voices were heard was through the traditional practice of allowing the condemned to give a public speech prior to a hanging. In many cases the condemned urged the gathered throngs (as many as 20,000 at a Philadelphia execution in the 1820s) to "shun the paths of vice." But not always: a man condemned for killing a deputy sheriff coming to arrest him for nonpayment of debt in New York in 1797 used his speech to attack "those who used credit to destroy the honest working man."[9]

In the 1850s, political prisoners dominated the creative expression coming from behind prison walls. In part this was a result of the repression of a wide range of political activism. Slavery abolitionists and antirenters wrote, although at the same time those seeking to maintain the status quo wrote stories that sought to turn political crimes into conventional crimes—thus subverting the political content of slave revolts. The best-known of these is *The Confessions of Nat Turner*, which Turner was forced to present to Thomas R. Gray—a white recorder

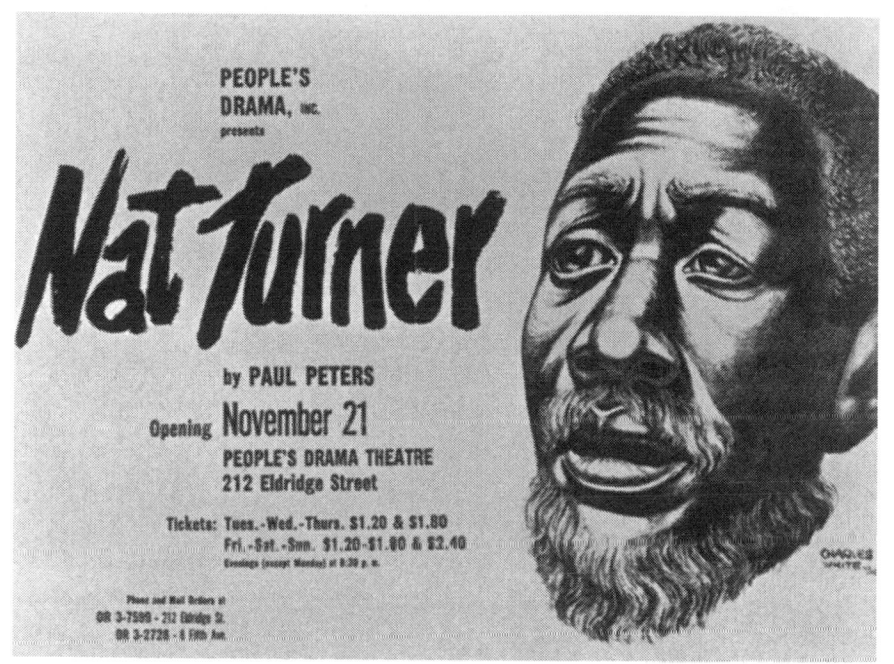

From an off-Broadway production of *Nat Turner,* 1950

and publisher—before his execution in the 1830s. Gray never missed a chance to interject descriptions of "ferocious miscreants," "remorseless murderers," and the observation that "no cry for mercy penetrated their flinty bosoms."[10]

Following these early texts, an explosion of prison texts emerged in relation to the rise of the modern penitentiary in the late 1800s and early 1900s. It is important to see creative expression by convicts in relation to these social and political changes rather than as a response to Hollywood stereotypes. This helps us to see writing and films as a form of protest of the inhumanity of torture in and by the prison system. Rather than seeing the problems of U.S. cities as either attractive or pathological, we see the emergence of prisoners describing themselves, as H. Bruce Franklin has argued, as a "new class of being" created by the shared experience of imprisonment. This had a racial dimension in that although it might have been new for poor whites, it was not new for African Americans who had written similar stories as slave narratives.[11] Gerald Toole, a white man imprisoned for murder in Connecticut in 1862, wrote in his *Autobiography*: "In the shop were about thirty men whose pale, emaciated looks showed that the very life blood was being worked out of them. They were all working at boot making. The coffers of unblushing contractors are filled from the labors of these poor convicts who work from dawn to dark."[12]

In this way prisoners help students locate the link between industrial production and incarceration. More than titillation or outrage, these texts promote socially engaged criticism of injustice. In addition, they take a page from the tradition of slave narratives by focusing on the brutality of prison life and downplaying the dull banality of daily life behind bars. For example, Dale Woodcock wrote in *Ruled by the Whip* that "I was given twenty-seven lashes as I lay on the concrete floor. The warden threw his weight behind each lash and pulled on the whip as it struck my buttocks, thus twisting and tearing the skin. Soon blood and skin together were flipped away at every blow. Blood was pouring from my rectum."[13] This is the tradition from which Jack London, author of the children's classic *Call of the Wild*, emerged. His story "Pinched," about being arrested for vagrancy and sentenced without the benefit of trial, appeared in—of all places—*Cosmopolitan*, but it was released later in the collection *My Life in the Underworld*.

In addition to raising comparative questions based on student exposure to mass-media texts, I would encourage discussion about the specific artistic and ideological qualities of these works. Some questions to consider include: (1) What are the unique qualities of context? (2) How does writing literature or making films behind bars differ from making them outside? (3) Where do you see evidence of limited access to materials, expertise, or mobility in the aesthetic choices made by the convict? (4) Conversely, how might prison be conducive to creative expression? One incarcerated painter in Walpole, Massachusetts, told an interviewer, for example, "Seg [segregation] is the best art studio."[14] Others discuss the power of creative expression to promote self-respect or simply kill time. Numerous documentary and feature films fit the bill. Some are by people who go into prison specifically to make a film. These include Arthur Dong's *Licensed To Kill* (1997) about hate crimes that target gay men—a grim premonition of the Matthew Shepard murder. In addition, both Errol Morris's *The Thin Blue Line* (1988) and Joe Berlinger and Bruce Sinofsky's *Paradise Lost* (1996) center on wrongful convictions.

Perhaps the most striking recent documentary about life behind bars centers on Rideau and Wikberg's Angola. *The Farm* (1998) is a documentary about Angola, the Louisiana State Penitentiary, that closely follows the experiences of a cross-section of inmates. What we see when watching *The Farm* is a far cry from most people's assumptions about daily life behind bars. We see a young man of eighteen entering the prison with the knowledge that he may never see freedom again. We see religious conviction, social engagement, and people in solitary confinement seemingly on heavy medication to mask mental instability. These are complicated images of people—some of whom committed horrible crimes—struggling to keep it together and make it through another day. The film also includes images of compassionate guards and a cynical parole board that has judged a convicted rapist before he presents his case. We see an elderly man who is dying say goodbye to inmates he has been friends with for the better part of four decades. In perhaps the most poignant scene in the film, we watch his family react to the news that he insisted he be buried behind the prison walls.

These individual stories are moving, but viewers are usually struck more by the historical connections the film makes. When prompted, many students recognize that Angola is also a country in Africa. The Louisiana State Penitentiary is named for the former plantation on which it stands, which in turn was named for the region of Africa from which many of its enslaved people came. We do not need to linger on old photographs of early-twentieth-century prison conditions to make this connection. The images of white and black guards on horseback and African American men stooping in the fields were filmed in the 1990s. A recent fiction film, *Slam* (1998), also strives to place itself within the long tradition of prison writing and creative expression.[15] Although *Slam* is about crime and prison, takes place in a poor African American community, features a rap soundtrack, and centers on a young male protagonist, it veers sharply from the representations Jones describes as "the new ghetto aesthetic."

Although both *Slam* and *The Farm* are clearly independent films, some qualifications about this status are necessary. Independent films often recapitulate the ideological positions of dominant cinema—even outdo them in some cases. Their lower production costs and emphasis on untested formulas, however, make them a refreshing forum for alternative visions. Second, saying a film is independent means little today. Disney owns the proverbial independent Miramax, and Time Warner owns New Line.[16] To further muddy the categories, the studios have incorporated independent voices and visions after they succeed on their own. Hollywood sometimes turns to convicts and ex-convicts for creative inspiration. Among the ex-convicts who have turned to acting and screenwriting within the studio system are Edward Bunker, Jimmy Santiago Baca, and Kim Wozencraft. Poet and screenwriter Jimmy Santiago Baca has written movingly about his feelings when he went to film a feature in San Quentin, the former site of his incarceration.[17]

Despite these qualifications, the distinction remains important. Although *The Farm* received funding from the cable television network A&E, the cooperation of the inmates and prison officials (Wilbert Rideau gets a production credit), its long form interviews, and its historical perspective make it a useful counterpoint to popular media representations. In addition, although Trimark—which is owned by a major studio—released *Slam*, it was produced independently and used many amateur actors, including prison guards and inmates. Despite the limitations of the performers and a budget of only $1.5 million, *Slam* won the 1998 Grand Jury Prize at Robert Redford's Sundance Film Festival and the Camera d'Or (awarded for best first film) at the Cannes Film Festival. In short, saying that a film is "independent" does not mean a film will represent a counterhegemonic voice or even that it was made outside of the

From *Malcolm X,* Warner Studios, 1992

studio system. What remains important is that we seek out voices and aesthetics that call into question student expectations for crime and punishment on the screen.

Despite narrative limitations and an ambivalent ending, *Slam* is one such film. The press release described *Slam* as a "coming to life" tale of a "street pharmacist" who finds salvation in his rhymes. Two of the screenwriters—self-described "middle-aged white dude" Richard Stratton and thirty-year-old African American journalist Bonz Malone—both spent time in prison. Stratton spent eight years in prison for drug trafficking (marijuana), and Malone has been in and out of New York's Rikers Island since he was a teenager. The plot places the film squarely in the tradition of prison literature, from slave narratives through *The Autobiography of Malcolm X,* by exploring the ways literacy and creativity can allow young black men to transform their lives and overcome subjugation.

The plot line is individualized, but the film—like the genre as a whole—does not skimp on structural critique. The filmmakers bring the hypocrisy of the court the court system to light with a clever cameo by beleaguered former Washington, D.C., mayor Marion Barry as the judge who throws the book at the main character, Ray Joshua (Saul Williams). Ray gets caught up in a drug deal gone bad and is sucked into the criminal justice system. Once behind bars, Ray becomes enmeshed in the internecine struggles among inmates. Instead of choosing sides or taking the self-destructive route of independence, Ray reads a carefully crafted poem meant to startle and provoke the audience—both the inmates on the screen and those watching the film. Ray begins by describing the events just prior to his arrest:

I stand on the corner of the block slinging
amethyst rocks
drinking 40s of Mother Earth's private nectar
stock
dodgin' cops
'cause five-0 be the 666
and I need a fix of that purple rain
the type of shit that drives membranes insane
oh yeah, I'm in the fast lane

snorting . . . candy yams

that free my body and soul

and send me like Shazam!¹⁸

These lines seem to imply that Joshua sought pleasure in the life of an outlaw, just another incarnation of the drug lord in *New Jack City* or the malt liquor–drinking boyz 'n' the hood. The correlation of the police with Satan indicates that he has pride in his vocation and a sense of moral superiority to the forces of law. As his rhymes stack up, however, he begins to sound like a teacher and a prophet, and he slowly rotates among the convicts who had initially threatened him but now look on in awe:

yeah, i'm sirius B
Dogon niggas plottin shit, lovely
but the Feds are also plottin' me
they're tryin' to imprison my astrology
put our stars behind bars
my stars in stripes
using blood splattered banners
as nationalist kites

but I control the wind

that's why they call it the hawk
i am horus
son of isis
son of osiris

worshipped as jesus
resurrected like lazarus

but you can call me lazzie

lazy
yeah, i'm lazy

'cause i'd rather sit and build
than work and plow a field
worshipping the daily yield of cash green crops

stealing us was the smartest thing they ever did
too bad they don't teach the truth to their kids

our influence on them is the reflection they see
when they look into their minstrel mirror
and talk about their culture
their existence is that of a schizophrenic vulture

Seeking to resurrect a sense of spiritual mission and a beatific past from the blood of nationalism and racism, Ray Joshua moves beyond simple depictions sold to audiences as reality-based megaplex fare. Instead he describes the political, historical, and economic forces that result in the destruction of poor African American communities and in self-deception for the politically powerful. His decision to deal drugs, he explains, should not be taken as a sign that he is simply an able-bodied young man too lazy to get a job. To the contrary, he hopes his listeners understand that what he is doing is a retreat from the corporate exploitation of poor people of color.

An award-winning poet in his own right, the actor who plays Ray Joshua (Saul Williams) won the Grand Slam Championship at New York's Nuyorican Poets Café in 1996. Williams said of this scene, "It was overwhelming. The first thing that came to mind entering prison was that it was like entering a slave ship. Everybody there looked like me. It seemed like it was nothing less than something calculated." In the climactic poem, Ray Joshua draws the connection between prison and slavery once again when he recites, "I don't want to have to go through the fucking middle passage to get to the new world!"[19]

Confronting the interaction among race, crime, and representation in the classroom presents unique challenges and opportunities. In a society segregated by race and class, Hollywood and the mass media influence or entirely shape the assumptions of students—particularly white students—regarding race and crime. Students frequently understand films about Asian gangs like *The Corrupter* (1999) or about poor African Americans like *Boyz N the Hood* as accurate depictions of people of color. Students frequently defend right-wing or progressive beliefs about incarceration and execution with vivid descriptions of crimes based in part or in whole on scenes from films—something teachers need to confront. In many states, prison populations contain wildly disproportionate numbers of African Americans and Latinos. Nationally, 63 percent of jail inmates belonged to racial or ethnic minorities in 1996, up slightly from 61 percent in 1989. Over a third of all inmates reported some physical or mental disability. A quarter of jail inmates said they had been treated for a mental or an emotional problem. An estimated 58 percent of federal inmates and 21 percent of state inmates in 1991 were serving a sentence for a drug offense; about 17 percent of federal inmates and 47 percent of state inmates were in prison for a violent offense. Forty-eight percent of jailed women reported having been physically or sexually abused prior to admission; 27 percent had been raped.[20]

In a media-saturated society, presenting students with the social and political contexts for crime and punishment goes far in creating informed judgments about volatile issues both on and off campus. Perhaps the most effective pedagogical strategy to counter mainstream visions of crime and race, however, is to present students with the cultural artifacts—art, music, and film—created or directly influenced by convicts. Students across racial and class lines have little and often no experience with alternative, independent visions coming from behind bars. Films like *Slam* and *The Farm* and books like *Cellblock Visions: Prison Art in America* and *Prison Writing in Twentieth Century America* force students to ask these questions about their previously held assumptions: (1) What insights might convicts' films, art, and writing offer about crime in the United States? (2) What relationship might exist between the cultural fascination with crime and punishment and the practices of the criminal justice system? (3) Does the representation of crime tell us something about the historically consistent and continually shifting inequalities based on class, gender, and race in the United States?[21]

NOTES

1. Daniel Bell, "Crime as an American Way of Life," *Antioch Review* 13 (September 1953): 131–154.

2. David Cole, *No Equal Justice: Race and Class in the American Criminal Justice System* (New York: New Press, 1999), 149.

3. Jacquie Jones, "The New Ghetto Aesthetic," *Wide Angle* 13, 3–4 (July-October 1991): 34; see also Ed Guerrero, *Framing Blackness: The African American Image in Film* (Philadelphia: Temple University Press, 1993).

4. Jones, "The New Ghetto Aesthetic," 34.

5. Assata Shakur, *Assata* (Chicago: Lawrence Hill, 1987), quoted in H. Bruce Franklin, *Prison Writing in Twentieth Century America* (New York: Penguin, 1998), 211.

6. Mumia Abu-Jamal, "Acting Like Life's a Ballgame," on her CD *All Things Censored: Huntingdon and SCI Greene Sessions* (San Francisco: Prison Radio/Quixote, 1998). Available through Prison Radio/Quixote, P.O. Box 411074, San Francisco, CA 94141.

7. Wilbert Rideau and Ron Wikberg, "Hollywood Comes to Angola," in their *Life Sentences: Rage and Survival Behind Bars* (New York: Times, 1992), 245. The *Angolite* regularly features stories about cultural activities in the prison.

8. Philip Kennison, quoted in H. Bruce Franklin, "A History of Literature by Convicts in America," in *Prison Literature in America: The Victim as Criminal and Artist* (Westport, CT: Lawrence Hill, 1978), 127–128.

9. Henry Tufts, quoted in ibid., 129.

10. Quoted in ibid., 133.

11. H. Bruce Franklin made this connection in *Prison Literature in America*. He also connects the songs of slavery to the songs of incarcerated people; see, ibid., 124–178.

12. Ibid., 136.

13. Dale Woodcock, quoted in ibid., 137.

14. Phyllis Kornfeld, *Cellblock Visions: Prison Art in America* (Princeton: Princeton University Press, 1997), 22.

15. *Slam,* dir. Marc Levin (Trimark Pictures, 1998). See also Richard Stratton and Kim Wozencraft, eds., *Slam* (New York: Grove, 1998).

16. Stuart Klawans, "Independents' Day," *The Nation* (3 April 2000): 46.

17. Kim Wozencraft, *Rush* (New York: Random House, 1990), was made into the film of that name. Jimmy Santiago Baca, *Working in the Dark: Reflections of a Poet of the Barrio* (Santa Fe: Red Crane, 1992).

18. Saul Williams, "Amethyst Rocks," in Stratton and Wozencraft, *Slam,* 216–217.

18. Mark Levin, Bonz Malone, Sonja Sohn, Richard Stratton, and Saul Williams, *Slam.* Screenplay in Stratton and Wozencraft, *Slam,* 249.

20. Cole, *No Equal Justice,* 149.

21. Kornfeld, *Cellblock Visions*; Franklin, *Prison Writing*; see also Bell Gale Chevigny, *Doing Time: 25 Years of Prison Writing* (New York: Arcade, 1999); Jeff Evans, ed., *Undoing Time: American Prisoners in Their Own Words* (Boston: Northeastern University Press, 2000); Rena Fraden, *Imagining Medea: Rhodessa Jones and Theater for Incarcerated Women* (Chapel Hill: University of North Carolina Press, 2001); Judith Tannenbaum. *Disguised as a Poem: My Years Teaching at San Quentin* (Boston: Northeastern University Press, 2000).

10

THE QUEERING OF CHICANA STUDIES
Philosophy, Text, and Image

Elisa Facio

The queering of Chicana studies since the early 1980s has generated theoretical and pedagogical dialogues regarding Chicana queer representation and voice.[1] As a Chicana professor intellectually, politically, and spiritually dedicated to Chicana studies and feminism, I recognize the significant and pivotal contributions of Chicana queer scholarship.[2] More important, on the level of human rights advocacy, the integrity and human value of queer Chicanas (also queer Chicanos and bisexual, lesbian, gay, and transgendered [BLGT] communities) must be respected and regarded as an integral part of society. To do otherwise is to leave students with an incomplete and biased history of queer communities in the United States. Additionally, students will remain ignorant, complacent bystanders and participants in the dehumanization of those communities.

This inquiry focuses on challenges for professors—granted heterosexist privilege—who impart Chicana queer studies. I argue that professors and teachers must critically assess and challenge the relationship between heterosexism and heteronormative pedagogy. More often than not, intentional and unintentional displays of heterosexism establish heteronormative classroom environments and spaces. Simply incorporating readings, inviting a guest speaker for "sexuality week," and casually viewing queer documentaries does not constitute inclusivity or a comprehensive curriculum. Rather, such pedagogical practices only perpetuate heterosexism by objectifying, or more likely sexually objectifying, both the subject matter and the individual. Such teaching techniques and approaches have become institutionalized, rendering critical discussions of heterosexism and heterosexist privilege as "other."[3]

My position in relation to deconstructing heterosexism and homophobia in the classroom is largely influenced by the interdependency of sexual orientation, racial and ethnic background, and gender. In this case my position as a heterosexual woman of Mexican descent determines a space in the classroom as both professor and student. Thus I argue that the deconstruction of heterosexism and homophobia in the classroom calls for a simultaneity of teaching and learning Chicana queer studies.

Given this pedagogical location, the second part of this chapter explores the simultaneity of teaching and learning Chicana queer studies through visual arts. The use of videos and films serves as an effective means for synthesizing course materials. Videos and films allow abstractions to take on realistic or real-life forms. Selection of videos and films should also reflect a conscientious process toward deconstructing heterosexist privilege and heteronormative classroom environments. For example, Chicana and Latina queer subject matter should be critically informed by Chicana and Latina queer standpoints.

The video *Tampon Thieves (Ladronas de Tampones)* (1996) focuses on two lesbians—one a biracial Latina, the other white—charged with stealing tampons. The film's title metaphorically represents lesbians claiming space as "women" who are lesbians rather than the traditional representation of the sexualized character and hierarchical placement of sexual orientation as secondary to gender. Additionally, themes of homophobia as well as homoerotic and racialized sexual identities are addressed in the film. The remainder of this chapter discusses the use of *Tampon Thieves* in deconstructing heterosexism for both professor and students as well as heteronormative pedagogy in teaching and learning Chicana queer studies.

POSITIONALITY AND PEDAGOGY

Imparting a Chicana feminism that is antiheterosexist and antihomophobic involves critical interrogation between positionality and pedagogy. First, it is important to place this discussion in relation to Chicana queer theory. This chapter does not address queer theory or even produce theory that it claims relates to queerness but instead defines itself as "diacritically against heterosexuality and not simply against the normative."[4] Nor is this chapter a marker of what Judith Butler has termed the "institutional domestication of queer thinking," that "normalizing [of] the queer [that] would be . . . its sad finish."[5] As a Chicana activist scholar, I have a genuine interest in Chicana queer theory for naming, describing, celebrating, criticizing, and honoring Chicana queer realities. Additionally, Chicana queer theory politically and intellectually challenges heterosexist and homophobic systems and ideologies. On a more speculative note, there is the surprised perplexity of recognizing "our own reflections in queer theory's mirror," thus moving beyond "constitutive otherness."[6] The challenge for heterosexual scholars lies in deciding how to articulate this recognition in a productive, nonappropriative manner.

The desire to impart an antiheterosexist, antihomophobic Chicana feminism is not to assimilate into queer theory or to assimilate queer theory into any governing framework; it is not to confiscate or seize queer theory's varied conceptual tools and put them to "straight" use. Heterosexual scholars should want even less to install themselves in a position of "comfort" relative to queer theory and no longer be called into question by its provocations. We should be suspicious of those who "want queer theory but want nothing from it."[7] And we should not want a queer theory that no longer troubles us; nor should we let our signs of engagement or association with queerness be read as proclamations of ownership. Thus the goal is not to appropriate queer theory but to proliferate its findings and insights. Gloria Anzaldua provided a very useful distinction when she wrote that "the difference between appropriation and proliferation is that the first steals and harms; the second helps heal breaches of knowledge."[8]

Second, the professor's positionality should be called into question. In my case the interdependent factors of sexual orientation (heterosexuality), race and ethnicity (Mexican), and gender (female) create a simultaneous and fluid positionality as both professor and student. As a professor, I intend to position myself as an antiheterosexist, antiracist Chicana feminist committed to deconstructing and transgressing heterosexism and homophobia, thus contributing to the queering of U.S. society. As a heterosexual woman of Mexican descent, I must recognize and take responsibility for heterosexist privilege. This involves claiming uncontested ownership of that privilege without guilt, apologies, or excuses. Professors must critically analyze how the damaging and dehumanizing system of heterosexism shapes not only the lives of queer Chicanas but their own lives as well. For professors, assuming a Chicana queer subjectivity is a patronizing and condescending gesture that only perpetuates heterosexism and sexual inequalities. Heterosexism and gender also grant "spaces" to explore and teach Chicana queer studies that may not otherwise be afforded Chicana queer professors without homophobic repercussions. In other words, Chicana queer professors are unquestionably sexualized or essentialized according to their sexual orientation, leaving little room to negotiate spaces of expertise in Chicana studies and feminism beyond "queerness."

Defining my position in antiheterosexist, antiracist Chicana feminist work has created a sense of uneasiness, which speaks to the place and space I must occupy. As previously mentioned, I cannot place myself in a position of comfort if my goal is to contribute to the deconstruction of heterosexism. Through this endeavor I have learned that I truly enjoy "female energies," meaning to live by female values and speak female discourse. We live in male systems, learn male rules, and speak male language when around men or we do not speak at all. Female energies and sites are the most progressive and radical spaces I have encountered. Unfortunately, the response from university colleagues, students, staff, and community members has been disappointing and hurtful. For example, various university community members have discouraged students from taking courses with me, and forms of lesbian baiting have been subtly employed toward my students and myself.

TEACHING AND LEARNING THROUGH VIDEO: *TAMPON THIEVES*

It was not until I had the unique opportunity to participate in the conference Beyond the Image: Crossing Cultures Through Film and Video at Colorado State University in March 2000 that I critically reflected on the use of films and videos as active pedagogy.[9] Students previously and currently enrolled in Chicana and Chicano studies have described course materials as "new," exciting, and relevant for some and boring, threatening, insignificant, and politically biased for others. Given the complexity of student reactions, implementing instructional means for assuring that students will gain and retain a reasonable understanding of Chicana queer studies (and Chicana and Chicano studies) is no doubt difficult. For many, this process begins with an assessment of the professor's relationship to course materials. In the classroom, questions can engage students in this process. For example, what privileges are granted to those who claim to be heterosexual and are consequently denied membership in BLGT communities? Students are asked to consider their places and spaces of daily interactions, gestures, and language.

As an activist scholar of Chicana and Chicano studies, I am passionately committed to teach students about the history and contemporary experiences of Chicana and Chicano communities from an active pedagogical standpoint. Given the controversial nature of course materials in Chicana and Chicano studies and the potential for an explosive classroom environment, race, class, gender, and sexuality are "named" the first day of class. The class is challenged to take individual and collective responsibility for recognizing that race, class, gender, and sexuality shape not only the classroom environment but—equally important—our own lives. Throughout the course, students take part in "counter-storytelling." Storytelling and narrative analysis are methodological tools used by critical race feminists and Lat-crit theorists to construct alternative social realities and protest against acquiescence to unfair arrangements designed for the benefit of others. I refer to this method as counter-storytelling because (re)construction of social realities is also involved in this process. Thus the goal of counter-storytelling is to move the student from objective observer to subjective participant in understanding the ideological, cultural, and political manifestations of race, class, gender, and sexuality.

My teaching is most effective when course materials are linked to students' personal lives as well as my own. The more effective the linkages, the more relevant and interesting the course becomes for student and professor, and constructive investment in the course continues to develop throughout the semester. According to Malcolm Collier and Lane Ryo Hirabayashi, "Visual media provides one means to help generate student interest . . . [and] obtain a fuller understanding and retention . . . of materials presented." Furthermore, they argue that "good visual media brings the content of courses out of the realm of words and abstractions and into the arena of real people through whom the students can make more personalized intellectual and emotional connections to course materials."[10]

In my effort to critically confront homophobia and my resistance to relinquish heterosexist privilege, I have used the video *Tampon Thieves* in Chicana and Chicano studies courses. The video is a 1996 production by the Colombian Jorge Lozano. A limited number of videos and films focus specifically on the Chicana queer community. Gay white male–oriented films have experienced some success, including *The Birdcage* (1995), *Love! Valour! Compassion!* (1997), and *Billy's Hollywood Screen Kiss* (1997). A common theme in these films is the depiction of the token "gay Latino" as exotic, one-dimensional, and even hypersexual. The complex love lives of gay white men are addressed, whereas gay Latinos become caricatures or cartoons. It is their job to make moviegoers experience both laughter and hatred. The gay Latino "savagely" disregards the sanctity of monogamy and long-term relationships in exchange for his selfish sexual interests. Thus a video such as *Tampon Thieves* is useful, as it addresses the harsh realities queer communities of color face in trying to live and survive in a racist, homophobic culture. The four major scenes in this twenty-two-minute video are described, followed by questions and critical commentary that can be addressed in classroom discussion.

Zena and Tita are due in court for stealing tampons because they refuse to pay for the privilege of menstruating. They live in an abandoned warehouse on the edge of Toronto and pay for college by selling phone sex. Both are on the verge of losing their *abuelas,* or grandmothers. During a night out with Tita's two dark-skinned, queer Colombian cousins, they are gay- and race-bashed. Zena feels guilty because she is white. Tita, a biracial Latina, is able to reconcile her two racial identities and comfort her friend, whom she loves. *Tampon Thieves* weaves reflections of family with the topic of love between friends who tell a story of how queer women and gay men of color are treated in a racist, homophobic culture.

Before viewing the video, students are led in a discussion of the social construction of sexuality and the invention of heterosexuality. Ruth Hubbard has argued that "Western thinking about sexuality is based on the Christian equation of sexuality with sin. . . . Sexuality must be intended for procreation, and thus all forms of sexual expression and enjoyment other than heterosexuality are invalidated."[11] Jonathan Katz has traced the historical process by which heterosexual ideas were created as ahistorical and taken for granted. Katz argues that by not studying the sociohistorical construct of heterosexuality, scholars "continue to privilege the 'normal' and 'natural' at the expense of [the] 'abnormal' and 'unnatural.' Such privileging of the norm accedes to its domination, protecting it from questions."[12] By making the normal the object of a thoroughgoing historical study, we simultaneously pursue a pure truth and a subversive goal: we upset basic preconceptions. Studying the history of the social construction of heterosexuality challenges its power.

ADMIRATION

Through the use of narrative, the video introduces Zena and Tita, with Tita describing the development of their relationship. Tita affectionately refers to Zena as her friend, someone with whom she can converse and in whom she can confide. The importance of this opening scene, and of the video in general, is that their relationship is not sexualized. The revelation of their intimacy informs the viewer of a lesbian relationship rooted in the love of women's energies. The power of this opening segment challenges stereotypes of queer communities solely engaged in eroticized, sexual acts and essentializing queer identity based on sexuality. This is a tender scene, one of admiration of one woman for another.

The tension of sexualized and asexualized representations is probed at this point. In an attempt to avoid essentializing lesbians along the issue of sexuality, one can fall into the trap of presenting lesbian unions as asexual. Lesbian sex is argued to be *valid* and powerful sex. Lesbian sex and desire should be discussed from the standpoint of lesbians. Carla Trujillo's book *Chicana Lesbians* includes a section titled "The Desire" in which Chicana lesbian writers embrace passion in its totality.[13] Additionally, works by Ana Castillo, Cherrie Moraga, Gloria Anzaldua, and Monica Palacios are introduced to students.

In general, Chicana-Latina representations have been dichotomous (e.g., virgin-whore duality) and essentialized (e.g., prostitute, housemaid, and Vata Chola gangster). In Rosa Linda Fregoso's article "Chicana Film Practices: Confronting the Many-Headed Demon of Oppression," she lists the numerous barriers Chicana filmmakers face. For one, they are intentionally excluded from Chicano film festivals, and their short films are criticized because they are not feature-length. Fregoso states, "In a phallocentric society, power is measured by *big-ness* [as in feature-length films] and *penetration* [as into the Hollywood industry]. . . . In this respect, there is little evidence among Chicana filmmakers of big-ness, penetration, or of coming into the mainstream on dominant culture's terms."[14]

RECLAIMING OUR ALIENATED SELVES

At this point the class should be uncomfortable "viewing" a young biracial lesbian couple who admire and spiritually care for one another. Given a supposed transition of the classroom viewing lens, students should be able to embrace and better appreciate subaltern spaces and locations for queer Chicanas and Latinas.[15] The video follows the young couple to a nightclub where bisexual, lesbian, gay, and transgendered communities converge. This subaltern space defines BLGT communities, culture, and societal boundaries and provides validity, comfort, and affirmation for Tita and Zena as a biracial lesbian couple. As the nightclub scene features Latino cross-dressers and drama queens, one may be compelled to dismiss the expression and interpretation as "flamboyant." Frances Negron-Muntaner's article "Drama Queens: Latino Gay and Lesbian Independent Film/Video" discusses four important Latino gay and lesbian independents that destabilize an essential gay and lesbian brown identity. She states, "Latino gay and lesbian films/videos suggest that drama queens continue to question and invent ways of representing the complexity of queer cultures and the contradictory pleasures of our 'selves.' "[16]

Heterosexist repercussions of homophobia and racism are played out in the following scene in which Tita, Zena, and her two gay cousins (Mario and Lalo) are violently attacked by three young men on their way home from the nightclub. Homophobic acts of violence against the queer community and racism toward Latinos are discussed among the four friends the following day at Tita and Zena's apartment. Tita, while massaging Zena's neck, thanks her partner for protecting her and her cousins. Tita states, "I'm so proud to be a woman." Mario and Lalo go into detail as to why they were singled out for a violent attack. One young man states he was attacked because he is Latino; the other exclaims that the violence occurred because he is a queer. A distinction between homophobic acts of violence toward men and those toward women is mentioned. Given that patriarchy does not allow for any form of feminine expression or appearance, any "deviation" from masculine characterizations is controlled through brutal force. For example, given his appearance, Lalo mentions that people assume he will either rob them, sell them drugs, or seduce them. Generally, female bonding—but with clearly defined boundaries—is more "acceptable."

The healing process continues with a discussion of Zena and Tita's court date for stealing tampons. Initially, they are teased by Mario and Lalo, and they revert to a discussion of the politics of menstruation. Zena rhetorically but adamantly asks why women have to pay to menstruate. She further notes that the arresting officer, a male, "didn't have a single female hormone in his body." The healing process, the location of resistance and struggle in recapturing their alienated selves, brings the group to reflect on their relationships with their grandmothers. Each person mentions the foods their grandmothers prepared, how they were taught to "make tortillas, prepare *arepas,* and eat with their hands." The scene ends with a dance in honor and celebration of *abuelas.* Zena, Tita, Mario, and Lalo are draped in women's clothing, symbolically representing their respective grandmothers and dancing without inhibitions to music.

GRANDMOTHER'S DANCE

A major theme throughout the video is that of family or, more specifically, grandmother-granddaughter relationships. That relationship leads us to discuss how the institutions of family, patriarchy, and Catholicism perpetuate heterosexism and homophobia and relationships among and between women. At the beginning of each scene throughout the video, Zena and Tita refer to their grandmothers. As previously mentioned, both Zena's and Tita's grandmothers are dying. Tita can only imagine her grandmother's struggle with death because she lives in Colombia, whereas Zena visits her hospitalized grandmother regularly. In reflecting about their grandmothers, both *abuelas* describe oppressive marital relationships and finding solace in the company of other women. Both grandmothers tell of how their respective husbands accused them of being "lesbians" because of their spiritual connections to female world(s).

Tita's narrative memory of her grandmother is introduced as a direct dialogue-conversation between the two women. Tita's grandmother describes in detail her husband's expectations of rigid gendered lives and his subsequent abusive treatment of her if those expectations were not met satisfactorily. Tita's *abuela* expresses confusion at having supposedly failed her husband as she describes rigorous days of cleaning, cooking, and rearing children. Her *abuela's* monotonous daily routine, tainted with abuse, leads her to establish friendships with women in the neighborhood. She finds comfort, solace, support, and strength in the company of women living similar lives. More and more time is spent with friends; thus gendered expectations are questioned and subsequently challenged. Her husband, Tita's grandfather, builds a gate around the house, locking the wrought iron bars behind him every day as he leaves for work. Tita's grandmother falls ill with depression until her granddaughter is born. Her grandmother ends the dialogue with words of encouragement and support for Tita. Tita's grandmother accepts Tita—a Latina lesbian—without judgment, thus providing Tita with the strength, courage, and pride to live and be queer. Both Zena and Tita comment on their grandmothers' acceptance of queer women.

Interestingly, the grandmother-granddaughter relationship becomes a site of acceptance, validation, and nurturing of lesbian identity and life. Chicana scholars such as Yolanda Chavez Leyva and Diane Alcala have written of their relationships with their grandmothers and of telling "secrets."[17] Much to their surprise, they find their *abuelas* accept their homosexuality. I speculate that the sexual positionality of older women in Chicana-Chicano communities is represented as an asexual space, thus somehow projected as "safe" and "secure." Whether Chicana and Latina grandmothers think of themselves as asexual is not being debated. Largely because of Catholicism and manifestations of patriarchy in Chicana-Chicano communities, however, grandmothers are expected to assume a space of asexuality. Unfortunately, many Chicanas and Latinas do not question notions of sexuality among older women, *nuestras abuelas*. Hence, "telling secrets" to one's grandmother leads to interesting speculations about grandmother-granddaughter relationships in interrogating, defining, and (re)constructing sexual identities and practices.

It is also important to mention that the institution of the family plays a pivotal role in the dialectic of lesbian identity. According to Trujillo, Chicana lesbians take on the sacred contexts of religion and family. Generally, there is stress and pull, an interchange that goes on when a woman deals with the confines of her family and her religion. Trujillo states:

> [For Chicana lesbians, family and religion represent] a two-sided coin, both simultaneously presenting a means of love, understanding, and support, while stressing conformity and, ultimately, control. For our own survival, Chicana lesbians must continually embark on the creation or modification of our spirituality and familia, usually implying alteration of the traditional, since these institutions, by their very nature, profess to be antithetical to the Chicana lesbian existence.[18]

The heterosexist and sexist nature of the family and Catholicism are further explored in class following the viewing of the film. In particular, the categorization of La Malinche, La Llorona, and La Virgin de Guadalupe are understood in their historical contexts, as are the ways such categorization has served to control and manipulate all women to engage in heterosexism.

CONCLUSION

Through implementation of the described pedagogical process, both professors and students should gain a better understanding of how the intersectionality of race, class, gender, and sexuality influences, shapes, and determines heterosexism and homophobia in Chicana and Chicano communities. Additionally, it is important to note that the Chicana lesbian experience is not compared with that of white lesbians. The Chicana lesbian experience is examined in relationship to, but is not compared with, dominant systems and institutions. When Chicana and Latina research or scholarship is considered, we are confronted with "comparative scholarship." We are asked to validate our "scientific" findings and the inferences of our scholarship by comparing our experiences with those of white women. This places white women at the center of intellectual discourse and once again marginalizes and disempowers Chicana and Latina experiences. When we do engage in comparative work, white feminism has traditionally minimized racial difference by taking comfort in the fact that we are all women or all lesbians and that we thus suffer similar sexual-gender oppressions. There is an attempt to seek a complete, totalizing identity. These unacknowledged or unarticulated differences only widen the gap between white women and women of color rather than seriously dismantling racism and heterosexism. It has taken tremendous perseverance to maintain the little space we have managed to usurp from the dominant culture in academia. And we are determined to continue to work at building Chicana and Latina studies as activist scholarship. Chicana and Latina scholarship, whether written with a heterosexual or a lesbian voice, in many respects has been our salvation. It has taught us about ourselves and told us what others would not and could not tell us. Therefore, works by Chicana lesbians are highlighted and discussed throughout my course to place the Chicana lesbian voice at the center of intellectual discourse in transgressing heterosexual boundaries.

Second, a critical understanding should be developed of how the social constructions of these concepts determine social organization, resources, and privileges. Both professors and students should be challenged to consider the subject matter in relation to themselves and to the queer community, as well as the implications of these relations for the larger society. I must therefore theoretically position myself as a "heterosexual" woman who is not speaking for Chicana queers but is attempting to present material from an informed and critical perspective. The injustices and inequalities of heterosexism can be mapped out with discussions of state policies (e.g., denial of same-sex marriage and benefits), acts of violence against BLGT communities (e.g., the Matthew Shepard case), and daily manifestations of heterosexism through our actions, discourse, and social relationships (campus politics and environment). Those in academia are challenged to accept their heterosexist privilege and to understand that such privilege is granted at the expense of someone else's livelihood. Are we comfortable perpetuating heterosexism and homophobia? How will we react when a friend or family member discloses that he or she is lesbian, gay, bisexual, or transgendered?

NOTES

1. Deena Gonzalez provides an excellent critique of the fallout from being a Chicana feminista and on experiences of intellectual practice and its complex interrelations in "Speaking Secrets: Living Chicana Theory," in *Living Chicana Theory*, ed. Carla Trujillo (Berkeley: Third Woman, 1998), 46–77. As for positioning Chicana queer studies within the larger context of Chicana studies, see Cherrie Moraga and Gloria Anzaldua, eds., *This Bridge Called My Back* (Watertown, MA: Persephone, 1981); *Making Face, Making Soul?*

Haciendo Caras; Gloria Anzaldua, ed., *Creative and Critical Perspectives by Feminists of Color* (San Francisco: Aunt Lute, 1990).

2. Anzaldua, *Making Face, Making Soul;* Gloria Anzaldua, *Borderlands/La Frontera* (San Francisco: Aunt Lute, 1987); Cherrie L. Moraga, *Loving in the War Years* (Cambridge: South End, 1983); Emma Perez, *The Decolonial Imaginary* (Bloomington: Indiana University Press, 1999); Carla Trujillo, ed., *Chicana Lesbians/The Girls Our Mothers Warned Us About* (Berkeley: Third Woman, 1991); Trujillo, *Living Chicana Theory.*

3. For an elaboration of the term *otherness,* see Cherrie Moraga, "La Guerra," in *Race, Class and Gender: An Anthology,* ed. Margaret L. Andersen and Patricia Hill Collins (Belmont: Wadsworth, 1998), 21–27.

4. Andrew Parker, "Foucault's Tongues," *Mediations* 18, 2 (Fall 1994): 80.

5. Judith Butler, "Against Proper Objects," *differences* 6, 2–3 (1994): 21.

6. Calvin Thomas argues this point effectively in *Straight With a Twist,* ed. Calvin Thomas (Urbana: University of Illinois Press, 2000), 1–3; quotation is on p. 3.

7. Quoted in ibid. Joseph Aimone made these remarks during a special session at the Midwest Modern Language Association Conference in November 1994.

8. Gloria Anzaldua, "Haciendo cara, una entrada," in *Making Face, Making Soul,* xxi.

9. Malcolm Collier and Lane Ryo Hirabayashi discuss the casual use of videos in classroom instruction in the context of passive pedagogy. Given the critical attention to the use of videos as transformative pedagogy, I use the term *active pedagogy* similarly to Collier and Hirabayashi. For a more detailed discussion of moving toward an active pedagogy of documentary videos, see Malcolm Collier and Lane Ryo Hirabayashi, "Video Constructions of Asian America: *Teaching Monterey's Boat People,*" *Education/Pedagogy/Cultural Studies* 21, 1 (1999): 79–94.

10. Ibid., 80.

11. Ruth Hubbard, "The Social Construction of Sexuality," in *Race, Class, and Gender in the United States,* 4th ed., ed. Paula S. Rothenberg (New York: St. Martin's), 52.

12. Jonathan Ned Katz, "The Invention of Heterosexuality," in *Race, Class, and Gender in the United States,* 55–56.

13. Carla Trujillo, "The Desire," in *Chicana Lesbians,* 55–75.

14. Rosa Linda Fregoso, "Chicana Film Practices: Confronting the Many-Headed Demon of Oppression," in *Chicanos and Film: Essays on Chicano Representation and Resistance,* ed. Chon A. Noriega (New York: Garland, 1992), 168–182; Rosa Linda Fregoso, "The Mother Motif in *La Bamba* and *Boulevard Nights,*" in *Building With Our Hands,* ed. Adela de la Torre and Beatriz M. Pesquera (Berkeley; University of California Press, 1993), 175.

15. Emma Perez, "Irigaray's Female Symbolic in the Making of Chicana Lesbian *Sitos y Lenguas* (Sites and Discourses)," in *Living Chicana Theory,* 87–101.

16. Frances Muntaner-Negron, "Drama Queens: Latino Gay and Lesbian Independent Film/Video," in *The Ethnic Eye: Latino Media Arts,* ed. Chon A. Noreiga and Ana M. Lopez (Minneapolis: University of Minnesota Press, 1996), 59.

17. Yolanda Chavez Leyva, "Listening to the Silences in Latina/Chicana Lesbian History," in *Living Chicana Theory,* 429–434; Diane Alcala, "La frontera," in *Chicana Lesbians,* 196–197.

18. Trujillo, *Chicana Lesbians,* x.

11

THE MATRIX

Using American Popular Film to Teach
Concepts of Eastern Mysticism in the College Classroom

JEFFREY B. HO

From the latest exercise trends—such as Yoga retreats on the beaches of Hawaii and Tai Chi classes in the mountains of Colorado—to spiritual seminars that talk about everything from Buddhism and meditation to Sufism and the path of love, to a growing interest in "alternative" health-care treatments such as herbal remedies, acupuncture, and chiropractic care, Americans are clearly becoming more interested in both the secular and spiritual practices of Eastern mysticism. Although the teachings of Eastern mysticism have been around for thousands of years, their popularity in the United States has grown rapidly in recent decades. Americans are sincerely curious about this "exotic" and "mysterious" topic.

Teaching concepts of Eastern mysticism in the U.S. college classroom is difficult, to say the least. Eastern mysticism, like any mystical teaching, is incredibly difficult for most people to understand. Because concepts of Eastern mysticism are so radically different from Western ways of thinking, many people quickly give up trying to understand the teachings. To teach concepts of Eastern mysticism to U.S. college students more effectively, teachers must be willing to meet students mentally in a familiar and comfortable place. One way teachers can do this is by incorporating American popular films into their discussions of Eastern mysticism.

The cultural scholar bell hooks points out that film is powerful not only as a social educator but as a pedagogical tool as well:

> Movies not only provide a narrative for specific discourses of race, sex, and class, they provide a shared experience, a common starting point from which diverse audiences can dialogue about these charged issues. Trying to teach complicated feminist theory to students who were hostile to the reading often led me to begin such discussions by talking about a particular film. Suddenly students would be engaged in an animated discussion deploying the very theoretical concepts that they had previously claimed they just did not understand.[1]

As hooks states, popular film is an excellent way to get students talking about subjects that are abstract, unpopular, or difficult to understand. Because the majority of U.S. college students are unfamiliar with Eastern mysticism, popular films offer students a way to start talking about this abstract topic—one they may be unable or unwilling to discuss otherwise.

The variety of alternative, foreign, independent, and documentary films relevant to discussions of Eastern mysticism is much wider than that for American popular films. Although a college teacher could use a PBS documentary on Buddhism or the Hungarian film *Simon the Magician* (1998)—which tells the tale of a contemporary mystic—to help students understand Eastern mysticism, most college students are less willing to view these unfamiliar films than they are to view American popular films.

If popular films are used correctly as a teaching tool, the results can be astonishing. Eric Harrison of the *Los Angeles Times* reported on this phenomenon when he interviewed a college instructor about his use of popular film in the college classroom: "Lance Olsen . . . teaches writing and literature at the University of Idaho and finds it remarkable how intensely his students relate to the films. Mention it [*Star Wars*] in class, he says, and they come instantly alive."[2]

Most of the writing and scholarship that make connections between American popular film and mysticism have tended to focus on Western mystical concepts and theories. One of the most popular films used to explain concepts of Western spirituality and religion is George Lucas's *Star Wars* (1977). Joseph Campbell, one of the first scholars to make such comparisons, labeled *Star Wars* the "monomyth"—a story that all people can somehow relate to and find meaning in.[3]

For years, audiences, scholars, and critics have been aware of Lucas's use of mystical theories and concepts. Writers frequently refer to Luke Skywalker as the "Ulysses," "King Arthur," "Moses," and "Jesus" figure in *Star Wars*. Scholars rarely, if ever, however, talk about *qi*, enlightenment, or thought dynamics—Eastern mystical concepts that are also dominant themes throughout the film. For instance, the "Jedi mind trick"—the ability of a trained Jedi knight to influence the thoughts and actions of another being—is a concept Yogi philosophers have known about for centuries.

Yogi Ramacharaka explains the concept of thought dynamics (the Jedi mind trick) in this way:

> The man [or woman] of strong will sending forth a vigorous positive thought . . . sends with it a supply of Prana [vital life energy] proportioned to the force with which the thought was propelled. Such thoughts are often sent like a bullet to the mark, instead of drifting along slowly like an ordinary thought emanation. . . . A strong, vigorous thinker, whose thought is charged strongly with Prana, often creates what are known as Thought-Forms. Such thought-forms . . . possess almost the same power that the person sending them would possess were he present, urging his thought upon you in an earnest conversation.[4]

Additionally, the concept of "the force"—a major theme in all of the *Star Wars* movies—is nearly identical to the Taoists' concept of *qi*. "The force," like *qi*, is a mystical energy present in all things. A good way to explain the concept of *qi* to Western audiences would be to use *Star Wars* as a starting point for discussion.

A few writers and scholars are making connections between mysticism and contemporary American popular films,[5] but the vast majority tend to frame their discussions within a Western perspective. Although some Hollywood filmmakers use themes and concepts from Eastern mysticism in their films, they rarely incorporate the people and cultures from which the philosophies came. For example, in the *Star Wars* series, which clearly borrowed many of its ideas and concepts from Eastern mysticism, George Lucas created neither clear nor positive representations of Asian culture. In fact, the closest thing to Asian people the audience ever sees are the antagonistic viceroys in *Episode I: The Phantom Menace*—who happen to speak with a poor pseudo-Asian accent.

When American filmmakers do incorporate Eastern mysticism and Asian philosophies into their films, Asians and Asian cultures are still represented as the "other"—as inferior to white American culture. Hollywood has not strayed far from the days when *The Karate Kid*'s Mr. Miyagi was one of the only mediated images of Asian people, Eastern mysticism, and Asian philosophy to be found in American theaters. In fact, before production on the sequel to *The Matrix—The Matrix Reloaded* (scheduled for release in May 2003)—began, the producers negotiated with martial arts actor Jet Li to play a role in the film. After contract negotiations with Li failed, the producers approached *Crouching Tiger, Hidden Dragon*'s female lead, Michelle Yeoh, with a similar offer; she also declined the role. If Li or Yeoh had signed on for the sequel, they would have played the stereotypical Asian villain—Kung fu–kicking, cold-blooded killers. Hollywood has taken a large step forward by exposing Western audiences to basic concepts of Eastern mysticism; however—sadly—looking at American popular film today, one still clearly sees racialized representations of Asian people.

Some may argue that because American popular film is created in a society founded predominately on Western philosophies, it only seems fair that we seek to understand popular film in Western ways of thinking. To satisfy the American public's growing curiosity about Eastern mysticism, however, writers and scholars must challenge themselves to find new ways of discussing this complex topic. If the teachings of Eastern mysticism are as universal as they claim to be, concepts of Eastern mysticism should be found in films regardless of the society that created them. Obviously, some American popular films are better suited for discussions of Eastern mysticism than others.

THE MATRIX: A GOOD PLACE TO START

The 1999 film *The Matrix* was incredibly popular with a wide range of audiences. "It's becoming a 'dream' movie," said the film's producer, Joel Silver, "a four-quadrant movie [it appeals to older, younger, male, and female audiences]. That's the Holy Grail, a movie that gets everybody."[6] Although no specific figures are available on how many American college students saw the movie, it can be assumed that because of its massive popularity and cutting-edge style, teachers should have no difficulty finding students who are familiar with the film. It was reported that *The Matrix* was so popular that some college students showed up at theaters dressed like characters from the film.[7] Because of its popularity, "mythical" nature, and "Forcelike mysticism,"[8] *The Matrix* is an excellent film to use for teaching college students concepts of Eastern mysticism.

Like *Star Wars,* most writers and scholars have analyzed and discussed *The Matrix* by referring only to Western religious and spiritual concepts—almost always talking about the lead character, Neo, as "the Messiah" and the "Christlike" figure of the narrative.[9] Obviously, clear examples of Western religious, spiritual, and mystical concepts are present in the film; however, much of the narrative clearly draws from the teachings of Eastern mysticism. By using *The Matrix* to teach concepts of Eastern mysticism, American students—who will likely be familiar with the Western mystical concepts in the narrative—will have to make sense of the conceptual dualities that exist between Western and Eastern mystical perspectives.

Here are some examples of how college teachers can use *The Matrix* to teach key Eastern mystical concepts such as awakening, the tyrannical nafs, universal knowledge, and *qi* in the classroom.[10] Numerous Eastern mysticism concepts could be discussed using this film, but these four concepts lend themselves well to an introductory discussion. Although Eastern mysticism may seem difficult to grasp, it is amazing how accessible it can become when placed within the context of American popular film.

Awakening

The difference between a normal state of consciousness and enlightenment is that in one we are asleep and in the other we are awake. One day soon after the Buddha became enlightened, he was walking down the street when a group of holy men, recognizing that he was not an ordinary person, asked, "Are you a god?" He replied, "No." They then asked if he was an angel or some other type of spirit, and again he said no. Finally they asked, "So what are you?" And the Buddha replied, "I am awake." Indeed, the word Buddha means The Awakened One.[11]

According to the teachings of Buddhism and many other Eastern mystical schools, the majority of the human race is asleep. We believe we are awake because we think "sleep" is only a physiological state rather than a spiritual or psychological one. Because we do not even realize we are in a state of slumber, most of us have no desire to "wake up" spiritually. Those who manage to wake up are considered to be "enlightened" beings—people who have an objective view of absolute reality. Many teachings explain that waking up is difficult because it forces us to look at ourselves and the world around us with greater clarity, often making us painfully aware of the intense misery and massive suffering we and the people around us endure.

Explaining this to someone unfamiliar with Eastern mysticism is difficult. Even people who have studied Eastern mysticism for decades have difficulty understanding what awakening really is. Discussing this concept in a class of forty college students at a state university in the midwestern United States poses even greater challenges. Because our minds cannot fathom things greater than we are—another basic premise of all mystical teachings—we need to use examples from the human world to try to explain mystical concepts.

The Matrix is a metaphor for the illusory reality that we mistakenly believe is absolute reality. Neo, played by Keanu Reeves, is asleep. Because of his search for higher truth—represented by his computer hacking, a metaphor for seeking greater clarity of a perceived reality—however, he is offered the opportunity to "wake up." From Neo's journey into absolute reality, we learn that the Matrix is actually a computer-generated illusion. In contrast, the real world is a bleak, desolate, and barren wasteland. The "enlightened" beings live on a massive, industrial ship that is constantly in danger of being detected by cyborg "demons." Those who are not "enlightened" have no idea that they are living in an illusion manifested in their own minds.

In the world that we, the viewing audience, live in, most everyone is "asleep." We have no idea what absolute reality is. In the same way, the "sleeping" people in the Matrix have no idea that human beings are being used as batteries to power the computers that rule the earth. Although we have developed many theories to explain our existence, we, too, have no idea of our true purpose on this planet. No matter how flawless our religious arguments are or how well supported our scientific theories may be, absolute reality can only be experienced; it can never be accurately explained in words alone.

Morpheus, played by Laurence Fishburne, is an enlightened being. He is awake and fully conscious of absolute reality. Early in the film, Morpheus offers Neo two pills: a red pill, which will allow him to experience absolute reality, and a blue pill, which will make him forget his interactions with Morpheus and allow him to go back to "sleep." Being a seeker of absolute truth, Neo takes the red pill and chooses to "wake up."

The Eastern mystics explain that, like Neo, we can also choose whether we want to wake up. Of course, it is not simply a matter of taking a pill. In fact, most of us do not even know we have a choice, either because we have no interest in bettering our lives or because we are too afraid to question popular notions of reality. Neo is offered the opportunity to wake up because he has demonstrated that he wants greater understanding about his life. As a computer hacker—a nonconformist who knows there is something more to the computer illusion in front of him—Neo questions the very system that defines his existence.

The Tyrannical Nafs

> When most Sufi authors use the term *nafs,* they refer to our negative traits and tendencies. We all struggle to do those things we clearly know we should do. . . . Even when we are convinced of what is right, there is some part of us that tries to get us to do the opposite. That part is the lower self, in particular, the lowest stage of the nafs, the tyrannical nafs.[12]

The tyrannical nafs represent our lower ego, which generally rules our lives. Most of us let our tyrannical nafs tell us what to do. Whether we want more money, power, sex, or fame, we rarely understand where those urges and desires come from. Sufis have long understood the existence and power of the tyrannical nafs. As Robert Frager says in the quotation at the start of this section, we know what is best for us, but we do not do it; and we know what is not good for us, but we still do it. According to the teachings of Eastern mysticism, one of our major life goals is to understand and control our lower ego, our tyrannical nafs. This is extremely difficult because most of us do not even know that our tyrannical nafs exist; therefore, we take no action to control and conquer the entity that causes so much of our misery and suffering.

Looking at *The Matrix,* we find several excellent metaphors for the tyrannical nafs. The antagonist, Agent Smith (Hugo Weaving), is one representation of the tyrannical nafs. By stopping Neo and the other "enlightened" beings from showing other humans the illusion of the Matrix, he fulfills his basic function (making sure none of the human beings wakes up). He does everything in his power to keep people from seeing absolute reality because—like the tyrannical nafs—his very existence depends upon human beings never waking up. If they do, they will realize that the computer-generated agents are holding their minds captive, and they will try to destroy the agents to set themselves free.

Our tyrannical nafs behave in the same way. They want us to remain asleep because then they will remain in control of our lives. No matter how hard Neo and his cohorts try, they cannot destroy Agent Smith and his gang of computer-generated villains—Agent Smith cannot be killed even by a machine gun or a speeding train. This is exactly like the tyrannical nafs: no matter what we do, we never totally conquer our egos. Although we may have control of our lower selves, our egos will never be completely destroyed. Once our "higher selves" become the master of our beings, however, our tyrannical nafs become a tool for us to use rather than the cause of our suffering.

Another example to explain the tyrannical nafs is the character of Cypher (Joe Pantoliano). Throughout the narrative Cypher continually tries to go back to sleep. At one point in the film, Cypher tells Neo he wishes he had taken the blue pill Morpheus offered him so he could have remained asleep. Eastern mystics tell us how difficult it is to wake up because the spiritual path requires much hard work and can actually be more dangerous and painful than remaining asleep. The tyrannical nafs fight hard to keep us asleep because the pain and effort required for us to gain enlightenment are too much for most of us to handle.

Cypher betrays his friends so he can be rewarded by going back to sleep, forgetting all he has seen of absolute reality. To get this reward he loses all sense of remorse and compassion, coldly killing his companions and jeopardizing the potential freedom of the entire human race. This illustrates how painful it was for Cypher to wake up; it shows how desperately he wanted to go back to living a life of illusions. In the scene where he makes a deal with Agent Smith to betray his friends, Cypher says he knows the filet mignon he is eating is not real, but he would still prefer to live in a world of blissful illusion than in the harsh world of absolute reality.

This is the function of our tyrannical nafs; they do everything in their power to keep our higher selves from gaining control. We want to indulge in eating fine food, having lustful sex, and being rich and famous—even if we know these things are only illusions. By letting our tyrannical nafs rule our lives, we choose to ignore absolute reality.

Universal Knowledge

> Then there is experienced an intellectual illumination, or a pouring in of "knowing," impossible to describe. The soul becomes conscious that it

possesses in itself absolute knowledge—knowledge of all things—the "why and wherefore" of everything is recognized as being contained within itself. . . . Everything seems made plain—it is not a sense of an increased ability to reason, deduce, classify, or determine—the soul simply knows.[13]

Unlike many Western teachings, Eastern mystical teachings believe one gains knowledge by eliminating, not accumulating, information. The Western belief in the accumulation of information results from the fact that other human beings, who likely do not understand absolute truth themselves, usually generate almost all of the information we accumulate. Even those who do understand absolute truth could never accurately explain their knowledge in words alone. The Eastern mystics believe that if we want real knowledge and true wisdom, we have to empty our minds of all of the artificial things we have learned—the more we can "empty our cups," the more "full" we will be.

The kind of knowledge Eastern mystics refer to is neither "book" knowledge nor the knowledge one gains from academic institutions or training seminars. In fact, as alluded to in the quote at the beginning of this section, mystical universal knowledge is both unexplainable and extremely powerful—a concept that is difficult to understand. The concept can be clarified, however, using *The Matrix* as an analogy.

One of the most spectacular and memorable scenes from *The Matrix,* one that helps clarify the concept of universal knowledge, is the scene in which Neo learns martial arts by being plugged into a computer and downloading the information. Within minutes, Neo uses his newly acquired skills against Morpheus with speed and power. The computer that downloads martial arts skills into Neo is like the IT (call it God, the Tao, the Great Spirit, Science, or whatever works best for each teacher and classroom of students).[14] Only the IT can give a human being the divine, universal information and understanding represented by martial arts skills. Neo receives this bit of universal knowledge because he has chosen to wake up and is slowly conquering the fear and doubt created by his tyrannical nafs.

The cellular phone calls the "enlightened" people receive while in the Matrix could be thought of as metaphors for intuition—the divine connection a person has to universal knowledge. Because Neo sees the Matrix for what it is, an illusion, he receives phone calls that give him information he would not receive if he chose to live like everyone else who exists in a state of slumber.

In the beginning of the film, Neo finds out through a cellular phone what will happen before it happens. The cellular phone is his direct connection to Morpheus, the all-knowing being who can see everything taking place in the Matrix. Morpheus informs Neo that he will soon be getting a package. Within seconds, a stunned Neo gets the package. Morpheus then guides Neo to safety when the villainous Agent Smith tries to apprehend him. Neo's escape is only temporary, however, because he doubts Morpheus and everything he was told.

Because of his doubt, Neo is captured and forced back into his sleeplike existence within the Matrix.

According to many Eastern mystical teachings, intuition is only a small part of our ability to access universal knowledge. We often just "feel" something is right or wrong or have a "sense" that we should turn down one street instead of another. Most of the time, we do not know why we "feel" or "sense" these things, but we cannot deny the existence of the phenomenon. Many teachers say that if we ignore our intuition and follow our own sense of what we think is right, which is usually dictated by the lower ego, our intuition will eventually decay—as would any skill we do not use.

In the beginning of the film, when Neo first gets the cellular phone calls from Morpheus, he has doubts and has difficulty escaping the illusion of the Matrix. As the film progresses, however, Neo's faith in his intuition increases, and he is eventually able to overcome the pain and misery the Matrix creates.

Trinity (Carrie-Anne Moss), the lead female character, also has access to universal knowledge. She is guided out of numerous life-threatening situations by Tank (Marcus Chong), the computer operator who has a complete view of "reality." Tank also represents an all-knowing, omnipresent being. The information he and Morpheus provide to their cohorts in the Matrix is a metaphor for IT—which knows everything at all times. Because Trinity never doubts the information she receives over the cellular phone, she never faces difficulties navigating through the illusion of the Matrix. She has complete faith in her intuition.

Unlike Neo, Trinity knows she has unlimited access to universal knowledge. Toward the end of the film, while Neo and Trinity are rescuing Morpheus, Neo asks Trinity if she can fly the helicopter they find on a rooftop. Trinity immediately asks Tank to download a program that will give her the knowledge she needs to fly the helicopter. Within seconds, the duo is in the air. Because Trinity has no doubt about her connection to universal knowledge, she can instantly receive any information she needs. Neo and Trinity have a direct link to universal knowledge, and because they are "awake," IT guides them and gives them information unavailable to other human beings living in the illusion of the Matrix.

Qi

Qi has been the fundamental concept in Chinese philosophy. It is regarded as the only elemental substance that possesses force or energy in the universe. At the very original state of initiation of the universe, there was nothing but Qi. Because of the function and movement of Qi, the nature occurred and developed into the universe, so did the earth, man and everything else, all of which are interrelated, interacted, interchanged and interdependent.[15]

Qi has no equivalent concept in Western society. Quite simply, *qi* is the force that gives life to all things. Other Eastern mystical schools refer to this concept as *Prana,* life energy. We are born with a certain amount of *qi,* which our parents pass on to us. We also get *qi* from our environment—the food we eat, the water we drink, and the air we breathe. We can cultivate this energy, or force, through the practice of *qi gong,* or yoga, and other physical exercises. We can store it to prolong our lives. We can use it to improve our health or the health of others. We can use it to defend ourselves or to inflict great physical harm on others. One of the fundamental premises of Eastern mysticism is that *qi* is both good and bad—it creates and destroys, it can be both yin and yang.

The Western mind tends to think of human strength only in terms of muscle mass, but Eastern mystics have known for thousands of years that the development of *qi* can make a person far more powerful and healthy than the person who develops "external" muscle strength alone. The average U.S. college student has had little or no exposure to the concept of *qi,* and even most of those who have heard the term do not understand what it means. Regardless of whether the filmmakers of *The Matrix* intended to incorporate the concept of *qi* into their film, the film offers good analogies for explaining this Eastern mystical concept.

The martial arts sequences in *The Matrix,* choreographed by Yuen Wo Ping, demonstrate one of the filmmakers' obvious appropriations from Eastern culture. The three main characters—Neo, Trinity, and Morpheus—all know martial arts. In the scene in which Morpheus trains Neo to use his newly "programmed" martial arts skills, Neo tires quickly from defending himself against Morpheus's relentless barrage of attacks. Morpheus asks a physically exhausted Neo if he is really tired or if he just thinks he is tired. Neo briefly contemplates the relationship between mind and body and suddenly becomes recharged with energy. In a way, this scene helps to illustrate the concept of *qi.*

Many practitioners of internal martial arts—martial arts that emphasize the development of *qi*—focus on using *qi* instead of physical strength to defeat their opponents. They emphasize using the mind to move energy through the body, as opposed to relying on the physical body alone to generate force and power—something most "external" martial arts emphasize. By using *qi* to move the physical body—accomplished by harmonizing body, mind, and spirit— "discharging" power becomes effortless and much more powerful than any force that could be generated by muscular strength alone. By using *qi,* Neo, Morpheus, and Trinity can fight endlessly without tiring. By recognizing the illusion that limits their physical bodies, they discover the possibilities of using their minds to guide their physical actions.

In one scene, Morpheus has Tank place Neo into the "jump program" and challenges Neo to jump from the top of one building to the top of another—a feat that would be impossible for a normal (unenlightened) human being.

Morpheus shows Neo that it can be done by jumping across to the other build-ing with ease. After seeing this, a doubtful Neo attempts to jump across the great distance, but he fails and falls to the ground. As the film progresses, however, Neo begins to acquire superhuman physical abilities without any fur-ther "external" training or development—no weightlifting to increase his mus-cular strength, no running to improve his stamina, and no further martial arts training to develop his fighting abilities. In fact, it seems the only reason he gains such incredible physical power is because he slowly realizes the immense potential of using his mind to control his actions—he understands the concept of *qi*.

Those who are "awake" within the illusion of the Matrix realize the limits of conventional ways of thinking about the human body. They elevate their physical abilities to spectacular levels by challenging practical assumptions about how the human body generates power and force. Similarly, in Tai Chi and other Taoist internal martial arts, the way to power is through softness and relaxation, a concept that seems counterintuitive to the Western mind. Many legends in Chinese folklore, however, say the greatest fighters of all times defeated their opponents effortlessly, as if they were using some mystical power.

The Matrix is also one of the few American popular films that features a woman who can physically defend herself as well as any of the men. Trinity's power demonstrates the physical abilities women possess when they use *qi* instead of physical force. In Western thinking, males are usually thought of as inherently more physically powerful than females.[16] In Eastern mystical teach-ing, however, which places great value on feminine power, women are seen as equal to men in many ways—even superior in some cases. (This is not to say that greater gender equality exists in Eastern societies because, like any society, peoples' beliefs and actions often contradict one another.) In *Chronicles of Tao*, Deng Ming-Dao tells the story of women in China who developed incredible martial prowess:

> Taking into account the vulnerabilities and limited strengths of women, the nuns had devised unique forms of training internal energy. They evolved a sophisticated internal alchemy rooted in female chemistry. . . . Ma Sixing . . . displayed her own ability with *qinggong*. Wielding a split bamboo stick, she leapt out of her chair, covering over twenty feet with gliding jumps.[17]

Trinity epitomizes the possibility of yin, or feminine, power. She defeats all the men who attack her in the Matrix, regardless of their size and stature. Being physically smaller than all of her opponents, Trinity must harmonize her body, mind, and spirit to defeat them. As an "enlightened" being, she understands and develops her "internal" power—her *qi*—and breaks free from the accepted laws of physical power and fighting abilities that usually define women as the "weaker" sex.

LIMITATIONS OF USING AMERICAN POPULAR FILM
TO DISCUSS EASTERN MYSTICISM

Using American popular film to teach the concepts and theories of Eastern mysticism can be effective, but it is limited in the depth of understanding it can offer students. In addition to restrictions imposed by class size, the diversity of students' backgrounds, and the length of the course and class time, the U.S. college environment is not well suited for discussions of religion, spirituality, or mysticism. The university environment teaches students to be "intellectuals," providing them with formulas and methods—defined ways of thinking—to analyze and "think" about everything. This is in direct contrast to Eastern mysticism, which encourages people not to intellectualize but to break free from the confines of conceptual thought. By using American popular film to teach Eastern mysticism in the college classroom, teachers must accept that the integrity of the teachings will be sacrificed to some degree.

Although films such as *The Matrix* and *Star Wars* lend themselves well to discussions about Eastern mysticism, even these films do not fully and accurately illustrate Eastern mystical concepts. Therefore teachers must be familiar with both Eastern mysticism and media studies to make useful connections between the two topics and to fill in the conceptual gaps that will always be present in these discussions. Some concepts can be easily explained to the average U.S. college class. For example, students are usually comfortable with the concept of tyrannical nafs because they learned about the Western equivalent, the lower ego, during freshman psychology courses. Teachers need to stretch much further, however, to illustrate more profound or abstract concepts such as enlightenment—the Eastern mystics, of course, say these kinds of topics can never be accurately explained in words anyway. One of the dangers of trying to make connections that do not exist between American popular film and Eastern mysticism is that teachers risk giving college students an inaccurate or altogether false understanding of Eastern mysticism.

Another limitation of using American popular film to teach Eastern mysticism is that teachers are limited to the stories created by filmmakers who may or may not have any intention of incorporating concepts of Eastern mysticism in their films. Most of the American popular films teachers have access to contain very few examples or illustrations of such concepts. Because of this, teachers must use texts that are framed in a Western perspective to explain Eastern philosophies. Trying to transform a filmmaker's Jesus-like character into a Buddha in a typical U.S. college classroom can be quite challenging.[18]

Furthermore, by using American popular film alone for a discussion of Eastern mysticism, teachers are limited to the realm of the visual image. Although we come to different ways of knowing by studying different kinds of texts, I do not believe even the best film on Eastern mysticism could compare to a well-written book on the same subject. There is a level of understanding we cannot get from the visual medium that we can get from the written word.

Sometimes visual media give too much information, so the audience develops a preconceived way of thinking about and seeing reality. Students and audiences usually consume this "packaged" reality without considering how it supports or challenges the way they think about their own concepts of reality. Books, on the other hand, often require readers to focus more of their attention inward; books may even encourage them to use their minds proactively to be more aware of the way they conceptualize reality. At the highest level, Eastern mystics say that absolute reality, or ultimate truth, cannot be talked about or written down in words; it can only be experienced. Even concepts that seem relatively simple to explain, such as *qi,* cannot be fully understood by students until they have experienced these concepts themselves—perhaps by taking a Tai Chi or a yoga class.

Additionally, teachers have to deal with many of the negative aspects inherent in almost all American popular films. The majority of these films still incorporate poor representations of "difference." Racial and ethnic minorities, women, the underclass, homosexuals, and anyone who does not fit Hollywood's "ideal" image is rarely seen in the world American popular films create. Teachers need to understand and be prepared to talk about the impact American popular films have on society and the way individuals create their identities.

Even though *The Matrix* lends itself to discussions of Eastern mysticism, teachers must be vigilant about making students aware of both the good and bad messages the filmmakers send to the audience. In *The Matrix* we still find many stereotypical portrayals of women and ethnic minorities. Like the vast majority of other American popular films, the central character of *The Matrix* is a white male whose job is to rescue everyone else and resolve all major conflicts that arise. Yes, there are ethnic minorities in the film, but their very survival depends upon the actions of the central white male. Trinity is the only major female character who makes it to the end of the film alive, which challenges stereotypes of the typical female lead character; but true to the Hollywood narrative formula, she ends up being relegated to a romantic trophy for the white male central character.

In addition, *The Matrix* is teeming with glorified and unrealistic violence. Unlike the Taoists, who believe the use of weapons should be avoided unless absolutely necessary, the characters in *The Matrix* calmly and coldly wield their guns, blasting away at anything that moves without the slightest hint of compassion or remorse. When talking about Eastern mysticism and American popular film, teachers must be very cautious that students do not end up believing Hollywood represents some kind of intrinsically mystical and admirable nature—after all, filmmakers' goal is to make money.

POSSIBILITIES FOR THIS KIND OF TEACHING

One of the greatest advantages of using American popular film to teach concepts of Eastern mysticism is that students are familiar with the texts being analyzed and, more important, are willing to discuss the material teachers bring into the classroom. Furthermore, students feel more comfortable engaging in potentially threatening discussions when they have something tangible in front of them that they can use to illustrate their comments. Taking attention away from students' personal beliefs and placing the focus on a movie minimizes the risks students must take to engage in discussion. Although some students will still feel threatened by Eastern mysticism, approaching the subject from this perspective will be easier for many.

For better or worse, we are rapidly becoming a visual media society. Using popular film as a teaching aid in the college classroom can reach students who are more familiar and comfortable with visual media than they are with more "traditional" oral and written texts. Arguably, many college students would rather watch television or go to a movie than read a book. Three of the added benefits of using American popular film to teach concepts of Eastern mysticism are, first, as teachers, we can help make the consumption of visual media more interesting for students by adding an Eastern mystical perspective; second, we can encourage students to become more critical and aware of the images and messages that create and define reality for masses of people; and third, teachings about Eastern mysticism can also have an impact on students' notions about Asians and Asian culture.

At the end of my course, students have commented (in retrospect) on how distorted their views of Asian culture and religious traditions were. Through course materials they come to a much different understanding of how and why Asians and Westerners see the world from different but legitimate perspectives. Once this point has been made, I try to reinforce it in different ways and bring it "back home" by tying it to issues of cultural diversity in general. Most of my students come to realize that U.S. society usually operates from an extremely Eurocentric point of view. By exposing them to the existence and nature of other cultural perspectives, students are forced to think more seriously about what ethnocentrism is all about.

In this way we can help students find positive and inspiring messages within the overwhelming negativity of American popular film. It seems that today, more than ever, we are constantly bombarded with artificially constructed images that paint a cruel, cold, and uncaring picture of reality. Rather than becoming apathetic and discouraged with the world and saying "that's just the way things are, there's no point in trying to make it better," we need to start thinking about how we can use what we have in front of us as tools to help us wake up.

NOTES

1. bell hooks, *Reel to Real* (New York: Routledge, 1996), 2.

2. Eric Harrison, "The Mything Link," *Los Angeles Times* (14 May 1999): 1.

3. Quoted in ibid.

4. Yogi Ramacharaka, *Fourteen Lessons in Yogi Philosophy* (Chicago: Yogi Publication Society, 1903), 85.

5. "In the *Green Mile*, Mysticism on Death Row," *Newsweek* (13 December 1999): 86; "Vampire Cyborgs and Scientific Imperialism: A Reading of Science-Mysticism Polemic in *Blade*," *Journal of Popular Film and Television* 27, 2 (1999): 4.

6. Quoted in Richard Natale, "*Matrix* Casts Very Wide Net," *Los Angeles Times* (16 April 1999): 2.

7. Ibid. "There were stories of college-age males showing up at the film wearing long black leather coats [which were sported by several of *Matrix*'s central characters]."

8. Harrison, "Mything Link," 1.

9. Marshall Fine, "*Matrix* Most Imaginative Movie of the Year," *Journal News* [Hamilton, Ohio] (30 March 1999).

10. The examples have been used as lecture material in SP-100, Communication and Popular Culture, and ET-200, Ethnicity in America—two courses offered at Colorado State University

11. David Samuel, *Practical Mysticism* (Denver: Bakshi, 2000), 3.

12. Robert Frager, *Heart, Self, and Soul: The Sufi Psychology of Growth, Balance, and Harmony* (Wheaton, IL: Theosophical Publishing, 1999), 48.

13. Yogi Ramacharaka, *Advance Course in Yogi Philosophy and Oriental Occultism* (Chicago: Yogi Publication Society, 1904), 76.

14. When trying to get students to think in non-Western ways, I avoid using the word *God* when talking about this great mystical "thing." Teaching in environments that predominately include white, Anglo-Saxon, Protestant students, I also avoid using the terms *Tao* or *Buddha* because these words tend to create unneeded religious division—a sense of "us" and "them." This is why I refer to the concept simply as "IT."

15. Simon Wang and Julius Liu, *Qi Gong for Health and Longevity: The Ancient Chinese Art of Relaxation/Meditation/Physical Fitness* (Tustin, CA: East Health Development Group, 1995), 30.

16. When talking about the physical power of women and men in university classes, a student will inevitably say "men are just stronger than women, and that's the way things are," to which almost everyone in the room will nod their heads in agreement. Students often use the "firefighter" analogy, which says that when it comes down to a life-or-death situation, everyone would throw out their notions of gender equality and political correctness and want a man to rescue them instead of a woman. Because examples of physically powerful women are rare in U.S. society, most of us do not even question the assumption that women are essentially physically weaker than men.

17. Deng Ming-Dao, *Chronicles of Tao: The Secret Life of a Taoist Master* (New York: HarperCollins, 1993), 35.

18. Students will often resist discussions about Eastern mysticism in popular film by saying, "Well, of course the protagonist represents Jesus because that's what the filmmaker obviously intended," which is a fair argument to make because, admittedly, teachers do not know what the filmmaker's intention was.

12
BEYOND THE HOLLYWOOD HYPE
Unmasking State Oppression Against People of Color

BRETT STOCKDILL, LISA SUN-HEE PARK, AND DAVID N. PELLOW

In this chapter we will focus on the documentary film *The Panama Deception* (1992) to unpack the concept of "the state" and the differential impacts of various government actions on ethnic minorities. We do so by applying an analysis of social inequality to the film, a model that centers on four interrelated levels of inequality: the historical, institutional, ideological, and personal. Our informal survey of students clearly revealed they found these levels of inequality useful as a tool for developing a solid comprehension of state violence and social oppression.

Our goals are straightforward. First, we want students to develop a critical understanding of oppression and social inequality, including how these phenomena affect their everyday lives (e.g., issues of difference and privilege). Second, we also seek to create an appreciation among students for unequal relationships between and among nations. In the sociological tradition of C. Wright Mills, Avelardo Valdez and Jeffrey A. Halley write, "Linking film and social science texts enhances students' abilities to draw connections between practice and structure, personal problems and social issues."[1]

Brett Stockdill, Lisa Sun-Hee Park, and David N. Pellow

SCREENING RACISM AND STATE VIOLENCE

In conjunction with lectures, small-group discussions, interactive class activities, field trips, and other teaching techniques, we have found that film and video are useful tools for illuminating how racism and other forms of inequality shape the lives of people of color in the United States and around the globe. Films and videos facilitate students' understanding of the multiple layers of oppression embedded in dominant institutions such as the state. They also provide insight into how these systemic inequalities impact communities, families, and individuals—including the students themselves.

The typology of four interrelated levels of social inequality (historical, institutional, ideological, and personal) has helped us teach students to unmask a range of covert and overt forms of inequality and place them into larger institutional contexts. As in the broader society, most students conceptualize racism at the microsociological, or individual, level without recognizing its roots in history and contemporary social structures.[2] For many students—particularly white middle-class students—the concepts of structural-state violence, privilege, and institutionalized racism remain largely invisible or inaccessible. Furthermore, students of all races are seldom encouraged to delve deeply into how their community and self-identity are socially constructed within the context of a racist society. Students are rarely challenged to explore the reality that racist social structures have substantial costs for some and benefits for others.

Because institutionalized racism and other systemic oppressions are commonly mythologized out of existence by the mass media and the educational system,[3] most students find it difficult to comprehend ideas and theories foreign to their personal experiences. More often than not, students are not equipped to acknowledge the existence of, much less critically analyze, events that run counter to their worldview—a worldview shaped by a capitalist economy and a corporate-controlled media, educational system, and government.[4] Therefore the study of racially oppressed communities often requires a direct confrontation with assumed, mainstream notions about the social institutions that regulate our everyday lives.[5]

In this chapter we discuss the film *The Panama Deception,* which exposes the U.S. government's role in perpetrating specific racist policies and actions that have had devastating consequences on peoples' lives. This award-winning documentary helps to make "visible" that which has been hidden and distorted and that many students find unbelievable. This film can play a critical role in exploring the concept of institutionalized racism, particularly when studying the impact various oppressive and violent government actions have had on communities of color. After briefly examining salient theoretical and pedagogical issues, we will analyze this film using the four interrelated levels of inequality presented earlier.[6]

THEORETICAL AND PEDAGOGICAL ISSUES:
TEACHING ABOUT OPPRESSION AND RESISTANCE

How we analyze the world theoretically as sociologists and activists is intertwined with how we teach our students. As sociologists, we have conducted research and taught various classes in the fields of Asian American studies, African American studies, queer studies, women's studies, environmental studies, social inequality, and social movements. As individuals, we have faced racism, sexism, and homophobia in various forms. As activists, we have been involved in collective efforts in the areas of domestic violence, immigrant rights, environmental justice, indigenous rights, police brutality, and HIV/AIDS. Our work as educators is guided by constant efforts to make connections—connections between personal troubles and collective injustices, teaching and learning, knowledge and practice, and different forms of institutionalized marginalization.

Our theoretical understanding of racial inequality and other systematic inequities has been informed by the work of Angela Davis, Karl Marx, W.E.B. DuBois, Oliver Cox, Howard Zinn, Eduardo Galeano, Margaret Randall, and other scholars whose writings present foundational critiques of structural inequalities in the United States and around the world. We are conflict theorists who view social inequalities as relationships between and among groups that are structured systematically and over time in such a way that subordinate groups are denied basic civil and human rights, exploited economically, denigrated culturally, and denied equal access to health care, education, employment, and physical safety.

Our teaching is grounded in this theoretical framework. Furthermore, learning from black feminists[7] and other feminists of color,[8] we take an approach to scholarship that emphasizes using knowledge to expose systemic violence and oppression and to work for equality and justice. From a pedagogical standpoint, we follow bell hooks in "teaching to transgress."[9] We use the classroom as a vehicle for exposing systemic injustice in different forms, and we encourage students to critically analyze their relationships to these injustices.

One of the most pressing challenges we encounter in the classroom is students' tendency to look at explanations of social problems solely at an individual level. Indoctrinated with "trickle-down economics," the shredding of the national welfare safety net, assaults on affirmative action and civil rights, "family values," and "three strikes you're out," many students are resistant to developing a broader progressive sociological analysis. For this reason it is often difficult to guide students beyond narrow notions of individual responsibility and prejudice toward a more complex comprehension of social inequality—one that takes into account specific historical and institutional relationships between and among different groups.

The typology of four interrelated levels of inequality is particularly useful when teaching about stratification. Here is a more detailed description of these levels:

1. Historical: pivotal examples of inequality in U.S. history that are antecedents for contemporary oppression
2. Institutional: inequalities perpetrated by dominant social institutions such as the federal government, the criminal justice system, transnational corporations, and the mass media
3. Ideological: collective beliefs that rationalize and justify current social, political, and economic arrangements
4. Personal: the ways social inequalities affect individuals on the individual level, including both negative and positive consequences of inequality

PEDAGOGICAL ISSUES

It is important to point out some of the pedagogical issues involved in using film and video in the classroom. When used effectively, films and videos provide a refreshing complement to lectures and discussion, thereby engaging students' interest.[10] Films and videos help to personalize sociological issues. By putting a human face on a particular issue or sociological dynamic, films and videos can create emotional immediacy in the classroom.[11] This immediacy can open the door to a consideration of other viewpoints while also stimulating sociological thinking[12] and extracting sociological themes that previously may have been difficult to grasp.[13]

Films and videos also provide a forum for voices that may not be represented in traditional texts and curricula. Octavio Romano has asserted that "in Chicano studies, there is a long tradition of critiquing how social science paradigms produced social research that has distorted the experiences of this group."[14]

A film is only one component of the learning process, however. Students often enjoy films and videos because they represent a departure from the conventional college lecture approach. To maximize a film's effectiveness, however, it must be carefully placed within the larger course curriculum.

A film or video may be used to illustrate a particular scholar's thesis. In this case students read articles and books, hear a lecture, and engage in class discussion centered on the theory. After this point, a film could be shown to refute or support the thesis and, perhaps more important, to illuminate the fact that theories can actually be useful in making sense of our social world.

Instructors can draw on many pedagogical techniques to make film viewing more valuable for students. They include:

- Know when to show a particular film. At times it is useful to show a film to present visual images of a particular social problem before reading sociological research and theory on that problem. At other times it might be better to have students read a particular book or article or listen to a lecture and then show a video that bridges the gap between the abstract level of theory and the concrete reality of people's experiences.

- Provide background-historical information. Often students have little knowledge about a historical or geographic context or ethnic group. Providing this background information first may enhance learning.
- Provide discussion questions beforehand. Providing students with a conceptual framework that can be used during and after the film to tease out sociological dynamics or to "get the big picture" can further enhance the learning experience.
- Prepare students for graphic, disturbing scenes. It is extremely important to inform students beforehand if a movie has explicit scenes of violence, sexual abuse, or similar elements. Sometimes alternative viewing arrangements might be helpful, such as allowing students to watch particularly sensitive films at home.
- Provide students with resources, referrals, and contacts. Showing films about the exploitation of people may stimulate interest among students to get involved as advocates and activists or to seek emotional support (e.g., sexual assault counseling). Students often appreciate receiving information about related organizations and services.
- Facilitate discussion after the film or video. Engage as many students as possible when discussing the movie, and connect the film with readings, lectures, guest speakers, and other class discussions.
- Connect conceptual discussion with emotional reactions. Encourage students to share their emotional responses to the film. "Making it real" is a key aspect of the learning experience. Discussions should highlight places where students experienced a visceral response to the film, where they actually began to feel for the characters, care about the issues, and make connections to their own lives.
- Address frustration, guilt, and other negative emotions. When confronted with some of the historical and contemporary realities of oppression in the United States and elsewhere, students sometimes have very strong feelings including anger, frustration, guilt, and defensiveness. As we help students develop skills to work through these tough emotions, it is important to explain that learning about social injustice is an inherently uncomfortable, frustrating, and painful process, but it can also be inspiring and empowering.
- Be creative in facilitating discussion. Give students the opportunity to write anonymous reactions and questions that can then be read to the class and discussed. Small- and large-group discussions can be used as well—these often yield a range of additional discussion topics and create new dynamics between students.
- Keep the constraints of the film form in mind. Valdez and Halley remind us that "visual images also carry a greater surplus meaning than the written word and are susceptible to a wider range of interpretations. . . . The process of film making, including condensation and reconstruction, alters social facts."[15] This is undoubtedly a greater concern when showing

Hollywood feature films than when showing documentaries, but regardless, both professors and students should be mindful of the complexity of films and videos.

In the next section we look specifically at how we use *The Panama Deception* to challenge inaccurate perceptions of a benevolent U.S. government and to stimulate students to apply the knowledge they learn in class to make their communities more just and humane.

READJUSTING THE LENS: USING FILMS TO EXPOSE STATE VIOLENCE

Many students enter our courses thinking race, class, gender, and sexuality are immutable, transhistorical, and universal, so it is essential to deconstruct these categories before showing films. In mainstream media coverage and academic scholarship, social problems—such as military conflicts—are frequently divorced from economic exploitation, institutionalized racism, globalization, and neocolonialism.[16]

From our perspective, a crucial part of the educational process is to challenge mainstream perceptions of equality and justice in the United States. Piercing the veneer of "democracy and freedom" and exposing the brutality of multiple, interlocking oppressions is essential in helping students utilize their critical thinking skills to work for progressive social change. Film and video can be extremely useful tools in critiquing hegemonic ideology and reconceptualizing structural and systemic violence—including U.S. military actions—as criminal. This theme is a direct response to the dominant and growing trend in sociology, under the rubric of "criminology," to focus on so-called index crimes (e.g., theft, rape, murder, assault) to the near exclusion of the more heinous crimes committed by corporations and nation-states. Within this rubric, genocide and the destruction of cultures and ecosystems around the world are referred to as "conflicts" or "policies," whereas pickpockets and "gang bangers" are referred to as "recidivists," "felons," and "hardened criminals." The authors of a recent book on corporate malfeasance refer to the few corporate criminologists as scholars inhabiting "an academic Siberia."[17]

THE PANAMA DECEPTION

The Panama Deception evoked a very strong response in me. . . . The injustices and disregard for the people of Panama infuriated me, as did the lies that the American public were told.

—Tomy, a white female student

Many students are entirely unaware of the consequences of U.S. military interventions in the Third World. Although alarming, this lack of awareness is not surprising given the corporate-government control of the mass media[18] and the whitewashed curriculum in public schools and public and private universities and colleges in the United States.[19] *The Panama Deception,* a documentary by Barbara Trent, can be used to teach students about systemic racism and classism and how they operate on the international level. The film challenges the dominant perception that the U.S. government promotes democracy in other countries. It also demonstrates the brutal violence and callous disregard for human life the U.S. government employs to maintain cultural, political, military, and economic hegemony on a global level.

We find it is best to show this film late in the term because students have developed a conceptual framework that can be used to analyze the film. It also allows the class to develop a cohesion and rapport that will facilitate discussions of the more extreme and atrocious images of oppression depicted in the film. Before discussing *The Panama Deception* in detail, we will briefly describe one course in which we showed students the film.

We teach courses on social inequality that focus on a range of oppressions such as racism, classism, sexism, and homophobia. The primary objectives of these courses are to teach students:

1. To critically analyze contemporary social inequalities on four interrelated levels: historical, institutional, ideological, and personal
2. To understand the social construction of race, class, gender, and sexuality
3. To identify contemporary manifestations of inequitable power relationships in the areas in the previous point
4. To understand how different forms of oppression are interlocking and mutually reinforcing
5. To understand how their life experiences are related to systemic inequalities

To achieve these objectives, we use a combination of readings, lectures, discussions, small-group activities, films and videos, and creative group research projects. One point we reiterate throughout the course is that violence and bigotry have their roots in dominant social institutions—such as the state, corporations, and the media—rather than being an essential component of human nature. The four levels of inequality are also themes that run throughout the course. By midterm, most students—given a current event, reading, or film—can identify and discuss examples of the different levels of inequality.

The course is designed to provide students not only with theoretical explanations and "measurements" of social inequality but also with personal analyses and testimonies of those affected by particular forms of oppression. It is crucial to pay particular attention to the experiences and analyses of members of groups that are the principal targets of oppression. Women, people of color, poor people, and queers have historically been marginalized, not only in the larger society but within academia as well. Therefore it is imperative to challenge mainstream academic analyses that have often rationalized and reinforced inequality.

Students are encouraged to move beyond the purely academic approach and, to the extent possible, identify personally with specific forms of inequality. Students who are members of oppressed groups often comment that our classes help them put their own experiences into a broader historical and analytical perspective. Students who are members of privileged groups sometimes feel defensive, but they are usually able to move toward a fuller understanding of their privilege and complicity and toward a deeper sense of compassion and social responsibility.

Films are key components of the classes. As stated in the introductory section of this chapter, films and videos push students to actually *look* at images of inequality. Actually seeing human faces and listening to human voices within the context of social inequality has a powerful impact on students. John, a white middle-class student, wrote:

> [*The Panama Deception*] offered information on an emotional level. The learning process had more of a visual impact on me that I feel I will always remember. . . . Adding the visual effect really helped strengthen my recollection and emotional impact for which I think that I benefited more from the video than I would have from a traditional lecture.

At the end of the term, we show *The Panama Deception* because by that time students are emotionally and intellectually prepared. Many students are not even aware that the U.S. military invaded Panama in 1989. One student wrote in his survey: "[*The Panama Deception*] showed many things that you would not see on the ten o'clock news. For example . . . I was never aware of the atrocities that were committed on the part of the United States." Students who are familiar with the invasion tend to have vague recollections of Manuel Noriega and the War on Drugs as the reasons for the intervention. The vast majority of students have little or no knowledge of Panamanian history, the political and economic relationship between the United States and Panama, or the devastating impact of the invasion. The film addresses all of these issues.

Before showing the movie, we ask students to locate Panama on a map because many do not know where it is. Students are then asked to share anything they know about the invasion of Panama. Telling them the film won an Academy Award for Best Documentary Film is a strategic way of "legitimizing" the film for students who are particularly insistent on believing the United States is "the land of the free and the home of the brave." Students are told that Elizabeth Montgomery of *Bewitched* is the narrator and that rock stars Sting and Jackson Browne are on the soundtrack. Students are warned that there are graphic scenes of violence and mutilated and decayed corpses. We urge them to compare and contrast the violence and death they see in the documentary with the scenes of violence and death they see on prime-time television and in Hollywood movies.

In addition to reminding students to keep the four levels of inequality in mind as they watch the film, we provide them with six discussion questions to consider:

1. What has been the role of the United States in Panama historically?
2. What were the official (government) reasons for the invasion of Panama?
3. What were the "real" reasons for the invasion?
4. How was the invasion covered up and presented by the mass media in the United States?
5. What was the response of the international community?
6. Was the invasion a violation of international law?

After the film, we ask for general reactions. Students are typically horrified by the extent of violence and death and by the fact that the U.S. government carefully orchestrated the tragedy. Roxanne, a Chinese American woman, wrote: "*The Panama Deception* is very intense. I thought it was shocking the first time I watched it because I was totally unaware of what went on. After watching it, I was rather depressed."

The film provides students with the empirical evidence of racist, imperialist U.S. foreign policy and the fact that this action led to the deaths of literally thousands of predominately poor Panamanians—people of color. The film helps students develop a more critical analysis of U.S. claims of "freedom" and "democracy." Roxanne wrote:

> After watching it, I was much more cynical because I grew up on the belief that the United States was great and wonderful. . . . It shows how classes are constructed in the third world countries. It shows U.S. domination in Panama. It shows inequality by telling tales of indiscriminate killing, massive amounts of killing. . . . I think this film helped open people's eyes to what really goes on. I think this film is a good tool to use. . . . It relates to my life because it's what helped shape my views on many things.

During discussion, we point out that the invasion was conducted in "our" name, with "our" tax dollars. We explain that the United States has "intervened" in dozens of other countries to varying degrees (e.g., Nicaragua, El Salvador, Chile, Vietnam, Grenada, Guatemala, Iraq). After taking the course and viewing *The Panama Deception,* students are better able to see the patterns of U.S. military atrocities, toppled governments, and support for dictatorial regimes; and they understand the links between racism-classism and neoliberal political and economic policies. Discussion of the film can also lead into considerations of other racist corporate-government alliances—such as the North American Free Trade Agreement, the World Trade Organization, and the International Monetary Fund—as well as of current events in Chiapas, Cuba, and Iraq. Tina, a Chicana student, wrote:

U.S. soldiers searching Panamanians. From *The Panama Deception,*
Rhino Video, 1992

> I always used to think of negative things when I heard the name Noriega. I
> was so blown away when I learned that he was set up by the [U.S.] govern-
> ment because he wouldn't make a deal with Bush. It ticked me off so much
> when I saw the poor peoples' families being killed by the Americans. . . .
> Frankly it all made me feel very sick to my stomach. Now I wonder how much
> about Saddam [Hussein] is the truth. The media portrays this country as
> being the good guy but now I'm absolutely not buying that ideology.

Joyce, a Chicana lesbian, wrote:

> *The Panama Deception* was a prime example of how the United States of
> America is an absolute puppet of the Power Elite. The social inequalities that
> were presented in the movie are so devastating that it is very difficult for me
> to even write about. . . . At the time of the crisis, the government was quick
> to misattribute the reasons for being there instead of revealing the truth: they
> were there to protect the interest of the corporate network.

Students state that the film helps reveal the extreme bias of and distortion by the
mass media as they transform the murders of thousands of Panamanians into an
intervention for the sake of "democracy." Jeremy, a biracial (Japanese and white
American) student, stated:

> According to *The Panama Deception,* the United States, Ronald Reagan,
> George Bush, and the CIA [Central Intelligence Agency] were the bad guys.

The Neighborhood of El Chorrillo after the invasion. Panama, December 1989. From *The Panama Deception,* Rhino Video, 1992. Photo by Julio Cesar Guerra D

underneath the table and were not honest with the American people. However, as a youngster, I watched television and the news broadcasts and I saw the terrible army of Noriega terrorize innocent Americans. . . . I believed that our President was doing all he could to maintain world peace and end the drugs coming into the United States. I experienced *The Panama Deception.* I was led to believe in things that the U.S. government forced me to believe.

Throughout the term and especially following the viewing of this film, we provide time for students to express their emotional reactions to learning about state violence and other forms of oppression. After seeing *The Panama Deception,* students often express feelings of anger, sadness, shame, guilt, and so on. Diane, an upper-middle-class white woman, wrote: "I felt shame to be a part of the nation that does such horrible things to people. That these people were never considered or treated like they had feelings or families. I felt naive for not knowing that these things were occurring."

Students also report feeling overwhelmed at the depths of U.S. oppression, and they feel hopeless and helpless. We encourage them to explore those feelings, but we also remind them that Barbara Trent and others went to great lengths to make the film and that doing so was an act of resistance to U.S. imperialism. We also state that simply showing the film to friends and family is another act of positive social change. This can also be an opportunity to announce upcoming progressive political events and provide students with contacts from progressive organizations.

Overall, *The Panama Deception* has been an extremely powerful educational resource in exposing the calculated injustices of U.S. foreign policy; the inaccuracy, racism, classism, and ethnocentrism in the mass media; and the close ties between transnational corporations and the federal government. At the core of the film's effectiveness is the humanization of the Panamanian victims—the footage of mass graves and bombed neighborhoods, the interviews with survivors—juxtaposed with the lies of then-President George H.W. Bush, the violent machismo of U.S. troops, and the ethnocentric mainstream press coverage in the United States. A working-class Chicana student spoke of the film's incredible emotional impact:

> [The film] helped me better understand people who are in another social and cultural group, because in watching I felt that it reached a deeper part of my mind than oral lecture by the instructor. When I actually saw the mutilated bodies in the film it gave me a knot in my stomach and brought tears to my eyes. I felt that hearing the voices from the women who were crying out for help opened my mind to better understanding the suffering that goes on with other people in the world.

On a more analytical level, Ed, a middle-class Chicano student, wrote about the film's ability to transform U.S. "democracy" into an "Evil Empire." He stated that *The Panama Deception* provides a

> Powerful and revealing look into an unfettered American intervention for "democracy." It leaves many of the doubters about America being the "Evil Empire" with no choice but to begin to accept the nature of their government. Because [of] the civilian accounts along with [those of] other international affairs experts, I could feel an uneasiness in the room because of the disgust many felt with their government. A disgust that many up to that point had still been in denial that such an event was possible.

After watching the film, students develop a deeper understanding of state violence in its historical, institutional, ideological, and personal dimensions. Like many documentary films, *The Panama Deception* is graphic and disturbing, but these characteristics turn the usual film screening in a classroom into a transforming educational experience.

DISCUSSION

In addition to lectures, readings, and group discussion, films and videos add a strong component to students' overall understanding of the character of social inequality. As a social phenomenon, inequality can be discussed in innumerable ways that include race, class, gender, and sexuality. Whether we choose to emphasize one or more types of social inequality, we find ourselves returning to the historical, institutional, ideological, and personal dimensions embedded within each type. Understanding these four components is crucial if students are to grasp the multilayered nature of stratification. To this end, films and videos can present a visual "face" for students to examine the different forms of social inequality and institutional violence. They also enable students to literally see, hear, and (it is hoped) feel how systemic inequalities impact communities, families, and individuals. More specifically, when used effectively, films and videos challenge students not only to "readjust the lens" through which they view social life but also to reconceptualize the oppressive practices of dominant institutions as violent, immoral, and criminal.

The Panama Deception also makes it clear that events occurring thousands of miles away in other nations are often directly linked to our lives here in the United States. The film demonstrates, for example, that the U.S. military—supported by taxpayers—murdered thousands of Panamanians. In other words, soldiers who were not only U.S. citizens but disproportionately people of color killed thousands of other people of color in the name of democracy. For many of our students this revelation underscored the fact that people of color are valued much less than whites around the world and that, as citizens and taxpayers, they were unwilling accomplices to this tragedy.

In addition, we make sure students realize that the history of racial hierarchy and the prevalence of racism in Panama is similar to that in the United States. As Joy James has noted, "A form of apartheid was practiced by the U.S. military in the Canal Zone until the late 1960s."[20] For much of the twentieth century, an oligarchy of European families, supported by the United States, ruled over the "colored" Panamanians—indigenous, African, and mestizo. The U.S. involvement in Panama thus raises serious concerns regarding our involvement across national borders. Are we truly propagating "democracy," as the media would have us believe, through the "War on Drugs"? Or are we violating international law in our efforts to mold the polity of Panama into our own image, American-style? In the end, many of our students are not only furious about what the United States government did and the fact that the media covered it up; they also appreciate more fully that many different connections link the fate of Panama and the United States.

Thus, as Malcolm Collier and Lane Ryo Hirabayashi have argued, visual media help bridge different experiences, creating linkages that lead to in-depth understanding.[21] Through this new lens, the recent murder of Amadou Diallo, an African immigrant, by the New York City Police cannot be viewed as a random tragedy committed by a "few bad apples." Instead, students are now prepared to view Diallo's death as part and parcel of the historical dehumanization, intimidation, and murder of people of color and members of other oppressed communities.

In conclusion, when teaching about social inequality, one of the most difficult ideas to convey is its complex institutional nature. The multifaceted and interrelated aspects of social inequality are difficult to illustrate so students will remain comfortable enough to engage in a critical dialogue—particularly in classrooms where student demographics vary widely. One of the most effective ways to communicate this complexity is through films and videos.

NOTES

1. Avelardo Valdez and Jeffrey A. Halley, "Teaching Mexican American Experience Through Film: Private Issues and Public Problems," *Teaching Sociology* 27 (1999): 286–295; quote on p. 286.

2. Oliver Cox, *Caste, Class, and Race* (New York: Modern Paperbacks, 1948).

3. bell hooks, *Teaching to Transgress: Education as the Practice of Freedom* (New York: Routledge, 1994).

4. See Noam Chomsky and Edward S. Herman, *Manufacturing Consent: The Political Economy of the Mass Media* (New York: Pantheon, 1988); William Domhoff, *Who Rules America? Power and Politics in the Year 2000* (Mountain View, CA: Mayfield, 2000); Michael Parenti, *Democracy for the Few* (New York: St. Martin's, 1988).

5. See Christopher Bates Doob, *Racism: An American Cauldron* (New York: HarperCollins, 1993); Manning Marable, *How Capitalism Underdeveloped Black America* (Boston: South End, 1983); Alfredo Mirandé, *The Chicano Experience: An Alternative Perspective* (Notre Dame, IN: University of Notre Dame Press, 1985); Ronald Takaki, *Strangers From a Different Shore: A History of Asian Americans* (Boston: Little Brown, 1989); Patricia J. Williams, *The Alchemy of Race and Rights: Diary of a Law Professor* (Cambridge: Harvard University Press, 1991).

6. Our analysis is based on our collective teaching experiences at Northwestern University, the University of Illinois–Chicago, Northeastern Illinois University, University of California–Los Angeles, California State Polytechnic University–Pomona, and the University of Colorado–Boulder. In addition, we conducted a survey of approximately 100 undergraduate students in three classes (two Social Inequality classes and one Social Movements class) at California State Polytechnic University–Pomona. The survey asked students to evaluate the effectiveness of using film and video in their classes.

7. See Angela Davis, *Women, Race, and Class* (New York: Random House, 1983); Barbara Smith, *Home Girls: A Black Feminist Anthology* (New York: Kitchen Table–Women of Color Press, 1983).

8. See Gloria Anzaldua and Cherrie Moraga, *This Bridge Called My Back: Writings by Radical Women of Color* (New York: Kitchen Table–Women of Color Press, 1983); Gloria Anzaldua, *Making Face, Making Soul: Haciendo Caras* (New York: Aunt Lute, 1990).

9. hooks, *Teaching to Transgress.*

10. Emory C. Burton, "Sociology and the Feature Film," *Teaching Sociology* 16 (1988): 263–271.

11. Nicholas Jay Demerath III, "Through a Double-Crossed Eye: Sociology and the Movies," *Teaching Sociology* 9 (1981): 69–82.

12. Kathleen A. Tiemann and Dana Bickford Tipton, "Using Feature Film to Facilitate Sociological Thinking," *Teaching Sociology* 21 (1993): 187–191.

13. Stephen B. Groce, "Teaching the Sociology of Popular Music With the Help of Feature Films: A Selected and Annotated Videography," *Teaching Sociology* 20 (1992): 80–84.

14. Octavio Romano, "The Anthropology and Sociology of the Mexican American," *El Grito* 2 (1968): 13–26; the quote is cited in Valdez and Halley, "Teaching Mexican American Experience," 289.

15. Valdez and Halley, "Teaching Mexican American Experience,", 287–288.

16. Edward Goldsmith, "Development as Colonialism," in *The Case Against the Global Economy,* ed. Edward Goldsmith and Jerry Mander (San Francisco: Sierra Club, 1996), 253–266.

17. Russell Mokhiber and Robert Weissman, *Corporate Predators* (Monroe, ME: Common Courage, 1999).

18. Chomsky and Herman, *Manufacturing Consent*; Parenti, *Democracy for the Few.*

19. Doob, *Racism.*

20. Joy James, *Resisting State Violence: Radicalism, Gender, and Race in U.S. Culture* (Minneapolis: University of Minnesota Press, 1996), 64.

21. Malcolm Collier and Lane Ryo Hirabayashi, "Video Constructions of Asian America: Teaching *Monterey's Boat People,*" *Review of Education/Pedagogy/Cultural Studies* 21, 1 (1999): 79–94.

PART IV
RETROSPECT AND PROSPECTS

13

SELF, SOCIETY, AND THE "OTHER"

Using Film to Teach About Ethnicity and Race

JUN XING

The university classroom has traditionally been regarded as a place of objective, rational, and scientific learning—an attitude that has led to the exclusion of women and minorities, who have often been viewed as overly emotional and unable to control their feelings. As Elizabeth Ellsworth has explained, "Rational argument has operated in ways that set up as its opposite an irrational Other, which has been understood historically as the province of women and exotic Others."[1] In contrast, ethnic studies—often considered a highly politicized field—centralizes within its curriculum the construction and meanings of race and the history of racism. What is more, an ethnic studies classroom tends to attract a large number of students of color. As a result, screening a film and then discussing its racial stereotyping, oppression, and colonialism may be an emotionally charged experience for all students. Whereas minority students may respond to a film with anger and frustration, majority students may respond with feelings of guilt or hostility.

In my experience, encouraging students to express their feelings and emotions within the classroom presents both opportunities and challenges. Here are the three key issues I have faced: What is the best way to overcome students' inhibitions and encourage honest dialogue? Once students begin to openly share their feelings and responses, how will their raw emotions regarding controversial issues, such as racial stereotypes and misrepresentation, be handled? Finally, how can students turn their emotional reactions into opportunities for productive learning? In confronting these issues, I have developed a few experimental strategies that have proven effective; I discuss them in the following sections.

CLASSROOM CLIMATE

One of the most important pedagogical decisions teachers make concerns the classroom climate. To develop a successful class environment, it is important to build student confidence and create an honest and open atmosphere from the beginning of the semester. In a film-based ethnic studies class, it is particularly important to develop this climate of trust because film speaks to our emotions as well as our intellects. As I discussed in Chapter 2, film provides an emotional immediacy that engages students in the subject, and it may also elicit strong feelings. Furthermore, when students sign up for an ethnic studies class—particularly students of color—they make an emotional commitment because minority students may identify personally with the cultural groups discussed in class (and portrayed in the films used in the course). The greatest challenge for the instructor is to determine how to nurture students' commitment and maintain their interest in the class while at the same time validating minority students' emotional reactions and empowering them in the process.

To develop a classroom environment in which these sensitive emotional issues can be explored and confronted with honesty and depth, I believe the instructor must be personally and emotionally invested in the course. If students are to trust, take risks, and grow together along with the instructor, the instructor and students need to work together as a team. Because of the imbalance in power, the instructor will need to initiate the team-building process, making special efforts to personalize class interactions—particularly in film discussions. As Richard Lacey has explained, an instructor in a film-based course should take on the role of facilitator rather than moderator. A facilitator, according to Lacey, is more personally involved in the discussion than a moderator, whose main job is to keep the discussion on track. Lacy identifies the three major characteristics of effective facilitators: genuineness, caring and empathy, and good rapport with students.[2]

One of the first pedagogical decisions in a film-based course is whether to have students screen films in class or as an out-of-class assignment. During my first semester, I assigned the film screenings as homework to save class time, but I quickly changed to in-class screenings and have stayed with that format because I believe viewing films together should be central to the class experience. Students who enroll in ethnic studies courses typically have diverse backgrounds and experiences, and this diversity causes them to react to films very differently. Race, ethnicity, and gender are only the most obvious differences that contribute to classroom demographics and dynamics. When students view a film together, their learning experience includes hearing the laughter, whoops, wows, occasional curses, and hushed silences that emanate from various sections of the classroom. This shared experience initiates communication and understanding between students (or viewers) before formal discussions even begin and often enhances the postscreening discussions as well. Although a provocative film may touch off controversies, sparking heated disputes and convoluted discussions that never reach class consensus, resentment rarely occurs between students. When students process something as a group, they seem to understand that although they may not always see issues the same way, they should respect one another's differences.

Lee Mun Wah's *The Color of Fear* (1995) clearly illustrates this constructive dialogue. Unlike many other "liberal" multicultural films, this full-length documentary attacks racism head-on. Nine men—two Mexican Americans, two Chinese Americans, one Japanese American, two African Americans, and two European Americans—gather in Ukiah, California, for a weekend of dialogue about racism. At the beginning they all seem nervous and vulnerable. David, one of the white participants, is baffled by the painful experiences of racism among the minorities in the group. In a state of denial, he constantly questions the nonwhite members: "Why can't you just be American and not Chinese American" and "Why do these guys have such a problem with their color? Why can't they make a name for themselves?" One of the Chicano participants responds, "As a white man, he [David] doesn't have to think about his place in the world. He doesn't have to think about being a white person. . . . They don't have to deal with it from day one. . . . They step into the world that is theirs." Victor, who is black and the most articulate of the group, tells David, "I won't trust you unless you can become transformed by my [black] experience as much as I am transformed by your [white] experience every day." As the film progresses, each person's guard gradually goes down. Out of the intimate and intense dialogue among these men, a deeper sense of understanding and trust emerges.

Amazingly, the classroom dynamics in response to the film basically parallel what the film depicts. Initially, students' opinions of the film are very divided. Some believe it is the best film about racism they have ever seen, whereas others feel it is very biased. During one postscreening discussion, students engaged in a heated debate about the prevalence of racism in contemporary U.S. society, but as the dialogue progressed, the deeper problems of racism took root in the students' minds. For example, after many minority students shared personal stories (e.g., about racial profiling), which coincided with many of those documented in the film, white students in the class began to position themselves as minority students. For many white students it was the first time they had heard that being "white" carries inherent privileges. (Sometimes I hand out Peggy MacIntosh's essay as a "think piece" to clarify issues of white, male privilege.[3]) After showing the film, I try to direct class discussion to the central question of what we can do as individuals so that, as in *The Color of Fear,* every participant will leave the experience believing he or she can make a difference.

I have found that if I identify who I am, where I stand politically, and where my perspectives come from and encourage my students to do the same, suspicion within the classroom will dissolve as my students and I struggle to deal with the volatile issues of race, ethnicity, gender, and sexual orientation. Working as a team also helps the class grapple with the pedagogical issues of privilege, authority, and legitimacy in the classroom.

WARM-UP AND FOLLOW-UP EXERCISES

For a film-based course I suggest a longer session (i.e., meetings of at least ninety minutes) because the popular "bite-sized pedagogy" does not work well when showing films during class time. Forty-five-minute class sessions will break a longer film into two or even three screenings, breaking down class continuity and debilitating students' ability to remember everything that has happened. In addition, films may evoke a variety of strong emotions (as discussed previously), so we need to find ways to help students prepare for and then process films that deal with particularly sensitive and controversial issues. The longer-session format provides the opportunity to do warm-up exercises before and follow-up exercises after a screening.

For warm-up exercises prior to screening a film, I suggest assigning relevant readings, including film reviews and interviews with the director. After screening the film, students may be compelled to intellectualize, but it is important to help them first process their pent-up emotions—especially minority students, who often experience controversial films viscerally, with existential intensity. If students do not deal with those emotions right away, it may be difficult for them to discuss the film civilly. Many years ago, several African American students walked out of my class during a screening of *Ethnic Notions* (1987), but such a response is rare; silence is more common. If students are reluctant to speak, a dead silence may envelop the classroom. To break the ice, I have adopted the "image-sound skim" technique discussed by Lacey in his book *Seeing With Feeling.*[4]

The image-sound skim methodology involves cataloging prominent images and sounds from the film, which can serve as an excellent springboard for discussion. "Skimming" encourages students to share their feelings first, helping them to build a bridge between their feelings and thoughts, their intuitive responses and intellectual analysis. During the skimming exercise following a screening of *The Color of Fear,* for example, many students chose the word *anger,* but even more selected the word *pain.* After discussing these two words for just a few minutes, students became actively involved in the discussion as they concluded that for the minority students in the class, tremendous pain lay underneath their anger. To tie up the loose ends of the discussion at the end of class, I passed out a take-home list of short written questions about the history of the different ethnic groups represented in the film. This homework assignment leads to my third and final pedagogical point: contextualizing the films.

THREE CONTEXTS

Sau-ling Cynthia Wong's book *Reading Asian American Literature* calls for reading Asian American texts as "an emergent and evolving textual coalition," a two-pronged approach of contexts and intertexts.[5] According to Wong, the context "stresses the indispensability of historical knowledge to any responsible reading of the corpus."[6] I find Wong's approach compelling and have applied this literary reading strategy to the study of Asian American and ethnic films. In this strategy, reading ethnic films contextually is not just literary or aesthetic but is also a sociological, historical, and cultural enterprise.

The success of a film-based course in ethnic studies demands a pedagogical framework that provides three different contexts for the films: social, cultural, and biographical. With few exceptions, minority films and ethnic cinema do not receive critical attention because of their limited distribution by independent filmmakers, activist groups, and small, alternative companies. As a result, the majority of the films discussed in my class are not widely known by students or the general public, and this lack of public knowledge places a tremendous burden on the instructor to provide the sociological, historical, and cultural background for the class.

Context is integral to the study of film, and many films and video productions presuppose a certain basic historical knowledge. For example, to understand the plot and themes of Asian American movies, we need to know the history of Asian American immigration to the United States. Thematically, almost all of the independent features directed by Asian Americans—from Wayne Wang's mother-daughter sagas *Dim Sum* (1984) and *The Joy Luck Club* (1993) to Ang Lee's "father knows best trilogy" *Pushing Hands* (1991), *The Wedding Banquet* (1993), and *Eat Drink Man Woman* (1994)—are first and foremost family stories.

Critical questions to consider regarding these films include, What was the significance of this mode of narrative for Asian American filmmakers? Was its popularity a result of Asian cultural traditions or of an Asian American historical specificity? How did the special dynamics in Asian American family formation, mandated by longtime exclusionist policies and racism, become the thematic focus for Asian American artists? These questions serve as the starting point for my lecture on the history of Asian American exclusion. Tracing Asian American legal history brings these issues even closer to home, as students begin to realize that historical specificity rather than cultural traditions has determined Asian American filmmakers' thematic focus.

When I teach Asian American films, I always require that students read Stephen Gong's essay, "A History in Progress: Asian American Media Arts Centers, 1970–1990" from *Moving the Image: Independent Asian Pacific American Media Arts.*[7] This essay details the role of various Asian American media centers in nurturing the Asian American film movement. In documenting their history, Gong distinguishes media arts from the media industry: "The Asian American media arts movement from its inception was an alternative movement developed in opposition to mainstream strategies and structures in the film and television industries."[8] A perfect companion documentary, *Claiming a Voice* (1991), will provide students with a visual history of Visual Communications, the earliest and among the largest of the Asian American media centers.

In addition to social and historical contexts, cultural context is also critical to understanding ethnic films. I find Edward T. Hall's concept of "high-context" and "low-context" cultures particularly pertinent here. According to Hall, in low-context cultures the focus is on wording, or the language, and what is being said. High-context cultures, on the other hand, incorporate a great deal of shared, tacit information, and words should not be taken at face value. Instead, the focus of the words is placed on who said them to whom, when, and where. To understand what each word means, we must first grasp its context. In other words, "meaning" is found in the "process" rather than the "ends."[9] Hall's analysis becomes particularly pertinent when using ethnic material in an American classroom. For example, he contends, "Japanese novels are interesting and sometimes puzzling for Westerners to read. To the uninitiated, much of the richness as well as great depths of meaning pass unnoticed, because the nuances of Japanese culture are not known."[10]

To help bridge the gap between cultures, I have incorporated various cultural resources when using ethnic films in the classroom. For example, I have designed a "cultural hunting" assignment for my class. Before I screen *The Wedding Banquet,* students investigate aspects of core Chinese cultural traditions such as the wedding ceremony—including drinking games, fertility rituals, kinship roles, and Chinese etiquette and attitudes toward sexuality, which are skillfully interwoven into the movie's plot. Although I am very careful to avoid the "tokenization" of minority students in class discussions, students from one cultural or ethnic background sometimes act as cultural resources for the whole class. For example, with a subtitled film, speakers of the native language can add commentary vis-à-vis the nuances lost in the translation.

Finally, learning about the filmmakers' personal backgrounds helps students understand their perspectives. For example, I preface Trinh T. Minh-Ha's *Surname Viet Given Name Nam* (1989) with a biography of the Vietnamese

From *Surname Viet Given Name Nam,* a film by Trinh T. Minh-ha. Courtesy Women Make Movies

American director and theorist, along with a handout of her interview with Judith Mayne.[11] After screening this very complex film, students discuss their varied reactions. Some are puzzled about the film's meaning or message, expressing frustration at not being able to figure out the main story line. Others complain about the English subtitles, which are sometimes too small to read or, when larger, flow too quickly to follow. Some students complain that the restless camera is distracting. I refer students to the filmmaker's concept of Zen, which she discusses in her interviews. By approaching the film with the notion of Zen in mind, students begin to understand Trinh's techniques of using negative space both on- and off-screen. For example, in many of the interview sequences in the early part of the film, the camera shots of the women being interviewed are of bodies, chests, hands, and legs—making their "talking heads" literally headless. When the faces of the women do appear, the restless camera never remains on them but pans across the screen, creating a series of blank screens.

The framing also heightens the importance of off-screen space. Trinh uses very few full-frame images of the women, and in her half-face images she disconcertingly cuts the screen edges at the women's noses. She also frames old photographs and stills with disproportionately large black space, and she often uses extremely low lighting, which reinforces the dark screen space. In addition to Trinh's manipulation of visual images, the soundtrack is interrupted with empty spaces (silences), or "sounding holes." Trinh relates all these strategies to the notion of the Void, derived from Zen Buddhism: "People often don't even know what you are talking about when you mention the vitality of the Void in the relationships between object and non-object, or between I and non-I."[12] By the end of the discussion, the majority of students feel Zen Buddhism explains the unconventional techniques and provocative cultural practices Trinh uses in *Surname Viet.*

Independent films by minorities should not be mere audiovisual aids in ethnic studies classrooms because—in contrast to some dry and didactic educational films—as fresh, challenging, artistic, and political works, they are valuable resources in their own right. This chapter touches on a few pedagogical strategies for using these films in the ethnic studies classroom—and obviously a plethora of additional approaches exist, particularly given the number of quality films available and the interdisciplinary nature of the field. Some instructors, for example, use "experiential learning" methods, such as role-playing and simulations, with great success. What is important is that we think about the possibilities so our teaching will be as productive and effective as possible. The overwhelming positive responses from my students testify to the power of film as a teaching tool. For the past ten years I have used film in my ethnicity classes, and, in a sense, doing so has become second nature to me.[13]

NOTES

1. Elizabeth Ellsworth, "Why Doesn't This Feel Empowering? Working Through the Repressive Myths of Critical Pedagogy," *Harvard Educational Review* 59, 1 (1989): 301.

2. Richard A. Lacey, *Seeing With Feeling* (Philadelphia: W. B. Saunders, 1972), 57–58.

3. Peggy McIntosh, "White Privilege and Male Privilege: A Personal Account of Coming to See Correspondences Through Work in Women's Studies," in *Gender Basics: Feminist Perspectives on Women and Men,* ed. Anne Minas (Belmont, CA: Wadsworth, 1993), 30–38.

4. Lacey, *Seeing With Feeling,* 24–54.

5. Sau-ling Cynthia Wong, *Reading Asian American Literature: From Necessity to Extravagance* (Princeton: Princeton University Press, 1993), 9–11.

6. Ibid., 9.

7. Stephen Gong, "A History in Progress: Asian American Media Arts Centers, 1970–1990," in *Moving the Image: Independent Asian Pacific American Media Arts,* ed. Russell Leong (Los Angeles: UCLA Asian American Studies Center, 1991), 1–9.

8. Ibid., 8.

9. Edward T. Hall, *Beyond Culture* (Garden City, NY: Anchor, 1975).

10. Ibid., 114.

11. Trinh T. Minh-Ha, "From a Hybrid Place," in her *Framer Framed* (New York: Routledge, 1992), 137–148.

12. Ibid., 142.

13. For more details, see Jun Xing, "Teaching the Asian American Experience Through Film," in *Teaching Asian America: Diversity and the Problem of Community*, ed. Lane Ryo Hirabayashi (Lanham, MD: Roman and Littlefield, 1997), 217–231.

14

THE ISSUE OF REINSCRIPTION
Pedagogical Responses

Lane Ryo Hirabayashi and Marilyn C. Alquizola

REINSCRIPTION

In conclusion, we would like to revisit and expand upon three aspects of our chapter "Confronting Gender Stereotypes of Asian American Women: *Slaying the Dragon.*" These have to do with (1) the issue of reinscription, (2) recent "reception theory" and images of ethnicity and race, and (3) the importance of pedagogy vis-à-vis points 1 and 2.

The basic issue here is simple, and it is relevant to all of the other chapters in this anthology: How can we be certain we are not actually reinscribing racial and ethnic stereotypes when we screen them for our students? According to Darnell M. Hunt in his fascinating study *Screening the Los Angeles "Riots,"*[1] there is a serious reason to be concerned about this issue. In screening the same seventeen-minute videotape of a KTTV newscast dealing with the Los Angeles uprising to groups of white, black, and Latino informants, Hunt found serious differences in the perceptions as well as responses of the three groups. After careful, multidimensional analysis of the responses, Hunt concluded:

> In short, an individual-level analysis of racial effects supports the group-level findings: black-raced informants left the screening significantly more tolerant

of event-related looting, and significantly less supportive of event-related arrests than their white-raced and Latino-raced counterparts. Furthermore, socio-economic status and gender, net of raced identification, did *not* seem to be a major determinant of informants' attitudes toward event-based activities.[2]

Without getting into the complexities of Hunt's entire presentation, his basic message is clear: people bring concepts, assumptions, ideologies, and internalized reference groups with them when they come to the screening room to see a video or a film. If this is the case, how can we be sure that, in showing racialized stereotypes, we are not reinscribing, if not reinforcing, these pernicious images at a conscious or subconscious level?

Going back to Deborah Gee's video documentary *Slaying the Dragon* (1988), we would like to discuss how we have dealt with the issue of reinscription because we accept that it is a problem—especially in terms of Hunt's "reception theory" concerning visual media representations of race.

DEALING WITH REINSCRIPTION

Although we acknowledge that it is a problem worth considering, we believe that to ignore or sidestep the presentation of stereotypical images raises more issues than it solves, especially when there are ways to combat the reinscription of negative images. Four key points are germane here.

First, we need to identify and deconstruct stereotypical images (we explicated a method for doing this in our treatment of the first episode of *Slaying the Dragon*).[3] Second, when we deconstruct stereotypes, we provide viewers with tools of critical visual thinking that can help them recognize negative and racialized stereotypes. Accurate recognition, in turn, provides them with the opportunity to develop strategies that will oppose and resist these stereotypes. Readers should note that resistance might be tangible and immediate; just as important, however, it might also be a matter of rethinking past experiences. Whether these past experiences were personal or involved another person (i.e., things that were observed or heard about secondhand), rethinking disturbing incidents can be a powerful tool in the learning process. By resituating, reconceptualizing, and revisioning, students can forge a path toward alternative interpretations and responses while also adopting more satisfying perspectives about their lives and their options.[4]

Third, confronting these images gives us important insights into the tangible linkages between Asians and Asian Americans and thus into a whole range of significant cultural and political issues. However much Asian Americans may want to be seen as "Americans," the history of stereotyped incidents indicates that this cannot ever be assumed. Students might be reminded of the infamous Vincent Chin case.[5] In fact, if time allows, a screening of Christine Choy's powerful documentary *Who Killed Vincent Chin* (1987) would illustrate

From *The Barbarian and the Geisha,* Twentieth Century Fox, 1958

this point, since "car wars" (including Toyota-bashing contests and racist ads and cartoons) against Japan and Japanese auto imports were part and parcel of the social context in Michigan that led to Chin's murder.

Fourth, squarely confronting negative racial stereotypes in Hollywood movies and the dominant society allows us to juxtapose more historically accurate representations that are grounded in the history of Asians in America. This historically pitched response could be juxtaposed to fiction and fantasy, which in our view is what the racialized gender stereotypes of Asian and Asian American women entail. Perhaps the most powerful way to do this, if time allows, is to screen a number of biographical documentaries of "real" (as opposed to "reel," as Ward Churchill puts it) Asian American women in either historical or contemporaneous time periods.

We have used a number of excellent historical documentaries to contrast with the racial and gender stereotypes of Asian and Asian American women as quiet, passive, and subservient—or as virgins or whores. We have often shown the twelve-minute clip on Mary Paik Lee from Tom Kim and Chris Chow's film *Lest We Forget* (1985). What is so impressive about her biography is that Mrs. Lee—a pioneer in that she came to the United States from Korea with her family as a child in the early 1900s—was able to accomplish so much in spite of the fact that she began with so little. Still active in the Korean American community at the time of the interview, Mrs. Lee volunteered regularly at the Korean American Service Center, helping Korean newcomers adapt to their new homes.

For images of contemporary women, we enjoy documentaries about artists such as Nellie Wong and Mitsuye Yamada, who are featured in Allie Light's film *Mitsuye and Nellie: Asian American Poets* (1981), or Freida Lee Mock's deft portrait of the designer Maya Lin in *Maya Lin: A Strong, Clear Vision* (1994). For anyone who has ever thought of Japanese American women as quiet and subservient, it is important to learn about the longtime progressive activist Yuri Kochiyama in *Yuri Kochiyama: A Passion for Justice* (1993).[6]

My Mother Thought She Was Audrey Hepburn (1988) is a wonderful "fictional" short film by Sharon Jue that appears to be semiautobiographical. The film features "Suzanne," a third-generation Chinese American woman who grew up in the suburbs of San Francisco. In a series of sly and witty vignettes and a tender account of her mother's and grandmother's biographies, "Suzanne" struggles to reconcile racialized gender stereotypes with her own (somewhat ambivalent) self-image. The film does a terrific job of illustrating the point that Suzanne wants to recognize and accept who she is as a Chinese American woman but at the same time not be "hemmed in."

Concomitantly, a range of printed resources can be used to reinforce this point as well, such as *Making Waves* and *Making More Waves* (fiction and nonfiction pieces by Asian American women from Asian American feminist points of view) or "Grinding Tofu," an Asian American lesbian Web page.[7] It is important for students to be exposed to a range of sources about Asian American women, since their strength and diversity stand in marked contrast to racialized, stereotypical representations.

In sum, whether considering the past or the present, the tenacity of the racialized gender stereotypes of Asian and Asian American women is striking if not shocking, especially since these women had to struggle against many limitations to develop constructive and satisfying lives. It seems to us that we cannot supersede these stereotypes until, as Jun Xing puts it, we confront and smash them.

PEDAGOGY

Although we may want to smash stereotypes, we must acknowledge that there are complications—even dangers—if we are not careful and reflexive about our use of visual media. This is where we believe very strongly that pedagogy comes into play.

Theoretically, we hold that pedagogy centers on a special interaction between a teacher and a learner. This interaction, however, is also inseparable from content (that is, what is being taught), as well as from the learning process itself. To explicate exactly what this entails was one of the objectives of each of our contributors, as well as of the anthology as a whole.[8]

In this same spirit, it is appropriate to emphasize at this juncture that teaching is more art than science. Decades of experience and hundreds of classes suggest that "lessons" are necessarily negotiated. There is hope in this as far as the screening and analysis of visual media about ethnicity and race are concerned, however. As Hunt has observed, "The relationship at any given moment between raced identification and decoding—what I have termed 'raced ways of seeing'—is always a probabilistic one, never a deterministic one." He further notes that "moreover, as informants negotiated these ways of seeing, as they replayed intertextual memories and engaged themselves in discussions with network members, they also affirmed (directly or by default) their own raced subjectivities."[9]

A great deal of thought would go into planning how this could be done. A great deal of care and sensitivity must be exercised to implement a group-based viewing, analysis, and discussion of a given program. This is where pedagogy and the art of teaching go hand in hand. What we envision are new negotiations and sessions structured in such a way that intertextual memories are interrupted, new kinds of discussions and agendas emerge, and the members of an audience are facilitated and can interpolate themselves vis-à-vis difference in new and creative ways.

We have argued in *Reversing the Lens* that diversity in general in the United States—and ethnicity and race in particular—are emotional, even explosive topics. Acknowledging this, video and film provide an especially effective way to approach the exploration of ethnicity and race and other related forms of difference in terms of several points.

Visual media offer relief to "target" populations, such as people of color, in that they do not have to reveal or express themselves directly or otherwise confront their classmates. Similarly, "nontarget" populations may also benefit from the distanciation film provides. Nontarget populations may be able to absorb information about and analyses of racial prejudice or discrimination and not be as defensive or feel "put on the spot" as they might in an open-ended discussion between class members.

Our experience over the years indicates that students relate well to visual media. If productions are well crafted, they can inspire new insights and perspectives, to the extent that a given program can capture insiders' knowledge, views, and statements of self-representation. Concomitantly, well-crafted productions can also stimulate research outside the classroom to gain a command of the substantive dimensions of a given issue or population. We have even seen cases where a video or film can inspire sustained involvement in and commitment to social issues such as environmental pollution (and racism), exploitation of new immigrant women and women of color in sweatshops, redress and reparations for Japanese Americans and for Latin Americans of Japanese descent, the Leonard Peltier case, and so forth.

REVERSING THE LENS

We hope to have demonstrated that film is a useful and stimulating medium that can be used effectively to examine the thorny topics of ethnicity and race and related forms of difference. Because we believe this anthology is only the spark for what will necessarily be a long, collective dialogue, we now turn to future prospects.

We invite our colleagues—other professors who teach about ethnicity and race in community and state colleges and public and private universities—to add their voices to this discussion. In assembling this anthology we learned that our "neighbors" down the hall or at other institutions had terrific ideas about and methodologies for teaching films. Because we believe our common goal as instructors is to provide better instruction, we felt it was important to get these ideas into print and circulate them. We invite others to contribute to this effort.

We also emphasize to community leaders and organizers that even though this anthology is framed in terms of the university classroom, the same films and techniques could also be utilized in a public or community setting. Although it may take additional preparation and experimentation, we believe community activists could "educate" their constituents through video and film using similar approaches to those described in this anthology.

Finally, we welcome anyone who may be interested in video and film—who may want to explore self, society, and "the Other"—to watch some of the films discussed in this anthology and use these chapters as a self-study guide. Because it is often more stimulating and enjoyable to view and analyze films in a small discussion group, you may want to gather a "film club"—similar in format to a book group—and go through the anthology together. But we think those who are reflexive could learn much through thoughtful, solitary introspection as well.

In conclusion, we believe that even though they are social constructions, ethnicity and race are still the basis of profound divisions in our society and our world. It is imperative to analyze both the micro and macro of this reality—our inner feelings, the historical and sociocultural constructions of racialization, the manifestations of ethnicity and race in the world system—and one way to do this is through visual media. By reversing the lens, we believe open-minded viewers may begin to grapple with the bigotry and intolerance that have alienated and separated so many in our society.

NOTES

1. Darnell M. Hunt, *Screening the Los Angeles "Riots": Race, Seeing, and Resistance* (Cambridge: Cambridge University Press, 1997).

2. Ibid., 135.

3. See p. 141 in this volume.

4. Malcolm Collier and Lane Hirabayashi raise this point in the chapter "Embracing Diversity: A Pedagogy for Introductory Asian American Studies Courses," in *ReViewing Asian America: Locating Diversity*, ed. Wendy L. Ng, Soo-Young Chin, James S. Moy, and Gary Y. Okihiro (Pullman: Washington State University Press, 1995), 15–31.

5. The Vincent Chin case is discussed in a report by the U.S. Commission on Civil Rights, *Civil Rights Issues Facing Asian Americans in the 1990s* (Washington, DC: U.S. Government Printing Office, 1992), 25–26. An excellent visual program is Choy's *Who Killed Vincent Chin*.

6. A useful reading is Diane Fujino, "To Serve the Movement: The Revolutionary Practice of Yuri Kochiyama," in *Legacy to Liberation: Politics and Culture of Revolutionary Asian/Pacific America*, ed. Fred Ho with Carolyn Antonio, Diane Fujino, and Steve Yip (Edindurgh, AK, and Brooklyn, NY: Big Red Media, 2000), 257–266.

7. Along with the *Making Waves* anthologies (*Making Waves: An Anthology of Writings by and About Asian American Women*, ed. Asian Women United of California [Boston: Beacon Press, 1989]; *Making More Waves: New Writing by Asian American Women*, ed. Elaine H. Kim, Lilia V. Villanueva, and Asian Women United of California [Boston: Beacon Press, 1997]), an article by Susie Ling, "The Mountain Movers: Asian American Women's Movement in Los Angeles," *Amerasia Journal* 15 (1989): 51–67, is a good resource. It reminds us that although there are bona fide Asian American women heroes, there are also many Asian American women who have worked together in group settings, so their individual names and contributions may not be widely known. The interesting website for "Grinding Tofu" is <http://www.geocities.com/Tokyo/Towers/4289/>. Those investigating this site are forewarned that, as with many sites on the World Wide Web, "Grinding Tofu" seems to undergo periodic revision. When we first visited the site, interesting autobiographical accounts of Chinese American lesbians' "coming out" experiences were available. When we visited last, in early December 2000, only two general statements were posted at the site.

8. A more extended discussion of pedagogy in Asian American studies is found in Lane Ryo Hirabayashi, ed., *Teaching Asian America: Diversity and the Problem of Community* (Lanham, MD: Rowman and Littlefield, 1998).

9. Hunt, *Screening the Los Angeles "Riots,"* 144.

SELECTED FILMOGRAPHY

This anthology covers a large group of films and videos, both mainstream and independent. In compiling this list, we adopted four general guidelines:

1. The films should be independent productions with significant thematic focus on ethnicity, race, gender, class, and sexuality.
2. The films can be mainstream productions, but they should have an important impact on ethnic, gender, or class representation and constitute the focus of study by an author.
3. Some educational films—such as those by PBS—that address significant themes of race, ethnicity, gender, and sexuality are included.
4. If a film has been made more than once, only the most recent version is listed.

After each film we list the director/producer, the date of release, and the distributor. If a film or video has multiple distributors, only one is listed. When a film has no currently known distributor, it is marked unknown; please contact the filmmaker/producer directly. For the convenience of readers, we have also provided an index of distributors for all listed films.

FILM INDEX

Cheyenne Autumn, John Ford, 1964, Warner Home Video, Inc.

Claiming a Voice: The Visual Communications Story, Arthur Dong, 1991, Visual Communications.

The Color of Fear, Lee Mun Wah, 1995, Stir-Fry Productions.

Color Schemes, Shu Lea Cheang, 1989, Women Make Movies.

Colors, Dennis Hooper, 1988, Orion Home Video.

The Corrupter, James Foley, 1999, New Line Home Video.

Custer of the West, Richard Siodmak, 1967, CD Universe.

Dances With Wolves, Kevin Costner, 1990, Orion Home Video.

Davy Crockett, King of the Wild Frontier, Norman Foster, 1955, Baker and Taylor Video.

The Deer Hunter, Michael Cimino, 1978, Baker and Taylor Video.

The Deerslayer, Richard Friedenberg, 1957, United Entertainment.

Dim Sum: A Little Bit of Heart, Wayne Wang, 1984, Facets Multimedia, Inc..

Dr. Quinn, Medicine Woman, James Keach, 1992, Foxvideo.

Eat Drink Man Woman, Ang Lee, 1994, Hallmark Home Entertainment.

El Espejo/The Mirror, Frances Salomé España, 1991, Frances Salomé España.

Ethnic Notions, Marlon Riggs, 1987, California Newsreel.

The Farm, Jonathan Stark and Liv Garbus, 1998, unknown.

Flash Gordon, Mike Hodges, 1980, MCA Universal Home Video.

The Flower Drum Song, Henry Coster, 1961, MCA Universal Home Video.

The Flying Torpedo, D. W. Griffith, 1916, unknown.

Fort Apache, John Ford, 1948, Turner Home Entertainment Company.

Fort Massacre, Joseph M. Newman, 1958, unknown.

Fu Manchu, 1956, Discount Video Tapes, Inc..

The Gatling Gun, Robert Gordon, 1972, Hollywood Home Entertainment.

Geronimo: An American Legend, Walter Hill, 1993, Columbia Tristar Home Video.

The Good Earth, Sidney Franklin, 1937, MGM/UA Home Entertainment (MGM).

Gunga Din, George Stevens, 1939, Turner Home Entertainment Company.

Hi-Ho Silver, Stuart Heisler, 1956, MGM/UA Home Entertainment (MGM).

High Noon, Fred Zinnermann, 1952, Baker and Taylor Video.

In Cold Blood, Richard Brooks, 1967, Columbia Tristar Home Video.

Incident at Oglala: The Leonard Peltier Story, Michael Apted, 1992, Facets Multimedia, Inc.

The Indian Wars Refought, Theodore Wharton and Vernon Day, 1914, Colonel W. F. Cody Historical Motion Picture Company.

Jeremiah Johnson, Sydney Pollack, 1972, Warner Home Video, Inc.

The Joy Luck Club, Wayne Wang, 1993, Buena Vista Home Video.

The Last of the Dogmen, Tab Murphy, 1995, HBO Home Video.

Last of the Mohicans, Michael Mann, 1992, Baker and Taylor Video.

Lest We Forget, Tom Kim and Chris Chow, 1985, San Francisco State University.

Licensed to Kill, Arthur Dong, 1997, Deep-Focus Productions.

Little Big Man, Arthur Penn, 1970, CBS/Fox Video.

The Legend of the Lone Ranger, William A. Fraker, 1981, Panavision.

The Lone Ranger and the City of Gold, Lesley Selander, 1958, unknown.

Love! Valour! Compassion! Joe Mantello, 1997, Movies Unlimited.

A Man Called Horse, Elliot Silverstein, 1970, CBS/Fox Video.

The Matrix, Andy Wachowski, 1999, Warner Home Video, Inc.

Maya Lin: A Strong, Clear Vision, Freida Lee Mock, 1994, National Asian American Telecommunications Association.

Memory/All Echo, Teresa Cha, 1991, Women Make Movies.

Mi Otro Yo/My Other Self, Amy Brookman and Peter Brookman, 1988, National Latino Communications Center.

Mississippi Masala, Mira Nair, 1991, Facets Multimedia, Inc.

Mitsuye and Nellie: Asian American Poets, Allie Light and Irving Saraf, 1981, Women Make Movies.

Mi Vida Loca, Allison Anders, 1994, HBO Home Video.

Monterey's Boat People, Spencer Nakasako and Vincent DiGirolamo, 1982, National Asian American Telecommunications Association.

My Mother Thought She Was Audrey Hepburn, Sharon Jue, 1988, Filmakers Library, Inc.

New Jack City, Mario Van Peebles, 1991, Warner Home Video, Inc.

Northwest Passage, King Vidor, 1940, MGM/UA Home Entertainment (MGM).

One Flew Over the Cuckoo's Nest, Milos Forman, 1975, Facets Multimedia, Inc.

One, Two Man, Steve Wong, 1995, unknown.

The Panama Deception, Barbara Trent, 1992, Rhino Home and Video/Records.

Paradise Lost, Joe Berlinger and Bruce Sinofsky, 1996.

Pocahontas, Mike Gabriel and Eric Goldberg, 1995, Walt Disney Home Video.

Pushing Hands, Ang Lee, 1991, Triboro Entertainment Group.

Pushing Tin, Mike Newell, 1999, 20th-Century Fox Film Corporation.

Race, the Floating Signifier, Stuart Hall, 1996, Media Education Foundation.

Rambo: First Blood, George P. Cosmatos, 1985, Live Home Video.

Representation and the Media, Stuart Hall, 1997, Media Education Foundation.

The Return of a Man Called Horse, Irvin Kershner, 1976, CBS/Fox Video.

Rio Grande, John Ford, 1950, Republic Pictures Home Video.

Sa-I-Gu: From Korean Women's Perspectives, Elaine Kim, 1993, National Asian American Telecommunications Association.

Sayonara, Joshua Logan, 1957, CBS/Fox Video.

The Searchers, John Ford, 1956, Warner Home Video, Inc.

Seminole Uprising, Earl Bellamy, 1955, unknown.

Set It Off, F. Gary Gray, 1996, Movies Unlimited.

Shane, George Stevens, 1953, Paramount Home Video.

She Wore a Yellow Ribbon, John Ford, 1949, Turner Home Entertainment Company.

Skin Deep, Frances Reid, 1995, California Newsreel.

Slam, Marc Levin, 1998, CD Universe.

Slaying the Dragon, Deborah Gee, 1988, National Asian American Telecommunications Association.

Soldier Blue, Ralph Nelson, 1970, Columbia Tristar Home Video.

Son of the Morning Star, Mike Robe, 1991, Republic Pictures Home Video.

Squanto: A Warrior's Tale, Xavier Koller, 1994, Walt Disney Home Video.

Stagecoach, John Ford, 1939, Warner Home Video, Inc.

The Stalking Moon, Robert Mulligan, 1969, Warner Home Video, Inc.

Star Wars, George Lucas, 1977, CBS/Fox Video.

Surname Viet Given Name Nam, Trinh T. Minh-Ha, 1989, Women Make Movies.

Tampon Thieves (Ladronas de Tampones), Jorge Lozano, 1996, unknown.

They Died With Their Boots On, Rauol Walsh, 1941, MGM/UA Home Entertainment (MGM).

The Thin Blue Line, Errol Morris, 1988, HBO Home Video.

Thunderheart, Michael Apted, 1992, Columbia Tristar Home Video.

Tombstone, George P. Cosmatos, 1994, Hollywood Pictures Home Video.

Tonka, Lewis R. Foster, 1958, Walt Disney Home Video.

Two Lies, Pam Tom, 1990, Women Make Movies.

Ulzana's Raid, Robert Aldrich, 1972, MCA Universal Home Video.

The Unconquered, Cecil B. DeMille, 1947, MCA Universal Home Video.

Unforgiven, John Huston, 1960, MGM/UA Home Entertainment (MGM).

The Wedding Banquet, Ang Lee, 1993, CBS/Fox Video.

The White Buffalo, J. Lee Thompson, 1977, MGM/UA Home Entertainment (MGM).

Who Killed Vincent Chin, Christine Choy and Renee Tajima, 1988, Filmmakers Library, Inc.

Winchester '73, Anthony Mann, 1950, MCA Universal Home Video.

The World of Suzy Wong, Richard Quine, 1960, Paramount Home Video.

Wyatt Earp, Lawrence Kasdan, 1994, Warner Home Video, Inc.

Year of the Dragon, Michael Cimino, 1985, MGM/UA Home Entertainment (MGM).

Yuri Kochiyama: A Passion for Justice, Rea Tajiri, 1993, National Asian American Telecommunications Association.

DISTRIBUTOR INDEX

ABC Network/Video
Capital Cities/ABC Video Enterprises
1200 High Ridge Road
Stamford, CT 06905
(203) 968-9100/Fax: (203) 329-6464
Asian Immigrant Women Advocates
310 Eighth Street, 301
Oakland, CA 94607

Baker and Taylor Video
501 S. Gladiolus
Momence, IL 60954
(815) 472-2444/Fax: (800) 775-3500

Buena Vista Home Video
350 S. Buena Vista St.
Burbank, CA 91521-7145
(818) 562-3568/Fax: (818) 569-5900

California Newsreel
149 Ninth Street, Suite 420
San Francisco, CA 94103
(415) 621-6196/Fax: (415) 621-6522
E-mail: contact@newsreel.org
Website: www.newsreel.org

CBS/Fox Video
2121 Ave. of the Stars, 25th Fl.
Los Angeles, CA 90067
(310) 369-3900/Fax: (310) 369-5811

CD Universe
101 N. Plains Industrial Road
Wallingford, CT 06492-2360
(800) 231-7937 or (203) 294-1648/Fax: (203) 294-0391

Colonel W. F. Cody Historical Motion Picture Company
(Buffalo Bill Historical Center)
720 Sheridan Avenue
Cody, WY 82414
(307) 587-4771

Columbia Tristar Home Video
Sony Pictures Plaza
10202 W. Washington Blvd.
Culver City, CA 90232
(310) 280-5418/Fax: (310) 280-2485

Deep-Focus Productions
22-D Hollywood Avenue
Hohokus, NJ 07423
(800) 343-5540

Discount Video Tapes, Inc.
P.O. Box 7122
Burbank, CA 91510
(818) 843-3366/Fax: (818) 843-3821

Frances Salomé España
Holy Smoke Productions
P.O. Box 4044
Alhambra, CA 91803

Facets Multimedia, Inc.
1517 W. Fullerton Ave.
Chicago, IL 60614
(312) 281-9075/Fax: (312) 929-5437

Filmakers Library, Inc.
124 E. 40th St.
New York, NY 10016
(212) 808-4980/Fax: (212) 808-4983
E-mail: info@filmakers.com
Website: www.filmakers.com

Foxvideo
2121 Avenue of the Stars, 25th Fl.
Los Angeles, CA 90067
(310) 369-3900 or (800) 800-2FOX/Fax: (310) 369-5811

Hallmark Home Entertainment
6100 Wilshire Blvd., Suite 14000
Los Angeles, CA 90048
(213) 549-3790/Fax: (213) 549-3760

HBO Home Video
1100 6th Avenue
New York, NY 10036
(212) 512-7400

Hollywood Home Entertainment
6165 Crooked Creek R., Suite B
Norcross, GA 30092-3105
Hollywood Pictures Home Video
Fairmont Bldg. 526
500 S. Buena Vista St.
Burbank, CA 91505-9842

Live Home Video
15400 Sherman Way
P.O. Box 10124
Van Nuys, CA 91410-0124
(818) 988-5060

MCA Universal Home Video
100 Universal City Plaza
Universal City, CA 91608-9955
(818) 777-1000/Fax: (818) 733-1483

Media Education Foundation
26 Center Street
Northampton, MA 01060
(800) 897-0089 or (413) 584-8500/Fax: (800) 659-6882
E-mail: mediaed@igc.org
Website: www.igc.org/mef

MGM/UA Home Entertainment (MGM)
2500 Broadway
Santa Monica, CA 90404-6061
(310) 449-3000/Fax: (310) 449-3100

Movies Unlimited
6736 Castor Avenue
Philadelphia, PA 19149
(215) 722-8298 or (800) 523-0823

National Asian American Telecommunications Association
690 Fifth Street, Suite 211
San Francisco, CA 94107-1517
(415) 543-5738/Fax: (415) 543-5638

National Latino Communications Center
Educational Media
P.O. Box 39A60
Los Angeles, CA 90039
(323) 663-8294/Fax: (323) 663-5606
E-mail: emedia@nlcc.com
Website: www.nlcc.com
New Line Home Video
116 N. Robertson Blvd.
Los Angeles, CA 90048
(310) 967-6670/Fax: (310) 854-0602
Website: www.newline.com

New Yorker Video
16 W. 61st St., 11th Fl.
New York, NY 10023
(800) 447-0196/Fax: (212) 307-7855

Orion Home Video
1888 Century Park E.
Los Angeles, CA 90067
(310) 282-0550/Fax: (212) 282-9902

Paramount Home Video
Bluhdorn Bldg., 1st Fl.
5555 Melrose Avenue
Los Angeles, CA 90038
(213) 956-8090/Fax: (213) 956-1100

Republic Pictures Home Video
12636 Beatrice Street
Los Angeles, CA 90066-0930
(310) 306-4040

Rhino Home and Video/Records
10635 Santa Monica Blvd., 2nd Fl.
Los Angeles, CA 90025-4900
(310) 828-1980 or (800) 843-3670/Fax: (310) 453-5529

San Francisco State University
Media Access Center
1600 Holloway Avenue
San Francisco, CA 94132
(415) 338-1229

Stir-Fry Productions
3345 Grand Avenue, Suite 3
Oakland, CA 94610
(510) 419-3930/Fax: (510) 419-3934
E-mail: stirfry470@aol.com
Website: www.stirfryseminars.com
Triboro Entertainment Group
12 W. 27th St., 15th Fl.
New York, NY 10001
(212) 686-6116/Fax: (212) 686-6178

Trimark Pictures
4553 Glencoe Avenue, Suite 200
Marina Del Rey, CA 90292
(310) 314-2000/Fax: (310) 392-0252
Website: www.trimarkpictures.com

Turner Home Entertainment Company
Box 105366
Atlanta, GA 35366
(404) 827-3066 or (800) 523-0823/Fax: (404) 827-3266

20th-Century Fox Film Corporation
P.O. Box 900
Beverly Hills, CA 90213
(310) 277-2211

United Entertainment
460 Park Avenue South, 9th Fl.
New York, NY 10016
(212) 378-0400/Fax: (212) 378-2160

Video Connection
3123 W. Sylvania Ave.
Toledo, OH 43613
(419) 472-7727 or (800) 365-0449/Fax: (419) 472-2655

Vidmark Entertainment
2644 30th Street
Santa Monica, CA 90405-3009
(310) 314-2000/Fax: (310) 392-0252

Visual Communications
263 S. Los Angeles St., Suite 307
Los Angeles, CA 90012
(213) 680-4462/Fax: (213) 687-4848

Walt Disney Home Video
500 S. Buena Vista St.
Burbank, CA 91521
(818) 562-3560

Warner Home Video, Inc.
4000 Warner Blvd.
Burbank, CA 91522
(818) 954-6000

Women Make Movies
462 Broadway, Suite 500R
New York, NY 10012
(212) 925-0606/Fax: (212) 925-2052
E-mail: info@wmm.com

ABOUT THE CONTRIBUTORS

Adeleke Adeeko is in the Department of English at the University of Colorado, Boulder.

Brenda J. Allen is in the Department of Communication at the University of Colorado, Denver.

Marilyn C. Alquizola is in the Department of Ethnic Studies at the University of Colorado, Boulder.

Lee Bernstein is in American Studies at San José State University and has held visiting appointments at Vassar College and the University of Colorado, Boulder. He is author of *The Greatest Menace: Organized Crime in Cold War America.*

Ward Churchill is in American Indian Studies and chair of the Department of Ethnic Studies at the University of Colorado, Boulder, where he is also a graduate faculty member in the Department of Communications.

Malcolm Collier is in the Asian American Studies Department, College of Ethnic Studies at San Francisco State University.

Elisa (Linda) Facio is in the Department of Ethnic Studies at the University of Colorado, Boulder.

Lane Ryo Hirabayashi is in the Department of Ethnic Studies at the University of Colorado, Boulder.

Jeffrey Ho was formerly with the Department of Speech Communications and the Center for Applied Studies in American Ethnicity at Colorado State University, Fort Collins. He is presently living in Beijing, China.

Carmen Huaco-Nuzum is an independent researcher of film and ethnic studies currently based in Santa Cruz, California.

Lisa Sun-Hee Park is in Ethnic Studies and Urban Studies and Planning at the University of California, San Diego.

About the Contributors

David N. Pellow is in Ethnic Studies at the University of California, San Diego. He is also the director of California Cultures in Comparative Perspective, an international research initiative based at UCSD.

Brett Stockdill, born and raised in Colorado, is in the Department of Social Sciences at California Polytechnic, Pomona.

Jun Xing is in the Department of Ethnic Studies and director of the Difference, Power, and Discrimination Program at Oregon State University, Corvallis.

INDEX

Page numbers in italics indicate film stills.

Index

Index

Index

Made in the USA
Columbia, SC
08 January 2023

75785906R00159